The Attributes of God Volume 2
with Study Guide

A.W. TOZER

The ATTRIBUTES of GOD

VOLUME 2

Deeper Into the Father's Heart

WITH STUDY GUIDE
by
DAVID FESSENDEN

MOODY PUBLISHERS
CHICAGO

The Attributes of God Volume 2 with Study Guide
ISBN: 978-1-60066-791-6
LOC Catalog Card Number: 2006936042
The Attributes of God Volume 2
© 2001 by The Moody Bible Institute of Chicago
The Attributes of God Volume 2 Study Guide
© 2003 by David E. Fessenden

Previously published by Christian Publications, Inc.
First Christian Publications edition 2003
First WingSpread Publishers edition 2007
The Attributes of God Volume 2 was first published
by Christian Publications in 2001.
The Study Guide was added in 2003.
First Moody Publishers edition in 2015

Cover design by
Erik M. Peterson and
Design Source Creative Services, Inc.

5 7 9 10 8 6 4

Scripture taken from
The Holy Bible: King James Version.

Contents

Introduction

God's Character

And they that know thy name will put their trust in thee. (Psalm 9:10)

In the messages that follow we will consider that which is behind all things. There could be no more central or important theme. If you trace effect back to cause and that cause back to another cause and so on, back through the long dim corridors of the past until you come to the primordial atom out of which all things were made, you will find the One who made them—you'll find God.

Behind all previous matter, all life, all law, all space and all time, there is God. God gives to human life its only significance; there isn't any other apart from Him. If you take the concept of God out of the human mind there is no other reason for being among the living. We are, as Tennyson said, like "sheep or goats/ That nourish a blind life within the brain."[1] And we might as well die as sheep unless we have God in our thoughts.

God is the source of all law and morality and goodness, the One that you must believe in before you can deny Him, the One who is the Word and the One that enables us to speak. I'm sure you will see immediately that in attempting a series of messages about the attributes of God we run into that which is difficult above all things.

The famous preacher Sam Jones (who was a Billy Sunday before Billy Sunday's time) said that when the average preacher takes a text it reminds him of an insect trying to carry a bale of cotton. And when I take my text and try to talk about God I feel like that insect; only God can help me.

John Milton started to write a book on the fall of man and his restoration through Jesus Christ our Lord. He was to call his book *Paradise Lost*. But before he dared to write it, he prayed a prayer that I want to pray as well. He prayed to the Spirit and he said, "And chiefly Thou O Spirit, that dost prefer / Before all Temples th' upright heart and pure / Instruct me."[2]

I'd like to say, with no attempt at morbid humility, that without a pure heart and a surrendered mind, no man can preach worthily about God and no man can hear worthily. No man can hear these things unless God touches him and illuminates him. And so Milton said, "Instruct me, for Thou know'st; . . . What in me is dark / Illumine, what is low raise and support / That to the highth of this great Argument / I may assert th' Eternal Providence / And justifie the wayes of God to men."[3]

Who can speak about the attributes of God—His

self-existence, His omniscience, His omnipotence, His transcendence and so on—who can do that and do it worthily? Who is capable of anything like that? I'm not. So I only have this one hope: As the poor little donkey rebuked the madness of the prophet and as the rooster crowed one night to arouse the apostle and bring him to repentance, so God may take me and use me. As Jesus rode into Jerusalem on the back of the little donkey, so I pray that He may be willing to ride out before the people on such an unworthy instrument as I.

It is utterly necessary that we know this God, this One that John wrote about, this One that the poet speaks about, this One that theology talks about and this One that we're sent to preach and teach about. It is absolutely, utterly and critically necessary that we know this One, for you see, man fell when he lost his right concept of God.

As long as man trusted God everything was all right; human beings were healthy and holy (or at least innocent), and pure and good. But then the devil came along and threw a question mark into the mind of the woman: "And he said unto the woman, Yea, hath God said . . .?" (Genesis 3:1). This was equivalent to sneaking around behind God's back and casting doubt on the goodness of God. And then began the progressive degeneration downward.

When the knowledge of God began to go out of the minds of men, we got into the fix that we're in now:

Because that, when they knew God, they glorified him not as God, neither were thankful; but became vain in their imaginations, and their foolish heart was darkened. Professing themselves to be wise, they became fools, and changed the glory of the uncorruptible God into an image made like to corruptible man, and to birds, and fourfooted beasts, and creeping things. Wherefore God also gave them up to uncleanness through the lusts of their own hearts, to dishonour their own bodies between themselves: who changed the truth of God into a lie, and worshipped and served the creature more than the Creator, who is blessed for ever. Amen. For this cause God gave them up unto vile affections: for even their women did change the natural use into that which is against nature: and likewise also the men, leaving the natural use of the woman, burned in their lust one toward another; men with men working that which is unseemly, and receiving in themselves that recompense of their error which was meet. And even as they did not like to retain God in their knowledge, God gave them over to a reprobate mind, to do those things which are not convenient. (Romans 1:21-28)

That first chapter of Romans ends with a terrible charge of unrighteousness, fornication, wickedness, covetousness, maliciousness and all the long, black list of crimes and sins that man has been guilty of.

All that came about because man lost his confidence in God. He didn't know God's character. He didn't know what kind of God God was. He got all mixed up about what God was like. Now the only way back is to have restored confidence in God. And the only way to have restored confidence in God is to have restored knowledge of God.

I began with the text, "And they that know thy name will put their trust in thee" (Psalm 9:10). The word "name" means character, plus reputation. "And they that know *what kind of God thou art* will put their trust in thee." We wonder why we don't have faith; the answer is, faith is confidence in the character of God and if we don't know what kind of God God is, we can't have faith.

We read books about George Mueller and others and try to have faith. But we forget that faith is confidence in God's character. And because we are not aware of what kind of God God is, or what God is like, we cannot have faith. And so we struggle and wait and hope against hope. But faith doesn't come, because we do not know the character of God. "They that know what Thou art like will put their trust in Thee." It's automatic—it comes naturally when we know what kind of God God is.

I'm going to give you a report on the character of God, to tell you what God is like. And if you're listening with a worthy mind, you'll find faith will spring up. Ignorance and unbelief drag faith down, but a restored knowledge of God will bring faith up.

I don't suppose there is ever a time in the history of the world when we needed a restored knowledge of God more than we need it now. Bible-believing Christians have made great gains in the last forty years or so. We have more Bibles now than we've ever had—the Bible is a bestseller. We have more Bible schools than we've ever had, ever in the history of the world. Millions of tons of gospel literature are being poured out all the time. There are more missions now than we know what to do with. And evangelism is riding very, very high at the present time. And more people go to church now, believe it or not, than ever went to church before.

Now all that has something in its favor, there's no doubt about it. But you know, a man can learn at the end of the year how his business stands by balancing off his losses with his gains. And while he may have some gains, if he has too many losses he'll be out of business the next year.

Many of the gospel churches have made some gains over the last years, but we've also suffered one great central loss: our lofty concept of God. Christianity rises like an eagle and flies over the top of all the mountain peaks of all the religions of the world, chiefly because of her lofty concept of God, given to us in divine revelation and by the coming of the Son of God to take human flesh and dwell among us. Christianity, the great church, has for centuries lived on the character of God. She's preached God, she's prayed to God, she's declared God, she's honored God, she's elevated God, she's witnessed to God—the Triune God.

But in recent times there has been a loss suffered. We've suffered the loss of that high concept of God, and the concept of God handled by the average gospel church now is so low as to be unworthy of God and a disgrace to the church. It is by neglect, degenerate error and spiritual blindness that some are saying God is their "pardner" or "the man upstairs." One Christian college put out a booklet called "Christ Is My Quarterback"—He always calls the right play. And a certain businessman was quoted as saying, "God's a good fellow and I like Him."

There isn't a Muslim alive in the world who would stoop to calling God a "good fellow." There isn't a Jew, at least no Jew who believes in his religion, that would ever dare to refer that way to the great Yahweh, the One with the incommunicable name. They talk about God respectfully and reverently. But in the gospel churches, God is a "quarterback" and a "good fellow."

I sometimes feel like walking out on a lot that passes for Christianity. They talk about prayer as "going into a huddle with God," as if God is the coach or the quarterback or something; they all gather around, God gives the signal and away they go. What preposterous abomination! When the Romans sacrificed a sow on the altar in Jerusalem, they didn't commit anything more frightful than when we drag the holy, holy, holy God down and turn Him into a cheap Santa Claus that we can use to get what we want.

Christianity has lost its dignity. And we'll never get it back unless we know the dignified Holy God, who rides on the wings of the wind and makes the clouds His chariots. We have lost the concept of

majesty and the art of worship. I got a letter from
my good friend Stacy Woods, who was until recently head of InterVarsity. And he said this in the
closing lines of his letter: "The church is getting
away from worship. I wonder if it is because we are
getting away from God." I think he's right and I believe that is the answer.

And then our religion has lost its inwardness. For
Christianity, if it's anything, is an inward religion.
Jesus said that we are to worship in spirit and in
truth. And yet we've lost it because we have lost the
concept of deity that makes it possible. Even though
we've hung onto our Scofield Bible and still believe
in the seven main doctrines of the fundamental
faith, we've lost the awe, the wonder, the fear and
the delight. Why? Because we've lost God, or at
least we've lost our high and lofty concept of God—
the only concept of God that He honors.

And so the gains we have made have all been external: Bibles and Bible schools; books and maga-
zines and radio messages; missions and evangelism;
numbers and new churches. And the losses we've
suffered have all been internal: the loss of dignity
and worship and majesty, of inwardness, of God's
presence, of fear and spiritual delight.

If we have lost only that which is inward and
gained only that which is outward, I wonder if
we've gained anything at all. I wonder if we are not
now in a bad state. I believe we are. I believe our
gospel churches, our Christianity, is thin and anemic, without thoughtful content, frivolous in tone
and worldly in spirit.

And I believe that we are desperately in need of a reformation that will bring the church back.

I quit using the word revival because we need more than a revival. When the great Welsh revival came to the little country of Wales around the turn of the century, the Holy Ghost had something to work with. The people believed in God and their concept of God was lofty. But because the church has lost her lofty concept of God and no longer knows what God is like, her religion is thin and anemic, frivolous and worldly and cheap.

Compare the preaching of the church today with that of the Hebrew prophets, or even of men like Charles Finney—if you dare to do it. How serious these men of God were! They were men of heaven come to earth to speak to men. As Moses came down from the mount with his face shining to speak to men, so the prophets and preachers down through the years went out. Serious-minded men they were, solemn men, lofty in tone and full of substance of thought and theology.

But today the preaching to a large extent is cheap, frivolous, coarse, shallow and entertaining. We in the gospel churches think that we've got to entertain the people or they won't come back. We have lost the seriousness out of our preaching and have become silly. We've lost the solemnity and have become fearless, we've lost the loftiness and have become coarse and shallow. We've lost the substance and have become entertainers. This is a tragic and terrible thing.

Compare the Christian reading matter and you'll

know that we're in pretty much the same situation. The Germans, the Scots, the Irish, the Welsh, the English, the Americans and the Canadians all have a common Protestant heritage. And what did they read, these Protestant forebears of yours and mine? Well, they read Doddridge's *The Rise and Progress of Religion in the Soul.* They read Taylor's *Holy Living and Dying.* They read Bunyan's *Pilgrim's Progress* and *Holy War.* They read Milton's *Paradise Lost.* They read the sermons of John Flavel.

And I blush today to think about the religious fodder that is now being handed out to children. There was a day when they sat around as the fire crackled in the hearth and listened to a serious but kindly old grandfather read *Pilgrim's Progress,* and the young Canadian and the young American grew up knowing all about Mr. Facing-Both-Ways and all the rest of that gang. And now we read cheap junk that ought to be shoveled out and gotten rid of.

Then I think about the songs that are sung now in so many places. Ah, the roster of the sweet singers! There's Watts, who wrote "Oh, God, Our Help in Ages Past," and Zinzendorf, who wrote so many great hymns. And then there was Wesley, who's written so many. There was Newton and there was Cooper, who wrote "There Is a Fountain Filled with Blood," and Montgomery and the two Bernards—Bernard of Cluny and Bernard of Clairvaux. There was Paul Gerhardt and Tersteegen, there was Luther and Kelly, Addison and Toplady, Senic and Doddridge, Tate and Brady and the Scottish Psalter. And there was a company of others that weren't as big as these great stars, but taken together they made a Milky Way that circled the Protestant sky.

I have an old Methodist hymnal that rolled off the press 111 years ago and I found forty-nine hymns on the attributes of God in it. I have heard it said that we shouldn't sing hymns with so much theology because people's minds are different now. We think differently now. Did you know that those Methodist hymns were sung mostly by uneducated people? They were farmers and sheep herders and cattle ranchers, coal miners and blacksmiths, carpenters and cotton pickers—plain people all over this continent. They sang those songs. There are over 1,100 hymns in that hymnbook of mine and there isn't a cheap one in the whole bunch.

And nowadays, I won't even talk about some of the terrible junk that we sing. They have a little one that is sung to the tune of "There'll Be a Hot Time in the Old Town Tonight," which goes like this:

One, two, three, the devil's after me,
Four, five, six, he's always throwing bricks,
Seven, eight, nine, he misses me every time,
Hallelujah, Amen.

And the dear saints of God sing that now! Our fathers sang "O God, Our Help in Ages Past," and we sing junk.

This tragic and frightening decline in the spiritual state of the churches has come about as a result of our forgetting what kind of God God is.

We have lost the vision of the Majesty on high. I have been reading in the book of Ezekiel over the last weeks, reading slowly and rereading, and I've just come to that terrible, frightening, awful passage where the *Shekinah,* the shining presence of God, lifts up from between the wings of the cherubim, goes to the altar, lifts up from the altar, goes to the door and there is the sound of the whirring of wings (Ezekiel 10:4-5). And then the presence of God goes from the door to the outer court (10:18-19) and from the outer court to the mountain (11:23) and from the mountain into the glory.

And it has never been back, except as it was incarnated in Jesus Christ when He walked among us. But the *Shekinah* glory that had followed Israel about all those years, that shone over the camp, was gone. God couldn't take it any longer, so He pulled out His Majesty, His *Shekinah* glory, and left the temple. And I wonder how many gospel churches, by their frivolousness, shallowness, coarseness and worldliness have grieved the Holy Ghost until He's withdrawn in hurt silence. We must see God again; we must feel God again; we must know God again; we must hear God again. Nothing less than this will save us.

I'm hoping that you will be prayerful and that you'll be worthy to hear this, and that I'll be worthy to speak about God— the Triune God, the Father, Son and Holy Ghost—what He's like. If we can restore again knowledge of God to men we can help in some small way to bring about a reformation that will restore God again to men. I want to close with these words of Frederick Faber:

Full of glory, full of wonders,
    Majesty Divine!
Mid thine everlasting thunders
    How thy lightnings shine.
Shoreless Ocean! who shall sound Thee?
Thine own eternity is round Thee,
Majesty Divine![4]

One hour with the majesty of God would be worth more to you now and in eternity than all the preachers—including myself—that ever stood up to open their Bible. I want a vision of the majesty of God—not as that song says, "one transient gleam"—no, I don't want anything transient, I want the gleam of majesty and wonder to be permanent! I want to live where the face of God shines every day. No child says, "Mother, let me see your face transiently." The child wants to be where any minute of the hour he can look up and see his mother's face.

Timeless, spaceless, single, lonely,
    Yet sublimely Three,
Thou art grandly, always, only
    God in Unity!

Lone in grandeur, lone in glory,
Who shall tell thy wondrous story,
    Awful Trinity?

Splendours upon splendours beaming
    Change and intertwine;

Glories over glories streaming
    All translucent shine!

Blessings, praises, adorations
Greet thee from the trembling nations
    Majesty Divine![5]

This is the day of the common man—and we
have not only all become common, but we've
dragged God down to our mediocre level. What we
need so desperately is an elevated concept of God.
Maybe by faithful preaching and prayer, and by the
Holy Ghost, we can see the "splendours upon
splendours beaming / Change and intertwine."
Maybe we can see "Glories over glories streaming /
All translucent shine!" To God we can give "blessings, praises, adorations" that "Greet thee from the
trembling nations / Majesty Divine!"

Chapter 1

God's Self-Existence

And Moses said unto God, Who am I, that I should go unto Pharaoh, and that I should bring forth the children of Israel out of Egypt? And he said, Certainly I will be with thee; and this shall be a token unto thee, that I have sent thee: When thou hast brought forth the people out of Egypt, ye shall serve God upon this mountain. And Moses said unto God, Behold, when I come unto the children of Israel, and shall say unto them, The God of your fathers hath sent me unto you; and they shall say to me, What is his name? what shall I say unto them? And God said unto Moses, I AM THAT I AM: and he said, Thus shalt thou say unto the children of Israel, I AM hath sent me unto you. And God said moreover unto Moses, Thus shalt thou say unto the children of Israel, The LORD God of your fathers, the God of Abraham, the God of Isaac, and the God of Jacob, hath sent me unto you: this is my name for ever, and this is my memorial unto all generations. (Exodus 3:11-15)

The translators set the words in Exodus 3:14, "I AM THAT I AM," in capitals, for that is the name of God, and God's memorial throughout all generations. "I AM," of course, means "I AM the self-existent One." I want to speak about God's divine attribute of self-existence, or God's selfhood. I'll use both of those terms and probably some others. But before I go on, I ought to say a little bit about a divine attribute—what it is and what it isn't.

Now an attribute of God is *not* that of which God is composed. The very fact that God is God indicates that God isn't "composed" at all. You and I are composed. We're composed of body, soul, mind, spirit, imagination, thought and memory. We're a composition, because there was Someone there to compose us. God took clay and His own breath, and as an artist brings the paints to the canvas, God brought all of His genius to the matter and spirit out of which man is made and He composed man. And so the attributes of man are the component parts; they compose the man.

But when we talk about the attributes of God we have no such idea in mind at all, because He said, "I AM THAT I AM." Anything that is composed has to have been composed by someone, and the composer is greater than the composition. If God the Father Almighty had been composed, somebody greater than God would have had to be out there to "make" God. But God is not made! Therefore, we cannot say that the attributes of God are the parts of which God is made, because God is not "made" of parts.

God exists in simple unity. I'm a unitarian and I'm also a trinitarian, you see. I believe in the unity of God. And when we say that God is One, if we're scriptural we do not mean that there is only one God, although that also is true. But we mean that God is One with Himself, without parts. God is like a diamond; the diamond is one with itself. God is like gold; it is one with itself—only that's a poor, cheap illustration. God is infinitely above all that.

God's attributes are not God; that is, I say that God is self-existent, but that's something that I posit about God—that isn't God. I say that God is holy, but holiness is not God. I say that God is wisdom, but wisdom is not God. *God* is God!

Would you like a definition of attribute as I shall use it? It is something which God has declared to be true of Himself. And one thing God has declared to be true of Himself is, "I AM THAT I AM"—I exist. Not "I will exist," or "I did exist," but "I do exist." The philosophy of existentialism begins with the propositions "I exist" and "There is no God." But the Christian believes that God is the original existence, that He said "I AM." And because God is, everything else that is, is.

An attribute of God is something we can know about God. It is knowing what kind of God God is. In this study of the attributes we'll try to teach what God is like.

Reason must always fall short of God. I was talking to one of the greatest minds in the evangelical world recently and I asked him, "You don't believe, do you, that all that God is can be grasped by our intellects?"

He responded, "If I didn't, I would be an agnostic."

I didn't think to say it at the time, but afterward I thought, "Well, if you believe that everything that God is can be grasped by the intellect, you're not an agnostic, you're a rationalist." That is rationalism, pure and simple—the belief that I can understand anything God says and anything God is, if there is a God. The idea that my brain is the criterion of all things, that's rationalism. And rationalism almost always follows a rigid, hard orthodoxy, because it says, in effect, "I know God, I understand God, I can grasp God."

But the truth is that God rises transcendently above all that we can understand. The human mind must kneel before the great God Almighty. What God is can never quite be grasped by the mind; it can only be revealed by the Holy Spirit. If the Holy Spirit does not reveal what I am trying to tell you about God, then you only know *about* God.

The little song says, "More about Jesus would I know," but it isn't more *about* Jesus that the heart craves after, *it's Jesus Himself*! It is the knowledge *of* God, not the knowledge *about* God.

I might know all about the Prime Minister of Canada, but I don't know him—I've never met him. From what I hear and read and the speeches I've heard him make, I suppose he's a fine gentleman. If I were to live with him awhile—travel with him, eat with him, talk with him—I suppose I'd get to know him. But now I only know *about* him, that's all. I know about him—his age, background, etc.—but I don't know him.

And so, when we talk about the attributes of God, we're talking about His essential essence, of which He says, "I AM." But we're talking only about that which the intellect can grasp. Thank God, there are some things the intellect can know about God. And even though we can't know, except by the Holy Spirit, about God, yet the mind is never better employed than when it is seeking to know this great God Almighty.

And if even the imperfect knowledge that you and I can have of our Father which art in heaven raises us to such rapture, and satisfies so deeply the roots of our being, then what must it be in that day when we look on His face! What will it be in the day when we no longer depend upon our minds, but when, with pioneer eyes of our souls, we look without mediation upon the face of God Himself! Wonderful! It's good to get acquainted with God now so that at the end of time you won't be embarrassed in His presence.

I'd like to point out something here: Everything that is true of God is true of the three Persons of the Trinity. Did you know that there was a time when the idea of Jesus being God—being truly God—was believed by one branch of the church, but not by another?

A man named Arius came along and began to teach that Jesus was a good man, a superior man, but He wasn't God. And the leaders of the church met together, a council, they called it. They studied the issue and they gave us the Athanasian Creed. Here's what they arrived at, and I'll never get over thanking God for these wonderful, learned, godly men. They said, "We worship one God in Trinity, and Trinity in Unity."

I am a unitarian in that I believe in the unity of God. I am a trinitarian in that I believe in the trinity of God. And they're not contrary one to the other.

> We worship one God in Trinity, and Trinity in Unity;
> Neither confounding the persons nor dividing the substance.
> For there is one person of the Father, another of the Son, and another of the Holy Spirit.
> But the Godhead of the Father, of the Son, and of the Holy Spirit is all one, the glory equal, the majesty coeternal.

I don't know whether you'll agree with me or not, but to me it is just like music to hear these old, godly, serious-minded church fathers set this out for all the ages. For the last 1,600 years, the church has feasted on this:

> Such as the Father is, such is the Son, and such is the Holy Spirit.
> The Father uncreated, the Son uncreated, and the Holy Spirit uncreated.
> The Father incomprehensible, the Son incomprehensible and the Holy Spirit incomprehensible.
> The Father eternal, the Son eternal, and the Holy Spirit eternal.

Yet there are not three eternals, but one eternal.

As also there are not three uncreated nor three incomprehensible, but one uncreated and one incomprehensible.

So also the Father is almighty, the Son almighty, and the Holy Spirit almighty, yet there are not three almighties, but one almighty.

So the Father is God, the Son is God, and the Holy Spirit is God; and yet they are not three Gods, but one God.

Now that's what we believe, my brethren: we believe in the three Persons, but one God.

The three Persons are three, but the one God is One. And this we believe. So when I talk about God, I mean the three Persons of the Trinity. You can't separate them—"not dividing the substance," said these old fathers. You can't have God the Father except you have God the Son; you can't have God the Spirit unless you have the Father and the Son, "for the Spirit proceedeth from the Father and the Son." So when I'm talking about God, I'm talking about the Father, the Son and the Holy Spirit—not confusing their Persons, for there are three Persons. But everything that is true of the Father is true of the Son and the Holy Spirit. And everything that is true of the Son and the Holy Spirit is true of the Father. Let's get that settled before we go any further.

Self-Existent Selfhood

God is self-existent selfhood. Novation, the church father, said, "God has no origin." Just those four words, "God has no origin," would be an education to the average person. Origin, you see, is a creature word. Everything came from somewhere. One of the questions that every child asks is, "Where did I come from?" Then you have a job on your hands! It won't be enough to tell him he came from Jesus, because when he gets a little older he'll say, "How did I come from Jesus?"

Everything has an origin. When you hear a bird sing, you know that once that bird was packed in a tiny little egg. It came from somewhere; it came from an egg. Where did the egg come from? It came from another little bird. And that bird came from another little egg, and that egg came from another bird, and so on, back, back, back to the heart of God, when God said, "Let the heavens bring forth, let the earth bring forth, let the dry land appear," as it says in Genesis 1.

Origin is a creature word. The trees had an origin, space had an origin, the mountains, the seas—all things have an origin. But when you come back to God, you come back to the One who has no origin. He is the Cause of all things, the uncaused Cause.

Everything is a cause and effect. For instance, a man walking down the street with his little boy is the cause of the little boy. But the man is also an effect, he was caused by someone else—his father. It's cause and effect, cause and effect, down through the years, until you come to the Cause that is the Cause of all causes—God. God is the uncaused Cause of everything. He is the Origin that had no origin.

This same Athanasian Creed says:

The Father is made of none, neither created nor begotten.

The Son is of the Father alone; not made nor created, but begotten.

The Holy Spirit is of the Father and of the Son; neither made, nor created, nor begotten, but proceeding.

I want to think, pray, study and meditate on God and get to learn the language of the place where I am going. I'm going up there where the Father is, and the Son and the Holy Spirit. All the great company of the redeemed is there—the blood washed, the regenerated, the sanctified. And when I get there I want to be able to speak the language of that place —without an American accent!

I want to know the language of the place where I am going, and the origin of that language, the origin of heaven itself, is God. God Himself has no origin, but He is the originator of everything else. He is the uncaused Cause of everything. God is the original, the "I AM THAT I AM." The verb "to be" (as in "I AM") is the Latin root of the word "essence." God is the original, uncreated essence.

God is not derived from anything. Everyone is derived from someone else and everything is derived from some other thing. But when it comes to God, God is underived—uncreated. If God had derived from something else then that something else would have antedated God.

That's why one of the silliest expressions that was ever used in all the wide world is to say that Mary is the "mother of God." How could Mary be the mother of God, when God is the original essence? Mary wasn't back there before God was. She's the mother of the body of Jesus and she's nothing more than that.

It was in the holy womb of the virgin Mary that the great God Almighty compressed Himself into the form of a Babe, and so we honor her and respect her highly, for she's blessed among women as the one that God used as the channel to come into this world of ours. But before Mary was, God was! And before Abraham was, God was. And before Adam was, God was! And before the world was—the stars, the mountains, the seas, the rivers, the plains or the forests—God was! And God is and God will ever be. God is the originating Self. God's selfhood is His holy being—His unsupported, independent existence.

God's Selfhood and Prayer

Did you ever think about God without getting down on your knees and begging for something? Most of us, when we pray, we bring our grocery list and say, "Lord, we'd like this and this and this." We act as if we were running to the corner store to get something. And God has been dragged down in our thinking to nothing more than the One who gives us what we want when we're in trouble.

Now God does give us what we want—He's a good God. God's goodness is one of His attributes. But I hope that we'll not imagine that God exists simply to answer the prayers of people. A business-man wants to get a contract, so he goes to God and says, "God, give me." A student wants to get a good grade, so she goes to God and says, "Give me." A young man wants the girl to say yes, so he gets on his knees and says, "Father, give her to me." We just *use* God as a kind of source of getting what we want.

Our Heavenly Father is very, very kind and He tells us that we are to ask. Whatever we ask in the name of His Son He'll give us, if it's within the confines of His will. And His will is as broad as the whole world. Still, we must think of God as the Holy One, not just as the One from whom we can get things. God is not a glorified Santa Claus, who gives us everything we want then fades out and lets us run our own way. He gives, but in giving He gives us Himself too. And the best gift God ever gives us is Himself. He gives answers to prayer, but after we've used up the answer or don't need it anymore, we still have God. In God's self there is no sin. We creatures properly and rightly and scripturally have everything to say against self and selfishness—it's the great sin. But God's self is not sinful, because God was the originator of us all, and it is only our fallen selves that are sinful. Because God is the original, unfallen, holy God, God's self is not sinful. The poet says,

In Thy praise of Self untiring
    Thy perfections shine;
Self-sufficient, self-admiring,—
    Such life must be Thine;—
Glorifying Self, yet blameless
With a sanctity all shameless
    It is so divine![1]

God loves Himself—the Father loves the Son, the Son loves the Father and the Son and the Father love the Holy Spirit. They understood this in the olden times, when men were thinkers instead of imitators and they thought within the confines of the Bible.

Incidentally, in discussing God's attributes I am not trying to think my way up to God. You can't think your way up to God any more than you can climb a ladder to the moon. You can't think your way into the kingdom of heaven—you go in by faith. But after you're in you can think about the kingdom of heaven. You can't think your way to England, but after you get there you can think about England.

So God loves Himself. And He loves Himself because He is the God who originated love. He is the I AM of love, the essence of all holiness and the fountain of all self-conscious light. The words "I" and "I am" always refer to the self. I knew a dear old brother—God bless him, he's in heaven now and he'll wear a crown so big that it'll come down over my shoulders, I'm sure—he'd been a missionary to China and he didn't believe much in saying "I." He knew that "I" meant self, and a fallen self is a sinful thing, so he would always say "one." And he'd say things like, "When one was in China one said this, and one did this." He meant himself—he was afraid to say "I." I suppose if he'd been writing Psalm 23, he'd make it read like this: "The Lord is one's Shepherd, one shall not want. . . ."

There's nothing wrong with saying "I" or "I am."

But when you say, "I am," you always put "am" in lower-case letters. But when God said, "I AM," He put it in capitals—there's a difference. When God says, "I AM," it means He did not derive from anywhere. He started the whole business—He is God. But when I say "I am," I'm a little echo of God.

I believe that God is very, very proud of His children. I believe that throughout the vast reaches of this universe God is happy to call His people His people. Do you remember what God said about Job? The sons of God—the angels—were all passing in parade, and who comes with them but Satan himself. The brass, the arrogance that he had—traveling along with the unfallen sons of God! And when he got out before the reviewing stand, God said, "Have you seen my servant Job? He is a good man and eschews evil. Have you seen my servant Job?" (See Job 1:8). He was proud of Job.

God is proud of His people, and He's proud to have us say, "I am" in a little echo voice, because He is the original Voice who said "I AM THAT I AM." The doctrine of man made in the image of God is one of the basic doctrines of the Bible and one of the most elevating, enlarging, magnanimous and glorious doctrines that I know. There's nothing wrong with self-respect, there's nothing wrong with saying, "I am" and "I will" and "I do" as long as we remember we're saying it in lower-case letters, as an echo from the original One who first said, "I AM."

Strange, isn't it, that God the Son was called the Word and God enabled man to speak. And he enabled no other creature to speak. Not the finest-bred dog can talk, not the finest myna bird (they're supposed to talk, but they don't know what they're saying). Man alone can talk, because only man has this thing we call the *logos*—the Word.

The essence of sin is independent self. You see, God sat on the throne—the I AM. And along came man and said, "I will" and sought to rise above the throne of God. He disobeyed God and took the bit in his own teeth and became a little god in his own right. The sinful world says, "I am," forgetting that they are an echo of the One above and saying it in their own right.

Mussolini said, "I will make my life a masterpiece." What a masterpiece he was—that big, bloated, arrogant gorilla! And now he lies rotting in the clay and the worms are feasting on the man who used to stand on a balcony and make big, noisy, bombastic speeches. That is what sin is.

The definition of sin is fallen selfhood. God made us to be like planets—around and around they go, held by the magnetic attraction of the sun. In the same way, God is the great "Sun of righteousness" (Malachi 4:2). And around Him, warmed and healed and blessed and lighted by His Holy Person, all His creatures move—all the seraphim, cherubim, angels, archangels, children of God and watchers in the skies. And best of all was man, made in His own image. We revolved around God as a planet around its sun.

Then one day the little planet said, "I'll be my own sun. Away with this God." And man fell. That's what we call the fall of man. That's where sin came in—sin reached up and took God's self and said, "I'll be self myself." And God was ruled out. As the holy apostle said, they did not like to have God in their minds, therefore God gave them over to vile affections (Romans 1:26). All the evil that the police, educators, doctors and psychiatrists are worried about now—deviancy, sodomy, exhibitionism and all the rest—all came as a result of man not wanting to have this God in his mind or in his heart, not recognizing Him as being God. He went out on his own to be his own little god.

Isn't that the way the average sinner acts? He's his own little god. He's the sun. He puts himself in capital letters and forgets that there's anybody up there that'll judge him.

Sin has symptoms and manifestations, just as cancer has certain manifestations. I've seen a few cancer victims in my time; my own father died of cancer. They have symptoms, but the symptoms are not the cancer; if you clear up the symptoms, you still have the cancer. Sin also has manifestations—many manifestations. Paul gives a list of them in Galatians 5:19-21: "Now the works of the flesh are manifest, which are these; Adultery, fornication, uncleanness, lasciviousness, idolatry, witchcraft, hatred, variance, emulations, wrath, strife, seditions, heresies, envyings, murders, drunkenness, revellings, and such like."

And yet, he didn't tell us sin at all, he told us the symptoms of sin. These things are all symptoms of something deeper: our asserting self. It is asserting my created and derived self, putting myself on the throne and saying, "I am self: I am that I am."

I have read books on existentialism. I could shudder and grieve that men can be so tragically mistaken as they are, and yet I knew they were because I read my Bible. Existentialists say that man is—man wasn't created, man just *is*—and he has to start from there. He has no Creator, no planner, nobody that thought him out: he just *is*. They make man say what only God can say: "I am that I am." Man can say, in a modest humble voice, "I am," but only God can say in capital letters, "I AM THAT I AM." Man has forgotten that and that is sin.

It is not your temper that is sin; it's something deeper than your temper. It is not your lust that is sin; it's something deeper than that—that's but a symptom. All the crime in the world—all the evil, the robberies, the rapes, the desertions, the assassinations—they're but the external manifestations of an inward disease: sin.

And yet, it is not to be thought of as a disease so much as an attitude, a derangement. There sat God upon His throne, the I AM THAT I AM, the eternal self-sufficient, self-existent One. He made man to be like Him and gave him a will—He said, "Man can do as he pleases." He meant for man to circle around the throne of God as the planets circle around the sun. And I repeat, man said, "I am that I am"—he turned away from God, and fallen self took over. No matter how many manifestations sin may have, remember that the liquid essence in the bottle is always self.

That's why it's not always easy to get people to become real Christians. You can get them to sign a card, or make a decision, or join a church, or something like that. But to get people delivered from their sin is a pretty hard deal because it means that I've got to get off that throne. God belongs on that throne but sin has pushed God off and taken over.

Can you imagine it? The great God Almighty, Maker of heaven and earth, said, "This is My name throughout all generations, My memorial forever: I AM THAT I AM. I never was created; I was not made, I AM. I made you for My love. I made you to worship, honor and glorify Me. I made you to love you and hold you and give Myself to you. But you turned away from Me. And you made yourself god and you put yourself on that throne." That is sin.

That's why the Scripture says, "Except a man be born again, he cannot see the kingdom of God" (John 3:3). What does "born again" mean? Among other things, it means a renewal, a rebirth, but it also means getting off the throne and putting God on it. It means that the self-existent One is recognized for who He is.

Reverently and humbly, I kneel before His Son, who died and rose and lives and pleads, and I say, "Oh, Lord Jesus, I give up. I'm no longer going to sit on the throne and run my own life. I'm no longer going to trust in my own righteousness, which is only a filthy rag. I'm no longer going to believe in my good works or in my religious activities. I'm going to trust Thee, the God of grace, the God who gave Thy Son to die." And so the new birth takes place and I trust the Lord Jesus Christ, the Man in the glory, my Savior and Lord. And thus I am saved.

Long ago there was one by the name of Lucifer, to whom God gave a position higher than any other creature—at the very throne of God. One day pride took over and he said, "I will arise, I will set my throne above God's throne." And he became proud and God cast him down (see Isaiah 14:12-14).

That's the devil.

And it is the devil who is leading the world now, "the prince of the power of the air, the spirit that now worketh in the children of disobedience" (Ephesians 2:2), right out there among the leaders of society, our politicians, our literary men and all the rest. This is true not only in North America, but all over the world from the day Adam sinned. We're guilty of offending His majesty, of insulting the Royalty that sits upon the eternal, uncreated throne. We're guilty of sacrilegious rebellion.

It isn't as if you're doing Jesus Christ a favor by coming forward and signing a card with a big grin. It's a matter of realizing that you've been occupying a stolen throne—one that belongs to Jesus Christ, the Son of the Father. You've been saying, "I AM THAT I AM," in capital letters, when you should say meekly and reverently, "O God, I am because Thou art." That's what the new birth means. It means repentance and faith.

So what is God like? God is not like anything you know, in that God is self-existent and nothing else is.

Before the hills in order stood,
Or earth received her frame,

From everlasting Thou art God,
　　To endless years the same.[2]

When heaven and earth were yet unmade,
　　When time was yet unknown,
Thou in Thy bliss and majesty
　　Didst live and love alone!
Thou wert not born; there was no fount
　　From which thy being flowed;
There is no end which Thou canst reach:
　　But Thou art simply God.[3]

Our Father in heaven, Thou art God and Thy name is I AM THAT I AM forever. In Thy lovingkindness Thou hast created me, but I have sinned. "All we like sheep have gone astray"—that's the essence of sin. We have all turned to our own way, and our own way will end in hell. And our Lord said, "If any man follow Me, let him deny himself." Father, I recognize Thy right to run my business, Thy right to run my home, Thy right to guide my life, Thy right to be all in all to me. "Not I, but Christ be honored, loved, exalted; Not I, but Christ be seen, be heard, be known." Not I, but Christ.

Chapter 2

God's Transcendence

Thine, O LORD, is the greatness, and the power, and the glory, and the victory, and the majesty: for all that is in the heaven and in the earth is thine; thine is the kingdom, O LORD, and thou art exalted as head above all. (1 Chronicles 29:11)

Canst thou by searching find out God? canst thou find out the Almighty unto perfection? It is as high as heaven; what canst thou do? deeper than hell; what canst thou know? (Job 11:7-8)

Lo, these are parts of his ways: but how little a portion is heard of him? but the thunder of his power who can understand? (Job 26:14)

Great is the LORD, and greatly to be praised; and his greatness is unsearchable. (Psalm 145:3)

For my thoughts are not your thoughts, neither are your ways my ways, saith the LORD. For as the heavens are higher than the earth, so are my ways higher than your ways, and my thoughts than your thoughts. (Isaiah 55:8-9)

Who only hath immortality, dwelling in the light which no man can approach unto; whom no man hath seen, nor can see: to whom be honour and power everlasting. Amen. (1 Timothy 6:16)

The term *divine transcendence* may sound like something that takes a lot of learning or at least a lot of profound thinking to understand, but it doesn't. *Transcend* simply means to go above, to rise above, to be above. Of course, it's very difficult to think of God as *transcendent* and also as *immanent* or *omnipresent* at the same time. It is difficult to understand how He can be here with us, in us, pervading all things, but at the same time transcending all things. It looks like a contradiction, but as with many other apparent contradictions, it's not at all contradictory; the two thoughts are entirely in accord with each other.

God is always nearer than you may imagine Him to be. God is so near that your thoughts are not as near as God; your breath is not as near as God; your very soul is not as near to you as God is. And yet because He is God, His uncreated Being is so far above us that no thought can conceive it nor words express it.

I want to make it very clear that when I say "far above," I do not mean geographically or astronomically removed. It's an analogy. Because we are human beings and live in this world, we learn to speak by analogy.

Almost everything we say is by analogy. Everybody's a poet and doesn't know it, as the saying goes. A poet is someone who speaks by analogies, who sees eternity in an hour and the world in a grain of sand. You and I are always thinking and speaking in analogies. When we say that a man is straight, we are comparing the man with a ruler. When we say that the ruler is a foot long, we are comparing it with a man's foot.

We say a man is "off base"—that's from baseball. We say that he's "going down for the count"—that's from boxing. We say he "put all his cards on the table"—that's from gambling. Almost everything we say is an analogy taken from the world around us. Every phase of life gives us tools to think with.

So when we say that God is far above, we're using an analogy. We're thinking about a star that's way above, way out yonder in space—but that isn't what we really mean when we think about the transcendent God.

If you miss this point, you might as well stop reading, because this is critical to understanding what follows. When we say that God's transcendence is "farness above," we are not thinking about astronomical distances or physical magnitude. God never thinks about the *size* of anything, because God *contains* everything. He never thinks about *distance,* because God is *everywhere;* He doesn't have to go from one place to another, so distance doesn't mean anything to Him. We humans use these expressions to help us to think—they're analogies and illustrations.

Imagine, if you will, a child that gets lost in the mountains. The family is out having a picnic and the little one wanders off and disappears. So they send out search parties and bloodhounds—everything they can to find that little child. She's only a little tyke, maybe two years old. She hasn't been in the world long and doesn't know much; she hasn't much size. She may be, if she's good and plump, forty pounds in weight. As far as this world is concerned, she could disappear from it and the world would never know that she'd gone—except for a few bleeding hearts back home.

So there she is, lost on a mountain. Now that mountain weighs millions, perhaps billions, of tons. And there are ores and minerals in it worth thousands of dollars. There's timber on it and animals roaming it. It's a beautiful, vast and mighty thing—so mighty that we stand in front of the mountain as the Jews did and find a whole Sinai. We're stunned by the immensity of it.

And yet, one little two-year-old girl, weighing thirty-five or forty pounds, is of more value than that mountain. The mountain has size, but that's all it has. It can't say "Mommy" or "Daddy" or "Now I lay me down to sleep." It can't kiss you or throw its chubby arms around your neck. It can't pray, it can't laugh and it can't jump for joy. And it can't sleep relaxed and limp in its little bed at night. It lacks all that God values.

The mountain has stability, strength, weight,

mass, size, form, shape and color. But it doesn't have a heart. And when God thinks about people, He thinks about hearts, not sizes. So we talk about God being high and lifted up, elevated, lofty and transcendent. We think not about distance for that doesn't matter. It's quality of being that matters. It's what makes the child valuable and the mountain not. The mountain has being, but not a high, transcendent quality of being. A little child has less being but it has quality of being infinitely higher.

You may find this hard to believe, but God is just as far above an archangel as he is above a caterpillar. You know what a caterpillar is—it's a little worm the size of your finger, with a fur coat. And of course, it's not a very high-class thing. It's never been out in society. It doesn't amount to much—it's just a worm. And you have to watch it very carefully to know whether it's traveling west or east, because it looks the same all the way around. That's a caterpillar.

An archangel, on the other hand, is that holy creature that we see beside the sea of God, in the presence of God's throne. That mighty creature is a little higher than the angels, just as man was made for a time a little lower. That being can look upon the face of God with unveiled countenance. This is the archangel. It never was in sin, and no one knows how vast it might be. And yet God is just as far above that archangel as He is above the caterpillar.

Why? Because both the archangel and the caterpillar are creatures. And God is the uncreated One who had no beginning, the self-existent One who was never created, but who was simply God, who made all things. The archangel is a creature; God had to put it together, God had to speak and say, "Be," and it became what it is—a creature. It isn't God and never can become God, and God never can become it.

There is a vast gulf, an all but infinite gulf, fixed between that which is God and that which is not God—between the great I AM and all created things, from the archangel down to the tiniest virus that cannot be seen with the naked eye. God made all that and is just as high above one as the other. God's uncreated quality of life causes Him to be transcendent, to rise high above all creatures.

We have to be careful not to think of life in evolutionary terms—and even Christians are guilty of this at times. We think life begins with a cell, then becomes a fish, then a bird, then a beast, then a man, then an angel, then an archangel, a cherub, a seraph and then God. That simply puts God on the top heap of a pyramid of creatures—and *God isn't a creature*. God is just as high above the seraph as He is above the cell, because God is God. God is of a substance wholly unique.

But how can I go on—how can any man go on? How can I speak of that which escapes all human speech? How can I think about that which is above all thought? And how can I talk when silence would become me better? Saint Augustine said, "O God, when I would speak of Thee I can't, and yet if I did not, somebody must speak." And so he burst out and spoke.

I wonder if some holy creature, who has spent centuries looking upon the holy face of God, ever listens to our speech—our vain and idle words, the chatter of earth's busy tribes of men and the meaningless talk of the pulpits. How strange and how welcome such talk as this would be, though it would have no more relation to the high truth of it all than a two-year-old child playing a violin would have relation to fine music. And yet any father would smile if, in obedience to his suggestion, his little one took up the violin and tried to play. Any father who's away from home knows what it is to get a letter written in block letters by a child in school—misspelled and run down the edge and all the rest—but it's a letter from home, from the little one that he loves very much.

I suppose that this message about God's transcendence is far from being all that it ought to be or could be. And yet I think God is pleased because, compared with all the chatter of the world, it is at least an effort to talk about the great and Holy One, high and lifted up.

I wonder if some holy one, some watcher who had spent centuries by the throne of God, if he came to earth and stepped into one of our pulpits, if he would be allowed to speak. I suppose that if he spoke here, he would say very little of what we usually hear. I suppose that he would charm our ears and fascinate our minds and cheer our hearts by his talk about God—the great God, the rapturous God, the One that gave His Son to die for us, the One in whose presence we expect to live while the ages roll.

And I suppose that after we heard such a being speak about such a God, we would never consent again to hear a silly, "timely" sermon preached out of *Time* magazine. I imagine we would insist that anyone who dares to take up our time preaching to us should not try to settle the political or economic problems of the world, but would talk about God and God alone.

> We praise Thee, O God: we acknowledge Thee to be the Lord.
> All the earth doth worship Thee, the Father everlasting.
> To thee all angels cry aloud: the heavens and all the powers therein.
> To Thee cherubim and seraphim continually do cry, Holy, Holy, Holy: Lord God of Sabaoth;
> Heaven and earth are full of the majesty of Thy glory.
> The glorious company of the apostles praise Thee.
> The goodly fellowship of the prophets praise Thee.
> The noble army of martyrs praise Thee.
> The holy Church throughout all the world doth acknowledge Thee;
> The Father of an infinite majesty;
> Thine honorable, true, and only Son;
> Also the Holy Ghost: the Comforter.[1]

Thus sang our fathers in what is known as the *Te Deum*. We've forgotten it now, because we're not spiritually capable of understanding it. We want to hear talk that will tickle our ears.

Now the holy man of God said, "Lo, these are parts of his ways: but how little a portion is heard of him?" (Job 26:14). All that we can think or say is rational. But God rises above rationality. He rises as high above the rational as He does above the physical. God is of an essence and substance the like of which nothing else exists in the universe. He is above it all—and yet we can know a little portion of God's ways. When I preach on the being of God, the attributes of God, when I talk about what God is like, and what kind of God He is, I approach it respectfully, from afar. I point with a reverent finger to the tall mountain peak which is God, which rises infinitely above my power to comprehend. But that is only a little portion. The paths of His ways cannot be known; the rest is super-rational.

I believe that we ought to get spiritual mysticism back into the church again. I believe that we ought to come back to the effort to walk and talk with God, to live in the presence of God. We have full-gospel Christianity down until its been programmed. Gifted and talented people and men with personality have taken over the holy place, and we've forgotten that we are here to worship God. God is the source and center and foundation of all. As the hymn says,

How shall polluted mortals dare
To sing Thy glory or Thy grace?
Beneath Thy feet we lie afar,
And see but shadows of Thy face.[2]

And even in our church services we can see only the shadows of God's face. For God transcends and rises so high above it all that the very angels in heaven veil their faces. And the living creatures cover their faces and cry, "Holy, holy, holy [is the] Lord God Almighty" (Isaiah 6:2-3; Revelation 4:8).

How terrible it is that, in the presence of this awesome, awful God, some people are untouched by it all! How frightful, how awesome, how awful it is! We don't want to hear about God. We want to hear about something that can tickle our fancy, that can satisfy our morbid curiosity or our longing after romance. But the great God is there and we're going to have to face Him now or face Him then.

This mighty God, like a great burning universe, will burst upon us someday, breaking down our defenses and destroying everything we've put up around ourselves, and we'll have to deal with Him. And yet the average man isn't worried about it at all. He sleeps well at night and thinks of his job and does it by day. He eats, sleeps, lives, breeds, gets old and dies, never having given a good, high thought about the great God who transcends all.

This is the God about whom it is said, "Thine, O LORD, is the greatness, and the power, and the glory, and the victory, and the majesty: for all that is in the heaven and in the earth is thine; thine is the kingdom, O LORD, and thou art exalted as head above all" (1 Chronicles 29:11). And yet we care so very, very little about Him. How tragic it is that men will follow their lusts and pride, living for money, business, appetite and ambition!

No additional proof needs to be given for the spiritual death that lies in the hearts of men. "She that liveth in pleasure is dead," says the Scripture, "while she liveth" (1 Timothy 5:6). And he that liveth in ambition, lust, appetite and pride, who lives for money and fame, is dead also. Though he may be young, trim and athletic, intelligent and well-to-do, he is still dead—and rotting in his death. He is like a blind man who cannot see the sun rise, because the great God rises above the horizon of his understanding and he doesn't know the sun has come up. And like a worm in a cave or a toad under a rock, he lives out his life and forgets that he's got to deal with God someday—the great God Almighty!

I live for that day, when God will crash in upon me, past my human understandings and every defense I might have put up. That can also happen right now, in this world. That's partly what conversion is—to be saved, to repent, to be forgiven of your sin, to see a vision of God in your heart, to see Jesus Christ on His cross and on His throne, to be brought into the presence of this holy God.

You can go through the whole routine of the church and never have an experience at all like this. You can learn to say, "God is love" when you're a wee little thing; you can get a Bible for passing from one grade to another; you can get big enough to make a speech in a Sunday school program; you can get old enough to sing in the choir, join the church and be baptized. You can teach a class, entertain missionaries and learn to tithe, giving of your money to the work of the Lord. You can be faithful and yet never have an experience of the great God breaking in upon your consciousness, but living always once removed from God.

In the Old Testament, when Absolom returned from exile, he went for two full years without ever seeing the king's face (2 Samuel 14:28). And that's what happens in the churches. But when God becomes real to us, we are affected; we are touched by what is called the *mysterium tremendum*—a tremendous mystery—that is, God.

I just read this week that somebody said, "I never read Tozer. He's too negative." Well, my brother, before there can be any healing there has to be diagnosis. When you go to see a doctor, he can't just smile and look up from his coffee break and say, "Take pill number nine." Maybe you don't need pill number nine; maybe that'll kill you. Maybe what you need is to go under the knife.

You have to have diagnosis, though sometimes I think diagnosis is worse than the disease. I've had more trouble finding out what is wrong with me (and sometimes finding it wasn't) than I've had with the treatment. What I preach may be negative, I don't know. If God—the God who is high and lifted up, whom I can love and worship and in whose presence I can live and pray and be with forever—is negative, give me a whole basketful of negatives!

The Dread of God

One thing that comes to us when we meet God is dread. People don't like that; they don't want to dread anything. They want to go to church to be cheered up—it's one of the silliest things I ever heard in my life! I'd rather preach to twenty-five people upstairs over a barber shop than to a church full of people who give their money and ride me around in a limousine—but don't want me to embarrass them by talking about God.

Concerning the dread of God, remember that Jacob said, "How dreadful is this place!" (Genesis 28:17). And Peter said, "Depart from me; for I am a sinful man, O Lord" (Luke 5:8). Down through the years, wherever a man looked upon God, even dimly and briefly, it affected him terribly. And the dread I'm talking about is not physical danger.

When you meet God, you get over the dangers and fears of this world. But the fear, the dread that is God, is not a sense of danger. It's a sense of being in the presence of someone very awful, very wonderful, transcendent and highly lifted up. It's a sense of creature consciousness. This was what Abraham expressed when he said, "Behold now, I have taken upon me to speak unto the Lord, which am but dust and ashes" (Genesis 18:27).

If Abraham were in some of our gospel churches and heard somebody lead in prayer, he undoubtedly would be shocked at what he heard. He wasn't as fluent as we are. Sometimes I think our very fluency is from education, not from being near to God. We're just repeating what we've learned. We criticize Roman Catholics for reading out of prayer books, but at least what they read is good English; it is fluent and beautiful. We pray prayers that are just as embalmed as those prayers are, only we make them up as we go along.

Those prayers are just as dead because there is no sense of creature consciousness. There's no feeling that I'm in the presence of this great God before whom angels fold their wings and shut up their mouths, only to open them again and cry, "Holy, holy, holy." That sense of creature consciousness, that sense of abasement, of being overwhelmed in the presence of that which is above all creatures— we ought to return to that again. I'd rather have a church of twenty-five people like that than twenty-five hundred that are simply there as religious socialites, meeting socially in the name of the Lord.

They tell me that Martin Lloyd-Jones, one of the greatest English preachers of them all, once in a while travels all the way to Wales and gathers with twelve or fifteen people. There he recharges his batteries before he goes back to his great London pulpit where he preaches to fifteen hundred or more people. But he wants to go up there. And he says, "After I have been with those simple-hearted worshipers for a little while, I'm a better man. And I come back to London better prepared to preach." I believe that this is what we need in this hour.

Another thing that comes to us when we meet God is a feeling of awful ignorance. There is a certain cult abroad (I'm not going to mention the name because I don't want to advertise it) that says we can answer any question there is in the Bible. And I have run into a lot of people that feel the same way. I think it was Cicero who said that some men would rather die than seem to be in doubt about anything. But the closer we come to God, the less we know— and the more we know we don't know.

I'm concerned about our flippancy these days. It is a terrible sin in the presence of a holy God. What if you and your friends were in the presence of the Queen of England, and someone started trying to be funny by telling jokes about queens? How shameful, how horrible it would be! No one would do such a thing. And yet, she's only a woman, a human being like you. How much more terrible that we can be so flippant in the presence of the great God, who is Lord of all lords and King of all kings!

We need to recover that feeling of ignorance. We know too much. There should be a speechless humility among us in the presence of the Mystery Inexpressible.

When we meet God we also have a sense of weakness. I don't think you will ever be strong until you know how utterly weak you are. And you will never know how utterly weak you are until you have stood in the presence of that great plentitude of strength, that great fullness of infinite power that we call God. When for an awful, happy, terrible, wonderful moment the eyes of our hearts have gazed upon the transcendent God, high and lifted up with His train filling the temple, then we will know how weak we are.

God never works out of human strength. The strongest man is the weakest man in the kingdom of God, and the weakest the strongest. The holy apostle said, "when I am weak, then am I strong" (2 Corinthians 12:10). You can turn it around and say, "When I am strong—whenever I feel that I can do it—then am I weak."

I've been preaching since I was nineteen years old and now I'm sixty-three. And yet, after all these years of preaching, I come into the pulpit shaking inside—not because I fear the people, but because I fear God. It's the fear and trembling of knowing that I stand to speak of God and if I don't speak rightly about God, what a terrible error it will be. If I speak evilly of God, what a frightful crime! It is only when I speak well of God that I dare sleep at night without asking forgiveness.

Weakness was what Daniel felt after he had been talked to by God: "I set my face toward the ground, and I became dumb. . . . there remained no strength in me, neither is there breath left in me" (Daniel 10:15, 17). That's the effect: self-depreciation and a sense of impurity. Isaiah said, "Woe is me! for I am undone; because I am a man of unclean lips" (Isaiah 6:5). It is a feeling of absolute profaneness.

You may say, "Must I live all of my life in a state of dread, of ignorance, of weakness, of impurity?" No. But you must arrive at that conviction about yourself and not just be told that by someone else. I grew up being taught that I was born in sin. They said, "There is none righteous, no, not one" (Romans 3:10); "all our righteousnesses are as filthy rags" (Isaiah 64:6). I believed it and when I began to preach, I told other people, "Your righteousnesses are filthy rags." But I thought their filthy rags were filthier than mine, that their sins were worse than mine!

You can be as orthodox as John Calvin and believe in total depravity as much as any Baptist and still be proud and selfrighteous. If you had asked a Pharisee, "Are all men sinners?" they would have said, "Yes—except for us!" And they looked down upon the publican and the harlot. But Jesus looked down upon the Pharisee, for He knew that they were just as sinful. The Pharisee, who to his knowledge had never broken the law, was just as sinful as the harlot who had broken it every night.

And yet, is there anyone who has never broken the law? No, I didn't say that. I said that the Pharisee may have never *consciously* broken the law. If you strike a compromise with your own conscience, you can learn to look at yourself in the glass and see something better than is there.

Old wise Aesop, who wrote so many great fables, told of a man who was walking with two bags tied together and thrown across his shoulder, one across his front and the other across his back. Those who met him asked, "What is in those bags?"

"Well," he said, "in the rear bag are my faults, and in the front bag are my neighbors' faults." He had his neighbors' faults out in front of him, where he could see them, but his own behind his back, where he couldn't see them.

This is how we live. But once we have been brought into the presence of God in true repentance, we will never again think of ourselves as good. We will never again think of ourselves as pure. We can only say, "Lord, Thou knowest"— that's all. And when God says to us, "Son, are you pure?" we can only say, ". . . the blood of Jesus Christ his Son cleanseth us from all sin" (1 John

1:7). We trust in what God said though we feel as if we were the worst of all men.

Saint Theresa, that dear woman of God, said that the closer we are to God, the more conscious we are of how bad we are. Oh, the paradox, the mystery, the wonder of knowing that God, that transcendent One who is so high above all others that there is a gulf fixed that no one can cross, condescends to come and dwell among us. The God who is on the other side of that vast gap one day came and condensed Himself into the womb of the virgin, was born and walked among us. The baby that tramped around on the floor of Joseph's carpenter shop, that got in the way and played with the shavings, was the great God so infinitely lifted up and so transcendent that the archangels gazed upon Him. There He was!

I remember hearing a song many, many years ago that is antiphonal [sung responsively between two groups of singers]. One man, who represents the sinner, sings,

> Which way shall I take, shouts the voice on the
>   night,
> I'm a pilgrim awearied and faint is my light.
> I seek for a palace that shines on the hill,
> But between us a stream lieth solemn and chill.

He goes on to ask, "How shall I bridge the gulf between me and the palace that I seek, knowing that I am so weak and He is so strong, I'm so bad and He is so good, I'm so ignorant and He is so wise? How can I bridge the gulf?" And then the other man speaks up and sings back,

> Near, near thee, my son, is the old wayside cross,
> Like a grey friar cowled and likened in moss.
> And its cross beams will point to the far distant
> strand That bridges the water so safely for man.

A great gulf lies between me and the transcendent God, who is so high I cannot think of Him, so lofty that I cannot speak of Him, before whom I must fall down in trembling fear and adoration. I can't climb up to Him; I can't soar in any man-made vehicle to Him. I can't pray my way up to Him. There is only one way: "Near, near thee, my son, is that old wayside cross." And the cross bridges the gulf that separates God from man. That cross!

God is transcendent. You'll never find Him on your own. Muslims can search for Him for a thousand years and not find Him. Hindus can cut themselves and lie on beds of glass and walk through fire and not find Him. Protestants can join churches and lodges and all other things and not find Him. Philosophers can rise on rung after rung of thought and not find Him. Poets can soar away on imagination and not find Him.

Musicians can compose heavenly music. When listening to Bach's Christmas oratorio, I think to myself that such music never was on earth. And yet we can listen to that and enjoy it until it breaks our heart and not find Him—never, never find Him!

I must needs go home by the way of the cross,
    There's no other way but this;
I shall ne'er get sight of the gates of light,
    If the way of the cross I miss.
The way of the cross leads home.[3]

So I offer you the cross. I offer you first of all that great God:

Lost in Thy greatness, Lord! I live,
    As in some gorgeous maze;
Thy sea of unbegotten light
    Blinds me, and yet I gaze.[4]

I point you to God the Transcendent One! And then I point you to the cross. But you will never know the meaning nor the value of the cross until God the Holy Ghost has done something within you to break you down and destroy your pride, humble your stubbornness, change your mind about your own goodness, blast away your defenses and take away your weapons. He will do what the Quakers call "meek" you—He will cause you to come down, to become meek.

What about you? You may be saved, or half-saved or badly and poorly saved. Perhaps you knew God wanted you but you wandered away; you compromised with your business or your school and now God seems so far away from you.

And He is far away, in one sense, but in another He is as near as your heartbeat, for the cross has bridged the gulf. Let the blood of Jesus cleanse us from all sin. He who is God the Transcendent One says, "Come unto me, all ye that labour and are heavy laden, and I will give you rest. Take my yoke upon you, and learn of me; for I am meek and lowly in heart: and ye shall find rest unto your souls" (Matthew 11:28-29).

Chapter 3

God's Eternalness

For thus saith the high and lofty One that inhabitath eternity, whose name is Holy; I dwell in the high and holy place, with him also that is of a contrite and humble spirit, to revive the spirit of the humble, and to revive the heart of the contrite ones. (Isaiah 57:15)

LORD, thou hast been our dwelling place in all generations. Before the mountains were brought forth, or ever thou hadst formed the earth and the world, even from everlasting to everlasting, thou art God. (Psalm 90:1-2)

I want to talk about something which everyone believes, but often without sufficient clarity and emphasis to make it worth their while. And if we can make the whole church see this truth, and can rouse others to preach about it, it will elevate the spiritual level of the church very markedly. I want to talk about the eternity of God.

In the first Scripture text above, God calls Himself "the high and lofty One that inhabiteth eternity." Eternity, of course, is a noun; it is the state of being eternal. There are those who say that such words in Scripture as "eternity" and "everlasting" do not mean "time without end" or "lasting forever," because God refers to "the everlasting hills" in Genesis 49:26. They say that we have read into these words the concept of everlastingness and endlessness, that it only means "to the end of the dispensation, to the end of the age." (The real reason men have taken that attitude is because the Scriptures say that hell is everlasting—and they can't bring themselves to believe that!)

If I thought that the word "eternal" as referring to God meant only "lasting until the end of the age," I'd just fold my Bible up and go home and wait for the end. If I had a God that only lasted so long, that didn't have eternity in His heart, I couldn't possibly find it worthwhile to preach. Why be a pro tem Christian and have a pro tem God? I believe that God is eternal.

The Old Testament Hebrew has exhausted itself —wrung its language as you wring a towel, to get the last drop of meaning out of it—to say that God is forever and ever endlessly, unto perpetuity, world without end. The New Testament Greek has done the same. There aren't any other words in the Greek language that can be used to mean "unto perpetuity, having no end, going on and on and on and on endlessly and forever." Then we come to the English language, which has the concept of endlessness.

And how could we have a concept of that which doesn't exist, a concept that is greater than the reality? That is plain foolishness, as anyone can see.

So we haven't any other words to use. Eternal, everlasting, forever, unto perpetuity, world without end—all of those words mean just what they say. When God talks about Himself, that's what He means—the High and Lofty One who exists eternally, forever, unto perpetuity, world without end.

And when we come to the second text—"from everlasting to everlasting, thou art God"—the Hebrew lexicon tells us that you could translate it "from the vanishing point to the vanishing point," because that's what it actually means: from the vanishing point of the past to the vanishing point of the future. But whose vanishing point? Not God's, but man's. Man looks back as far as he can, then turns around and looks forward as far as he can, until human thought falls exhausted and human eyes can no longer see—unto perpetuity, unto man's vanishing point, world without end. Other meanings of the word are "concealed" and "out of mind." From the time concealed to the time concealed, Thou art God. From the time out of mind to the time out of mind, Thou art God.

God Is Not Dependent

Shake your head to get all the wheels going and try to stretch your mind all you can, then think, if you can, about the past. Think your hometown out of existence. Think back to when there wasn't anything here but some Indians. Then go back and think all those Indians away, back to before the Indians got here. Go back before that and think away the North American continent. And then think away all this earth of ours. And then let's go back and think that there are no planets and no stars dotting the clear night sky; they have all vanished away and there is no Milky Way, no anything.

Go to the throne of God and think away the angels, the archangels, the seraphim and the cherubim that sing and worship before the throne of God. Think them all away until there is no creation: not an angel waves its wing, not a bird flies in the sky—there's no sky to fly in. Not a tree grows on a mountain, there is no mountain for a tree to grow on. But God lives and loves alone. The Ancient of Days, world without end, to the vanishing point back as far as the human mind can go—there you have God.

The great Augustine said,

What, then, art Thou, O my God—what, I ask, but the Lord God? For who is Lord but the Lord? or who is God save our God? Most high, most excellent, most potent, most omnipotent; most piteous and most just; most hidden and most near; most beauteous and most strong, stable, yet contained of none; unchangeable, yet changing all things; never new, never old; making all things new, yet bringing old age upon the proud and they know it not; always working, yet ever at rest; gathering, yet needing nothing; sustaining, pervading, and protecting;

. . . Yet, O my God, my life, my holy joy, what is this that I have said? And what saith any man when He speaks of Thee? Yet woe to them that keep silence, seeing that even they who say most are as the dumb? . . .

But Thou, O Lord, who ever livest, and in whom nothing dies (since before the world was, and indeed before all that can be called "before," Thou existest, and art the God and Lord of all Thy creatures; and with Thee fixedly abide the causes of all unstable things, the unchanging sources of all things changeable, and the eternal reasons of all things unreasoning and temporal) . . .[1]

God is not dependent upon His world, upon kings and presidents, upon businessmen and preachers, upon boards and deacons. God is not dependent upon anything. We have thought our way back until there's no history—back to God Himself, God the Eternal One.

God Has No Beginning

God never began to be. I want you to kick that word "began" around a little bit in your mind and think about it. "In the beginning God created the heaven and the earth" (Genesis 1:1), but God Himself never began to be! "Began" is a word that doesn't affect God at all. There are many concepts and ideas that don't touch God at all, such as the concept of beginning or creation, when God spoke and things began to be. "In the beginning God created"—but before the beginning, there wasn't any "beginning"; there wasn't any "before"! The old theologians used to say that eternity is a circle. Round and round the circle we go, but back before there was any circle, God was!

God didn't begin to be—God was. God didn't start out from somewhere—God just is. And it's good that we get that in our minds. Time, you see, is a creature word, because it has to do with things that are. It has to do with the angels, with the lake of fire, with the cherubims and all the creatures that are around the throne of God. They began to be; there was a time when there were no angels. Then God said, "Let there be," and the angels began to be.

But there never was a time when God was not! No one said, "Let God be"! Otherwise, the one who said "Let God be" would have to be God. And the one about whom He said "Let him be" wouldn't be God at all, but a secondary "god" who wouldn't be worth our trouble. God, back there in the beginning, created. God was, that's all!

God Is Not in Time

Time cannot apply to God. C. S. Lewis gave us an illustration which I'd like to pass on to you. If you can, think of eternity, of infinitude, as a pure white sheet of paper extending infinitely in all directions. Then think about a man taking a pencil and drawing a line, one inch long, on that infinitely extended sheet of paper. And that little line is time. It begins and it moves an inch and ends. It begins on the

paper and it ends on the paper. So time began in
God and will end in God. And it doesn't affect God
at all. God dwells in an everlasting now.

No age can heap its outward years on Thee:
Dear God! Thou art Thyself Thine own eternity![2]

You and I are creatures of time and change. It is
in "now" and "was" and "will be" and "yesterday"
and "today" and "tomorrow" that we live. That's
why we get nervous breakdowns, because we're always just one jump ahead of the clock. We get up
in the morning, look at the clock and let out a gasp
of dismay. We rush for the bathroom, brush our
teeth, tear downstairs for breakfast, eat a half-
cooked egg and rush out to catch the commuter
bus. That's time, you see—time is after us! But God
Almighty sits in His eternal now. And all the time
that ever was is only a tiny mark upon the infinitely
extended bosom of eternity.

God Has No Past or Future

God has no past! Now I want you to hear that.
And I want you to shake your head hard here, because this is an idea that the old church fathers
knew, but that we, their children, don't seem to care
much about. God has no past. You have a past; it isn't
really very long, although you may wish it wasn't so
long. But God has no past and no future. Why
doesn't God have a past or a future? Because past
and future are creature words, and they have to do

with time. They have to do with the flowing motion of time. But God is not riding on the bosom of time. Time is a little mark across the bosom of eternity. And God sits above time, dwelling in eternity: "from everlasting to everlasting, Thou art God."

It is a wonderful thought that God has already lived all of our tomorrows. God has no yesterdays and no tomorrows. The Scriptures say, "Jesus Christ the same yesterday, and to day, and for ever" (Hebrews 13:8), but it's not His yesterday—it's yours and mine. Jesus Christ the Lord is the One who came out of Bethlehem, out of Judea, whose goings forth have been even from everlasting. He can't have yesterdays and tomorrows, because yesterday is time and tomorrow is time, but God surrounds it all and God has already lived tomorrow. The great God who was present at the beginning when He said, "Let there be" and there was, is also now present at the end, when the worlds are on fire and all creation has dissolved and gone back into chaos— and only God and His redeemed saints remain. Remember that God has already lived our tomorrows.

I wonder if that could be the reason that men can prophesy. The ability to foretell with precision an event that will take place 3,000 years from now— how can that be? It might be that a prophet in the Spirit is up in God, seeing as God sees, "the end from the beginning" (Isaiah 46:10). So God way up there takes the end from the beginning and looks down. And that's where we ought to be—not down here looking up through the clouds, but up looking down.

Sometimes when I go here and there I take a plane. Once you get up in the air, you've got so much sunshine that if you want to read you've got to shut the little curtains to keep the sun off your book. But down below you see a solid carpet of thick clouds and you find it very difficult to understand how anybody can be down there saying, "Oh, what a cloudy, overcast, gloomy day this is!" It isn't cloudy and overcast and gloomy up where you are. You're looking down on it.

So if you insist on being down here looking up, you're always going to have an overcast sky—the devil will see to that! But if you remember that your life is hid with Christ in God then you'll be looking down on it, and not looking up.

The Scripture says in Psalm 90:12 that because God is eternal, we must learn "to number our days, that we may apply our hearts unto wisdom." God is in our today because God was in our yesterday and will be in our tomorrow. God is the One that you can't escape. You can't escape God by denying Him because He will be there anyway. You can't escape Him by redefining Him into something else because He will be there anyway. God is! And because God is, then God is here and God is now. God dwells in an everlasting and eternal now.

When God talked with Abraham, Jacob and Isaiah, He had already lived in the New Jerusalem, because the New Jerusalem is in the heart of God; all the things that will be are in God. God isn't subject to the flow of time.

Christ the eternal Son is timeless. When you

think about Jesus, you have to think twice. You have to think of His humanity and His deity. He said a lot of things that made it sound as if He wasn't God. He said other things that made it sound as if He wasn't human. He said, for instance, "Before Abraham was, I am" (John 8:58). That made it sound as if He antedated creation. Then He said, "I can of mine own self do nothing: as I hear, I judge . . . (5:30), and that made it sound as if He wasn't divine. He said, "my Father is greater than I" (14:28), and that made it sound as if He wasn't God. And He said, "I and my Father are one" (10:30), and that made it sound as if He wasn't human.

But the fact is, He is both. He talked about Himself as divine and as human. And when Jesus talked about Himself as human, He used humble, lowly words. When He talked about Himself as divine, He used words that startled and shook people. He said, speaking about the inspired Scriptures, "Ye have heard that it was said . . . but I say unto you . . ." (Matthew 5:21-22). He could talk like God and then He could talk like man. So we've always got to think about the Son of Man, Jesus Christ the Lord in two ways.

"But when the fulness of the time was come, God sent forth his Son, made of a woman, made under the law," (Galatians 4:4), that He might "deliver them who through fear of death were all their lifetime subject to bondage" (Hebrews 2:15). That means His humanhood.

And then He was "slain from the foundation of the world" (Revelation 13:8). What can that mean?

How could He be slain from the foundation of the world? When God laid the heaven and the earth and caused the grass to be upon the hills and the trees to be upon the mountains, when God made the birds to fly in the air and the fish to swim in the sea, God had already in His heart lived Calvary and the resurrection and the glory and the crown. So He was slain before the foundation of the world.

We pray to God sometimes as though God were panicky, as though God were in as great a distress as we are. And we pull out our watch and look at it. I refuse to wear a wristwatch; it's bad enough to have a watch in my pocket where it's difficult to get to. But if I had to look at the miserable thing all the time and know that time is getting away from me, I think I'd panic. But God never panics, because God never looks at clocks or watches. "The fulness of time" was the time when God had ordered it; when that time came, Mary gave birth to her Boy and He was born and lived and died, "the just for the unjust, that he might bring us to God" (1 Peter 3:18). So the eternal Son has lived through all time. He who was born in Bethlehem's manger did not take His origin in the womb of the virgin. The human Baby did, but the eternal Son did not.

Time Marches On

Now I don't like to be gloomy, but you might as well face the fact that

Time, like an ever-rolling stream,
    Bears all its sons away;

They fly, forgotten, as a dream
   Dies at the opening day.[3]

"Time like an ever-rolling stream" is carrying a
lot of people away. My wife and I were discussing
this some time ago and she said, "It looks as if every
time we get a letter from back home, somebody else
is dead." Well, it's natural; you can expect it, you
know. Everybody has to die. "Time, like an ever-
rolling stream, bears all its sons away."

Out in California I've seen the redwood, or sequoia, tree. And I wanted to know how big around
the thing was. I'm an old farmer and I don't have to
have a measuring tape; I can just pace it off. I
marked where I started in the dirt and then I walked
around that tree, hugging it as tight as I could. And
when I got around I had paced off fifty-one feet.
And I dimly remember enough mathematics to
know that it was seventeen feet thick. Now, that's a
sequoia tree! And it grows up as high as 300 feet—
thirty stories in the air.

How long did it take to grow that big? I don't
know, but the scientists say (I don't quote scientists
too often because they change their minds and leave
a man out on a limb) that some of those sequoia
trees go back as far as Abraham, and even before
Abraham's time. Not the species, but those very
trees. When Abraham left Ur of the Chaldees and
followed the gleam of faith downward to the Negev,
where he finally established his great nation in the
land we now call Palestine, those trees were growing out there in California—standing looking up at

the sun, nourishing themselves by their roots. Those trees were already there.

And when the Greeks took over the world (and not only militarily—they became the great minds of the ages) and were thinking their great thoughts and writing their funny plays, those trees were a little taller and still growing out there. And when Rome took over and became the iron kingdom and brought the world to her feet and the soldiers of Rome went everywhere, conquering and to conquer, the trees out on the California coast were a little bit taller. And when the British people got out of the woods and stopped eating acorns and began to wash behind their ears and clean up and look human, why, the trees were a little taller than they had been before.

And long before William the Conqueror had been across the channel and Columbus went sailing around and discovered a little piece of land and called it America, those trees were out there. And way back when George Washington crossed the Delaware, and long before there was any communism or fascism or Nazism, and long before there were airplanes or any of these modern things, the trees grew out there, looking down upon generation after generation of men.

For generation after generation, looking down from His everlasting now, is the eternal God, watching the little tribes of men live a little while and lie down and die and another generation come.

We Need God

Remember that God is to you a necessity. I preach the gospel of Jesus Christ and say, "Come unto me, all ye that labour and are heavy laden, and I will give you rest" (Matthew 11:28), quoting the lovely words of Jesus that warmed my heart when I was a boy and helped bring me to Him. When I quote those words and when I quote the words of the gospel that "whosoever believeth in him should not perish, but have everlasting life" (John 3:16), I'm doing you a tremendous favor—because you need God!

We are slaves to time; we find our immortality in God and nowhere else. We sing, "O God, our help in ages past"—what ages past? God's ages past? No, God lives in now. Our ages past—the brief race of men. "Our hope for years to come"—and your hope and my hope for years to come. And may this God "be Thou our guide while life shall last and our eternal home."[4] I need somebody to guide me. I can't go it alone. I'm too small and weak and stupid and vulnerable.

Microbes so small I can't see can get in my nose and start down my neck and the next thing you know it's in my lungs and I have pneumonia, and then I'm gone. That's us poor little creatures. Immortality and eternity you'll only find in God—and you'll only find God through Jesus Christ the Lord. I am not pleading the cause of One who failed. I am pleading the cause of One who has conquered absolutely and sits at the right hand of God now in eternity.

One time when I went to the museum, I wandered into the Egyptian room and looked at the mummies there. They'd taken some of them and partly unwrapped them to show them off— old fellows with their teeth fallen out and their chins meeting their noses. There were little babies there and one little chap who was probably seven years old. I looked down at that mummified boy and I began to grieve.

I walked from one crypt to the other looking at these mummified human beings. Some of them had been kings, incidentally, but now they were lying all wrapped up in gunnysacks, so dry that they had to keep the wind off them or they would have blown away. Dust! Dust! Dust! I saw sunken eyes and sunken cheeks and tough leathery arms that had been uncovered for the occasion. There they were— human beings who had lived before England was, before Greece was, before Rome.

I walked around down there till I got gloomy. I'm kind of sensitive and easily affected and I began to get gloomier and gloomier, feeling more miserable all the time. It was past noon and I was hungry and they had a restaurant that was just the next room over from the mummies. But I couldn't have eaten if they'd have given me caviar and hummingbird tongues. I was sick—sick in my heart, sick in my body, sick to think that men made in the image of God had to die and turn to dust.

When I walked out of there and headed home, I was about as gloomy as they come. I had a book of poems with me by an Englishman named Thomas

Campbell, so I read one called "The Last Man." I had just come from looking at dead men, and now I was reading a fanciful story-poem written by a man who believed in Jesus Christ. It was beautifully written, for he was a master craftsman, though not perhaps one of the greatest of the poets.

The poem was a dream or vision he had about seeing the human race down to the last man. There had been pestilences, famines, wars and all sorts of things that whittled the human race down till there was only one man left; everyone else was dead. This man was leaning on his elbow high upon a promontory looking out over the western ocean as the sun was setting. And he knew it would be the last sunset he would ever see, for the rattle of death had already come. And his eyes were getting glazed but he could still think and still talk a little. So as he gazed out at the setting sun, he began to talk to the sun, and he said,

> By Him recalled to breath,
>   Who captive led captivity.
> Who robbed the grave of Victory,
>   And took the sting from Death!

Then after he had reminded himself that there was One who had risen from the dead and had robbed death of its sting and taken away victory from the grave, he spoke to the sun and said,

> Go, Sun, while Mercy holds me up
>   On Nature's awful waste

To drink this last and bitter cup
    Of grief that man shall taste—
Go, tell the night that hides thy face,
Thou saw'st the last of Adam's race,
    On Earth's sepulchral clod,
The darkening universe defy
To quench His Immortality,
Or shake his trust in God!

He was saying, "Sun, when you are old and burned out and have gone to dust I'll still be living. Because I live in Him who captive led captivity and robbed the grave of victory and took the sting from death." Well, you know what that did for me? That lifted me up out of the miry clay and established me (my emotions at least) on the solid rock.

I had just come from seeing kings and queens and little babies and half-grown kids all done up in gunnysacks, all of them 3,000 years old. I thought, *Oh boy, is that where I'm headed?* Then I read this poem and I thank God that my soul was lifted up. I came back home a joyful man, remembering that no matter what you do to the body, no matter how much you wrap it up or embalm it, Jesus Christ recalled back the human breath and took the sting from death and gave victory to man.

You need God, for God is your eternity. You need God, for God is your tomorrow. You need Jesus Christ for Jesus Christ is your tomorrow. He's your guarantee of that which will be. He's your resurrection and your life. And when the sun has burnt itself out and the stars have been folded up like a garment, God will still be, for God dwells in an ever-lasting now that nothing can get to. And He takes His children who believe in His Son into His bosom, into the heart of the everlasting now.

That's why I believe in the communion of saints. I do not believe that one saint that leaves the earth goes anywhere but into the heart and bosom of God to be a timeless, endless, forever saint. And I believe that all these great Hebrew and Greek and English words that apply to God—eternity and forever and unto perpetuity and world without end—will apply to every man and woman who is in the bosom of God. I'll settle for that—won't you?

If somebody came along to me and said, "We're going to take you to heaven, but you can only be up there for twenty years," I'd be a miserable man. What's the good of getting used to a place like that and learn-ing to love it and then having to leave it in twenty years? But I accept for my own soul and for the souls of all the Lord's children these wondrous words: eter-nal, everlasting, forever, unto perpetuity, world with-out end. I accept the everlastingness of the saints.

Why can we believe in our own immortality? Be-cause God is eternal. That's basic to the doctrine of immortality. If God were not eternal there could be no immortality and no certain future for anybody. We would only be cosmic dust that somehow or other managed to get shifted into human beings or trees or stars—and then, only to be swept away again and blown into immensity and forgetfulness. But because God is eternal, we have our home in God. We can look forward with calm restfulness to the time that shall be.

Chapter 4

God's Omnipotence

And when Abram was ninety years old and nine, the LORD appeared to Abram, and said unto him, I am the Almighty God. (Genesis 17:1)

But Jesus . . . said unto them . . . with God all things are possible. (Matthew 19:26)

For with God nothing shall be impossible. (Luke 1:37)

And I heard as it were the voice of a great multitude, and as the voice of many waters, and as the voice of mighty thunderings, saying, Alleluia: for the Lord God omnipotent reigneth. (Revelation 19:6)

Out of a shining jewel case of luminous texts on the omnipotence of God—and there are many—I have chosen four. To Abraham (then called Abram) God said, "I am the Almighty God." Our Lord Jesus said, positively, "with God all things are possible." And the angel who appeared to Mary turned it around and said it negatively: "With God nothing shall be impossible." Finally, we hear the voice of the great multitude: "Alleluia: for the Lord God omnipotent reigneth."

I suppose the first thing to do would be to define omnipotence. It comes, of course, from *omni,* meaning "all," and *potent,* meaning "able to do and to have power." And so *omnipotent* means "able to do all and to have all power." It means having all the potency there is.

Then we come to a second word, *Almighty,* which is also in one of these Scripture passages. Now that means exactly the same thing as *omnipotent,* only it is from the Anglo-Saxon, while *omnipotent* is from the Latin. In the Bible, the word *Almighty* is used fifty-six times and is never used about anyone else but God. In our English Bible the word omnipotent is only used once and it refers to God. And there's a reason for this. *Almighty* means "having an infinite and absolute plenitude of power." When you use the words *infinite* and *absolute* you can only be talking about one person—God.

There is only one infinite Being, because infinite means without limit. And it is impossible that there should be two beings in the universe without limit. So if there is only one, you are referring to God. Even philosophy and human reason, as little as I think of them, have to admit this.

I read a review of a book of mine the other day, written by a doctor of philosophy; he was in favor of it, but not wholly so. He said that I was against scholarship, which I am not; I am just against big windbags, that's all. I am against fellows whose heads are inflated. I'm not against a real scholar such as Augustine or Paul or Luther or Wesley. But I'm against men who think they're scholars. But even reason has to kneel down and declare that God is omnipotent.

If you think you don't know a thing except by reason, you don't have knowledge. If you have knowledge by revelation— "holy men of God spake as they were moved by the Holy Ghost" (2 Peter 1:21)—then you have it. But once you have it by revelation then reason sometimes is forced to kneel down and say "the Lord God omnipotent reigneth," and admit that it's true. So I give you three propositions briefly here:

1. God Has Power

Proposition #1 is that God has power. Of course everybody knows that. David said, "God hath spoken once; twice have I heard this; that power belongeth unto God" (Psalm 62:11). And the man Paul, one of the greatest intellects that the world ever knew, said this: "For the invisible things of him [God] from the creation of the world are clearly seen, being understood by the things that are made, even his eternal power and Godhead" (Romans 1:20). You look up at the starry heavens above and see the eternal power of God there. God's power and Godhead are found there.

We used to sing a song which they still sing in some places:

The spacious firmament on high,
    With all the blue ethereal sky,
And spangled heavens, a shining frame,
    Their great Original proclaim.
Th' unwearied sun, from day to day,
    Does his Creator's power display,
And publishes to every land
    The work of an almighty hand.
Soon as the evening shades prevail,
    The moon takes up the wondrous tale,
And nightly to the listening earth
    Repeats the story of her birth:
Whilst all the stars that round her burn,
    And all the planets in their turn,
Confirm the tidings as they roll,
    And spread the truth from pole to pole.

In reason's ear they all rejoice,
    And utter forth a glorious voice;
Forever singing, as they shine,
    "The hand that made us is divine."[1]

God has power and whatever God has is without limit; therefore, God is omnipotent. God is absolute and whatever touches God or whatever God touches is absolute; therefore, God's power is infinite; God is Almighty.

2. God Is the Source of All Power

Proposition #2 is that God is the source of all the power there is. There isn't any power anywhere that doesn't have God as its source, whether it be the power of the intellect, of the spirit, of the soul, of dynamite, of the storm or of magnetic attraction. Wherever there is any power at all, God is the author of it. And the source of anything has to be greater than that which flows out of it.

If you pour a quart of milk out of a can, that can has to be equal to or greater than a quart. The can has to be as big as or bigger than that which comes out of it. The can may contain several gallons, though you may pour out only a quart. The source has to be as big or bigger than that which comes out of it. So if all the power there is came from God— *all* the power— therefore, God's power must be equal to or greater than all the power there is.

3. God Gives Power, but Still Retains It

Proposition #3 is that God delegates power to His creation, but He never relinquishes anything of His essential perfection. God gives power, but He doesn't give it away. When God gives power to an archangel, He still retains that power. When God the Father gives power to the Son, He keeps that power. When God pours power upon a man, He still keeps that power. God can't give anything of Himself away. God can't relinquish any of His power, because if He did, He would be less powerful than He was before. And if He were less powerful than He was before, He would not be perfect, for perfection means that He has all power. God can't "give away" His power.

A battery has only so much power in it and if that is slowly given away, the battery gets weaker and weaker. You've found that out on a cold morning sometimes, when you go out to the car, turn the key and there's a discouraged moan, but the thing won't turn over. You trusted your battery and your battery failed you. It used up its power. It has given it away, so that little by little it has become less than it was before. But when God gives power—to angels, archangels, redeemed men, mountains, seas, stars and planets—He doesn't relinquish anything. He does not become less than He was before; God's batteries do not run down.

Everything comes out from God and returns to God again. The great God Almighty, the Lord God omnipotent, reigneth. He has now the same amount of power that He had when He made the heaven and the earth and called the stars into being. He will never have any less power than He has now, nor will He ever have any more since He has all the power there is. That is the God we serve!

Therefore I cannot for the life of me see any reason in the world why anyone should be fearful and timid, saying, "I'm afraid I can't make it; I'm afraid God can't keep me." God can keep the stars in their courses and the planets in their orbits; God can keep all His vast display of might everywhere throughout His universe. Surely God can keep you!

It's like a fly perched on a seat in an airplane, moaning and trembling for fear that the plane can't carry its weight. That plane weighs several tons and it has several tons of people and baggage on it. That fly is so light that it's impossible, outside of a laboratory, to even weigh the little guy. And yet we can imagine him sitting there, flapping his little wings and saying, "I'm just afraid this plane won't hold me up!"

The great God Almighty stretches forth His broad wings and moves upon the wind. God will hold you up. He'll keep you if you turn yourself over to Him! He'll hold you when nothing else can; nothing will be able to destroy you.

God contains, perpetuates and sustains all things. He is "upholding all things by the word of his power" (Hebrews 1:3). It is God that holds all things together. Do you ever wonder why you don't cave in from fourteen pounds of air pressure on every square inch of your body? Have you ever wondered why you don't blow up from internal pressure? Because the great God Almighty has spoken His power into His universe and everything runs according to that power.

You may be thinking, "It's all well and good to say that God has all the power in the universe, but what about the laws of nature?" Well, let's look at that phrase, "the laws of nature." What is a law, anyway? The word has at least two meanings.

The first meaning is "an external rule imposed by an authority." If you don't think so, try parking by a fire hydrant sometime and go whistling off to do your business. When you come back, you'll go whistling off to pick up your car at the impound lot. It's a law imposed by an authority, the same as the laws against murder, assault and robbery. I wonder what they do with all the laws they crank out in our legislatures? Thank God we don't know even one-tenth of them or we would die worrying about it. Anyway, those are laws imposed by an authority from the outside. You either do it or else. And the "or else" part is a fine or jail time or something else. That's one kind of law.

Then there's another way the word law is used: by scientists, philosophers and the general public, but it's not properly a law. It's the path God's power and wisdom take through creation. That's what we call the laws of nature. It's the way things are. An eagle lays an egg and it hatches into an eagle instead of a mud turtle or a frog. We call that a law of nature, but nobody passed that law in any parliament or congress. It's just the way it is. It's phenomenon rather than law. It's just the way God's power runs through His creation. God moves through His universe, a free God moving through His creation, and the path He takes we call "the laws of nature." That's the way God works! Scientists study these phenomena and all science is based upon them, of course.

There are two things all scientists know, and one is the uniformity of these phenomena. They never change from year to year, century to century, millennium to millennium; they're always the same. God always acts the same way all the time. And that's one reason I can sleep at night: I serve a God who is always the same and acts according to Himself with uniformity, always. He takes the same path through the universe at all times. The resultant ability to predict that path is what scientists call the laws of nature. It is why we can have such things as navigation and engineering.

I heard of a sailor that was put in charge of steering the ship and was told by the navigator, "Now you keep that star yonder just a little off the port bow."

A couple of hours later, the officer came back and discovered that they were way off course, so he said to the sailor, "I told you to keep the star off the port bow!" And he responded, "Oh, we passed that star a long time ago."

Of course, this story is funny only because the navigator can depend on the star staying in a fixed point in space. The acts of God are uniform. Suppose that God were whimsical and the sun came up in the east on Wednesday, but on Thursday morning it came up in the south and on Saturday in the north. We would say, "What's happened to the world? Has the world gone drunk? The sun is rising and setting opposite to what it usually does!" But you don't need to worry about that. God doesn't work that way.

The great God who made heaven and earth works according to uniform "laws" or phenomena. He always takes the same path through His universe. You can always predict where God will be and always know how it is with God. That's why the Word of God stands secure. When you meet certain conditions, you can always be sure that there will be certain results because God is always taking that path through His Bible, always going by the same road through the Scriptures—always! God never backtracks or detours, but always goes the same way all the time.

When God makes a promise, God keeps that promise. If the promise is over here and you're over there, it will be a dead promise, but if you come over to where it is, it will be a live promise. If God makes a promise and puts conditions on it, and you don't meet the conditions but plead the promise, nothing will happen. You can pray for a lifetime and nothing will happen. But if you meet the conditions and go where God is, you'll find God right there all the time. That's the way it works! That's why you can have faith in God and know, absolutely, that God is there.

Engineering, astronomy, chemistry, navigation and all other fields of study are possible only because the "laws of nature"— the phenomena—are always predictable and uniform. One kind of scientist studies these phenomena and calls it "pure" science. He doesn't care what you do with the phenomena once he discovers them. Then along comes the applied scientist, who takes the work of the pure scientist and applies it to make a bomb to blow up a city or an engine to run a ship. It doesn't make any difference to the pure scientist—that is, objectively he should not care. He's simply finding out where God moves through His universe. He may not always call it God—I suppose usually he doesn't. But we who are God's children say, "That's the way God works. That's the way He does things in His universe."

Religion goes beyond science, further in and further on, and says, "I'm not stopping with the 'laws of nature,' the path of God through His material universe. I'm going back to God Himself—back to the source of it all, the cause of it all, to the master of these phenomena." And so Christ by the Holy Ghost takes us back.

Powerful, Yet Personal

We need to remember, of course, that when we think of that vast *mysterium tremendium,* that mysterious wonder that fills this universe, and all the other big words that philosophers use to describe God Almighty, He is the same God who called Himself "I AM THAT I AM" (Exodus 3:14). And His Son taught us to call Him "Our Father which art in heaven" (Luke 11:2). A king sits on a throne, inhabits a palace, wears a crown and a robe, and they call him "your majesty." But when his little children see him, they run to him and yell, "Daddy!"

I remember when the present Queen Elizabeth was growing up. I've followed her life since she was a wee little tot. One time when she was walking about the palace with her dignified but kindly old grandfather, George V, the old king left the door open. Little Elizabeth turned to him and said, "Grandpa, go close that door." And the great king of England went and closed the door at the voice of a little girl! He couldn't pull any of that "your majesty" business on little Elizabeth. She was just his granddaughter.

And so, no matter what awful terms the philosophers want to apply to the power that rules this universe, you and I can say, "Our Father which art in heaven, hallowed be Thy name" (11:2). We can get intimate with God, and God loves it.

The old dignified king smiled and closed the door. God Almighty is like that. He loves to have His people know that in spite of His greatness, His omnipotence and His power, He still said, "When ye pray, say, Our Father which art in heaven" (11:2). He's a Father to the fatherless, a Husband to the widow; He knows all our troubles. This great and mighty God who fills heaven and earth will "make all [our] bed in [our] sickness" (Psalm 41:3). Who is it that makes the bed, smooths the sheet, turns the pillow to keep it cool and gives you life when you're sick? It's God who does it, if you only knew it. He is the God who told us to call Him "our Father." And God joyfully calls Himself this.

God set the moon up there and set the sun down yonder. In between the two He made the earth and spangled the heavens with the stars. God made all this. But we go back, behind the "laws of nature," behind science, behind matter, back to God Himself. Christianity calls you to the knowledge of this God Himself. "And this is life eternal, that they might know thee the only true God, and Jesus Christ, whom thou hast sent" (John 17:3). You can know God Himself! Salvation means the knowledge of God Himself.

I happen to be a lover of Beethoven. I don't know Beethoven, but I know Beethoven's works somewhat. It would have been much better, I suppose, to know the man himself. They say he was a pretty tough customer, but he was a genius, towering above the geniuses of generations. It would have been wonderful to know him. I just listened today while we had our dinner to a sonata by Beethoven and it was beautiful. But I suppose it would have been more wonderful if I could have shaken hands with the great Beethoven and said, "It's an honor to shake your hand, sir. I consider you one of the greatest composers that ever lived—a genius!" He'd have shaken his great head and walked away. But I would have told my children and grandchildren that I shook hands with Beethoven. It would have been wonderful.

And so with Michaelangelo, the greatest artist of his day. If only I could have shaken hands with him, eaten with him and talked with him! Perhaps he would have called me by my first name and I could have called him by his first name. I would introduce him to my friends and say, "I'd like to have you meet the great Michaelangelo." That would have been better than knowing his works. I have seen his tremendous sculpture of Moses, but it would have been better if I could have seen the man himself.

So let men turn their telescopes on the heavens and their microscopes on the molecules. Let them probe and search and tabulate and name and find and discover. I can dare to say to them, "I know the One who made all this. I'm personally acquainted with the One who made it."

They may respond, "But what about the Milky Way galaxy— don't you know what it is?" Yes, I know what it is—it's great clusters of stars so far away that all you can see is a blur, like looking at the lights of a city a long way off. I know the One who put the Milky Way there! I know the One who put the ocean where it is and said, "Hitherto shalt thou come, but no further" (Job 38:11). The ocean has never dared move out of its banks.

We know God for Himself—God the Father Almighty, Maker of heaven and earth, and Jesus Christ, His only Son our Lord. That's why I can't understand why the gospel churches in our day are such a bunch of playing children. Jesus said to such as we are, "You're like children playing in the marketplace. First you decide to play funeral and you all sit around and cry. We walk by, paying no attention to you, and you don't like it because we don't cry with you. Then you decide to play dance, so you pipe a tune. We're busy and we don't pay any attention to you. Then you get mad because we don't stop and dance. We're grown-ups; we're serious-minded people. We've got things to do and we can't stop to play church or play funeral or play dance with you every time you get a notion." So said Jesus, in effect, to the people of his day (see Matthew 11:16-17).

The gospel churches over the last fifty years have become progressively worse. More and more, like children in the marketplace, they want to dance one day, play funeral another day and play church the next. I refuse to play church. I believe in the great God Almighty who made the universe, who has called me and whom I dare to call my own. He has deigned to say that we are "accepted in the beloved" (Ephesians 1:6). He has stooped to say that we're His children.

They used to say about a certain automobile that

it was "bigger inside than outside." I believe that all of God's children ought to be infinitely bigger inside than outside. I think that you and I ought to live high up yonder. Someone told me the other night after a service that he was on cloud nine. Well, that's where we belong! Our feet ought to be on the earth; we ought to have a good hard core of earthly reality in us. But we shouldn't stay down here and play in the marketplace. We ought to search for the power of God and the cleansing blood of the Lamb—to get to know the great God Almighty.

Is Anything Too Hard for God?

What does it mean to us, that God Almighty has all the power there is? It means that since God has the ability always to do anything He wills to do, then nothing is harder or easier with God. "Hard" and "easy" can't apply to God because God has all the power there is. Hard or easy applies to me. Suppose I have one hundred units of power. You set a task for me that uses twenty-five units and I've got seventy-five left; that's not hard. Set a task for me that uses fifty units and I have fifty left; I can still do it, but I don't like it. Set a task for me that uses seventy-five, and I'm straining. Set a task for me that uses ninety-five and I've only got five units left; I'm ready to go to bed and rest up.

But is God limited to so many units, so that God uses up His power? Did God make the world and then fall exhausted and say, "That took everything out of me"? What kind of silly talk is that, as if anything could take anything out of God? God, who has all the power there is, can make a sun and a star and a galaxy as easily as He can lift a robin off a nest. God can do anything as easily as He can do anything else.

This truth applies specifically to the area of our unbelief. We hesitate to ask God to do "hard" things because we figure that God can't do them. But if they are "easy" things, we ask God to do them. If we have a headache, we say "Oh God, heal my headache." But if we have a heart condition, we don't ask the Lord about that, because that's "too hard" for the Lord! What a shame! Nothing is hard for God—nothing whatsoever. Nothing! In all God's wisdom and power He is able to do anything as easily as He is able to do anything else.

A man told me one time that he had two diseases, one critical, possibly fatal, and the other merely chronic. So he went and was prayed over for healing. And—now this sounds silly and rather humorous, but it actually happened—he said to me, "Do you know what happened? I was healed of the dangerous one, but I still have the other one." He couldn't somehow believe that God could heal the chronic disease. "Oh God, I've had it too long, even You can't do it." That's no way to look at God. God can do anything—anything at all! You may say, "Oh, if you knew how tangled up my life is!" God can untangle your life just as easily as He can do anything else, because He has all the power there is and all the wisdom there is.

There was a Presbyterian preacher by the name of Albert B. Simpson, a Canadian from Prince Edward

Island. He was one of the great orators of his time; people came from everywhere to hear this man pour out his eloquence. But when he was only in his mid-thirties he began to get sicker and sicker until, he said, "Many a time I was called upon to have a funeral and I tottered on the edge of the grave while conducting the service, not knowing but what I would tumble in myself into the grave."

Finally, in deep discouragement, he decided to quit the ministry even though he was a highly successful minister. But one day he took a long walk in the woods and came upon a camp meeting. A black gospel quartet was singing a song which had this for a chorus:

Nothing is too hard for Jesus,
No man can work like Him.

Well, that educated, cultured preacher fell on his knees there among the pine trees and said, "Lord, if nothing is too hard for Thee, then Thou canst deliver me; deliver me now, Lord." And he knelt and gave himself over to the Lord and was instantaneously and perfectly delivered. He lived about thirty-six years after that and worked so hard that he put everyone around him to shame. The great God Almighty had done something for him, had come into his life and transformed him, because he dared to believe.

Do you see how the attributes of God are not ivory-towered theology that only scholars can get ahold of, but truths for you and me? What's your trouble? Got a mean wife you can't live with, or a mean husband that treats you like a dog? Nothing is too hard for Jesus. Got a boss at work who is so hard on you that you're afraid you will have a nervous breakdown? God can handle that boss.

Got a temper you can't control? God will take care of that if you let Him. There isn't anything God can't handle. There isn't a situation that God can't take care of. Nothing is too hard for Jesus and no man can work like Him.

His is an effortless power, because effort means I'm expending energy, but when God works, He doesn't expend energy. He *is* energy! With effortless power, God did and is doing His redeeming work. We stand in awe and speak in hushed tones of His incarnation. How could it be that the great God Almighty could be conceived in the womb of a virgin? I don't know how it could be, but I know that the Great God who is omnipotent, the Great God Almighty, could do it if He wanted to. The incarnation was easy for God. It may be hard for us to understand—a mystery of godliness—but it is not hard for God.

And what about the atonement? Jesus died in the darkness on that cross to save the whole world. Don't try to understand it—you can't. I know no more about how the blood of Jesus Christ can atone for sin than I know what God's nature is like. I only know it does. I only know that I'm reconciled to God through the blood of the Lamb. That's all I know, and that's enough.

I also know that God raised His Son from the

dead. I don't know how, but I know He could do that. And I know God can raise you from the dead. Have you ever stopped to think about the resurrection? What a hard thing it is to think about—all those people that died generations ago. How is God going to find all that dust? I don't know!

But I don't have to know. I put my hand in God's hand and He says, "You just come along and keep happy and I'll take care of everything. I can make creation and I can keep it and I can bring about incarnation, and I can bring about atonement, and I can bring about resurrection. And I can bring about your resurrection." So I'm not worrying. I can't visualize my resurrection, but I can believe it! Amen!

And so it is with forgiveness and cleansing from sin and the breaking of habits. That ugly sin that has been on you so long—you hate it so bad; it's been there so long; you wish you were free. But you just don't have the courage to believe. I appeal to you—dare to believe that the Lord God omnipotent lives and with Him nothing shall be impossible. He has all the power there is. Your need is nothing compared with the great things that God has done. And yet God pardons your sin and cleanses your spirit and gives you His nature, just as easily as He makes the heaven and the earth, because God is God!

God can deliver you from temper and pride and fear and hate and all other diseases of the soul, if you'll only trust Him.

Chapter 5

God's Immutability

For I am the LORD, I change not. (Malachi 3:6)

Wherein God, willing more abundantly to shew unto the heirs of promise the immutability of his counsel, confirmed it by an oath: that by two immutable things, in which it was impossible for God to lie, we might have a strong consolation, who have fled for refuge to lay hold upon the hope set before us. (Hebrews 6:17-18)

Every good gift and every perfect gift is from above, and cometh down from the Father of lights, with whom is no variableness, neither shadow of turning. (James 1:17)

Jesus Christ the same yesterday, and to day, and for ever. (Hebrews 13:8)

To announce that you're going to speak on the immutability of God is almost like putting up a sign saying, "There'll be no service here tonight!" Nobody wants to hear anybody talk about it, I suppose. But when it's explained, you'll find you've struck gold and diamonds, milk and honey.

Now the word *immutable*, of course, is the negative of *mutable*. And *mutable* is from the Latin, meaning "subject to change." *Mutation* is a word we often use to mean "a change in form, nature or substance." *Immutability,* then, means "not subject to change." I think we get a better idea of what we mean by *mutable* if we remember [Percy Bysshe] Shelley's little poem "The Cloud" that you may have learned in school. It starts out with a cloud talking and it says,

> I am the daughter of Earth and Water,
>   And the nursling of the Sky;
> I pass through the pores of the ocean and shores;
>   I change, but I cannot die.

That's the way a cloud is—it's a cloud today, it's rain tomorrow, it's fog the next day. Then it's a cloud again, snow the next day and ice the next day. It's boiling hot one day, but the next day it's cool. The next day it's vaporized and becomes a cloud again. It is constantly changing, passing "through the pores of the ocean and shores." It changes because it's mutable. But it cannot die.

Now there is in God no mutation possible. As it says in James, "with whom is no variableness, nei-

ther shadow of turning" (1:17)—there is no varia-
tion due to change. And there is also that verse in
Malachi: "I am the LORD [Jehovah], I change not"
(3:6).

They couldn't make it any plainer than that; there
isn't one trace of poetry, no figure of speech, no
metaphor. It is just as blunt and prosaic as for me
to say, "This is February 12, 1961, period." There
isn't any way to "interpret" that; you don't go to a
scholar and say, "What does this mean?" You don't
need to. "I am Jehovah, I change not!"

Incidently, He's the only One in the universe that
can say that. And He *did* say it! He simply says that
He never changes, that there is no change possible
in God. God never differs from Himself. If you get
ahold of this, it can be to you an anchor in the
storm, a hiding place in danger. There is no possibility of changing in God. And God never differs
from Himself.

One of the sickest pains that we know in our lives
is how people change. Men smile at you one day
and two weeks later they'll turn their face away. A
friend you used to write to once a week, you haven't
written to in five years, because a change has taken
place. They've changed, you've changed, circumstances have changed.

And little babies—they're tiny, soft things you can
pick up, but give them a little while and they'll
change. Their doting parents hold these tender little
things in their arms, admiring and loving them until
their love becomes a pain inside. They'll be startled,
confused and somewhat pleased one of these days

to see that little, fat body begin to lengthen out and those little dimpled knees becoming undimpled and getting bony. And that tendency to cling to Mama will disappear. The little guy will put his hands on his hips and back off; he is *somebody* now! And that's change.

My wife and I take out pictures of the family every once in awhile and just look at them. Such pretty little fellows they were, and so delightful. But they're great, long, lean fellows now, lanky, tall and bronze—not the way they were. And that's not the worst—give them forty years more and they won't be as they are now. There is always change—change and decay in all we see. The English poet said,

> O Lord! my heart is sick,
> > Sick of this everlasting change;
> And life runs tediously quick
> > Through its unresting race and varied range:
> Change finds no likeness to itself in Thee,
> > And wakes no echo in Thy mute Eternity.[1]

Only God does not change. "And all things, as they change, proclaim the Lord eternally the same."[2] That's a theological fact. That's something you can build on. That is revealed truth—it needs no support of poetry or reason. But once a truth has been declared and established, I like to reason it out. To quote Anselm, "I do not seek to understand that I may believe, but I believe in order to understand."[3] And so I'd like to show you, as briefly as I can, three reasons why God cannot change. That's reasoning within the Scriptures.

Now for God to alter or change at all, to be different from Himself, one of three things has to take place:

1) God must go from better to worse, or
2) He must go from worse to better, or
3) He must change from one kind of being to another.

Now that's so plain that anybody can follow it; there's nothing profound about that. (Occasionally somebody will say I preach over their head. All I can say is, they must have their head awfully low!) Isn't it reasonable to assume that if anything changes it has to change from better to worse, from worse to better or from one kind of thing to another?

An apple on a tree changes from green to ripe—that's from worse to better. Now if a little boy eats it when it's green, as I used to, he gets sick. I did it once or twice every year when I was a little chap on the farm and I went to bed with a tummyache. When it ripens it has changed from worse to better, from our standpoint. But let it hang there long enough and it'll change from better to worse. It will rot and fall away, and so it gets as worse from its better state as it had gotten better from its worse state. Anybody can understand that. If you can't, shake your head and see if you can wake up the brain cells in there!

Therefore, if God is to change, then God either has to get better or worse or different. But God can't go from better to worse, because God is a holy God. Because God is eternal holiness, He can never be any less holy than He is now. And of course, He never can be any more holy than He is now, because He is perfect just as He is. There will never be a change in God—no change is necessary!

Change is necessary in created things, but no change is necessary in God, therefore God does not change. And God, being the eternal, holy God, cannot change. He will not go from better to worse. You cannot think of God being any less holy than He is now, any less righteous than He is now. God must remain infinitely holy, fixed, forever unchanging in holiness. He cannot go from worse to better for the simple reason that God, being absolutely holy, cannot go beyond Himself. He cannot get any more holy than He is now, or go from less good to better.

You and I, however, can. Thank God we can! "He that is holy, let him be holy still," it says in Revelation 22:11. And I believe that since we are creatures and capable of mutation upward toward the image of God, we will become holier and wiser and better while the ages roll. But remember that in becoming holier and better and wiser, we will only be moving toward the perfect likeness of God, who is already all-wise and good and holy. God cannot become any better than He is.

These words that you and I use—holier, wiser, better—we use about ourselves. A man is a good man, another man is a better man. But you cannot say "better" about God, because God is already the apex, the fountain, the top. There are no degrees in

God. There are degrees in angels, I suppose. There are certainly degrees in people too. But there are no degrees in God.

That is why you cannot apply such words as "greater" to God. God is not "greater." God is great. "Greater" is a word applied to creatures who are trying to be like God. But you cannot say that God is greater, because that would put God in a position where He was in competition with someone else who was great. God is simply God.

You cannot say God is less, God is more, God is older, God is younger. You cannot say God is older because God has in His bosom all of time. Time casts no shadow on God and does not change God at all. God does not live according to the tick of the clock or the revolution of the earth around the sun. God does not observe seasons or days. He allows us to because we are caught in the stream of time. The sun that goes down at night and rises in the morning, and the earth that goes around the sun in 365 days always tells us where we are in time. But not God. God remains eternally the same, absolutely the same.

All the "direction" words that we apply to ourselves—back, down, up and all such words—cannot apply to God. God can't go "back," because He's already there, being omnipresent. He can't go "forward," because He's already there. God can't go "right" or "left," because God is already everywhere. "The heaven and heaven of heavens cannot contain him" (2 Chronicles 2:6). So we do not say, "God came from" or "God goes to." We may use these words about God, but we don't mean them in the same way we mean them about ourselves. Direction words haven't anything to do with God.

A week from next Monday I'm going to get on an airplane and fly to Chicago, then get on another one and fly to Wichita. Then I'll get in an automobile and go to Newton, Kansas—wherever that is. I'll preach a while there in a Bible conference. I will be going somewhere, I will be there and then I will be moving toward somewhere else. But God is not in one place moving toward another because God fills all places. And whether you're in India, Australia, South America, California or anywhere around the world, or even in outer space, God's already there. "If I ascend up into heaven, thou art there: if I make my bed in hell, behold, thou art there. If I take the wings of the morning, and dwell in the uttermost parts of the sea; even there shall thy hand lead me, and thy right hand shall hold me" (Psalm 139:8-10).

So these words—greater, lesser, back, forward, down, up—can't apply to God. God the eternal God remains unchanged and unchanging—that is, He is immutable.

God cannot change from better to worse or from worse to better. There is, however, a third way to change. A creature can go from one kind of being to another. That beautiful butterfly that you squeal over in the springtime—why, just a little while ago it was a miserable, hairy worm; you wouldn't have touched it. But now you say, "Isn't it beautiful!" There was a change from one kind of creature to another.

Moral changes can also take place. A good man

can change and be a bad man. And then, thank God, a bad man can, by the grace of God, change and be a good man. We sometimes sing the songs of John Newton. Did you know John Newton was, by his own confession, one of the vilest men that ever lived? Did you know that John Bunyan [author of *Pilgrim's Progress*] was, by his own confession, one of the vilest men that ever lived? Did you know that the apostle Paul was, by his own testimony, the chiefest of sinners (1 Timothy 1:15)? But these men became saints of God.

They changed. It's possible to change. There may have been a time in your life when you would have been bored to tears listening to all this talk about God. But you've changed! There's been mutation. Thank God, you are not immutable; you are able to change. You changed from worse to better. You went from one kind of creature to another kind of creature. But you can't think that about God. God cannot do that, it's unthinkable. The perfect and the absolute and the infinite God cannot become anything else but what He is.

In teaching the doctrine of the incarnation, we do not say that God became man, in the sense that God left His deity and took on humanity. Jesus Christ was both God and man, but His manhood and His Godhood, while mysteriously fused, never passed over into each other. The old Athanasian Creed makes that very clear. It says that God became man, not by the degradation of His Godhood into man, but by the lifting up of His manhood into God.

While Christ is God and was with the Father

before the world was, when Jesus was born of the virgin Mary, He took a tabernacle on Himself but His deity didn't become humanity. His deity was joined to His humanity in one person forever. But God the eternal and uncreated can never become created.

That which is not God cannot become God. And that which is God cannot become that which is not God. God can come and dwell intimately within His creatures, yet you do not become God when God comes into your nature and fills you with Himself. And God does not become you. That is pantheism. God is your Father and you're His child; He dwells in your heart, and experientially you are one. But actually and metaphysically you and God remain two beings.

Buddhists teach that we pass away into Nirvana, into the eternal sea of deity and cease to be, like a drop of water into the ocean. I wouldn't look forward to that! If I were on my deathbed and some priest came and said, "Well, brother Tozer, you're just about to pass on; your personality will cease to be and you will be lost and melted up into the vast personality that is God," I'd say, "I'm not looking forward to it. I'm going to hang on to my own personality as long as I can, because I like my dreams and memories, my thoughts and worship, my happiness. I like to see and hear and feel. I like being human and alive; I like having my own personality." I could never look forward to being dissolved in God and forgotten.

But I'll never be forgotten. God will always keep

me an individual, capable of memory, imagination, thought, drawing conclusions, capable of worship.

Always the Same

God is always the same. As the poet Faber put it,

Thine own Self for ever filling
    With self-kindled flame,
In Thyself Thou art distilling
    Unctions without name!
Without worshipping of creatures
Without veiling of Thy features,
    God always the same![4]

And when I say that God is the same always, I'm talking about all three Persons of the Godhead. You will remember that the Athanasian Creed says,

Such as the Father is, such is the Son, and such is the Holy Spirit.

The Father uncreated, the Son uncreated, and the Holy Spirit uncreated.

The Father incomprehensible, the Son incomprehensible, and the Holy Spirit incomprehensible.

The Father eternal, the Son eternal, and the Holy Spirit eternal.

Yet there are not three eternals, but one eternal.

As also there are not three uncreated nor three incomprehensible, but one uncreated and one incomprehensible.

You can run through the gamut of the attributes of God and what you say about the Father you can say about the Son without modification. What you say about the Father and the Son you can say about the Spirit without modification, for there is one substance that are together to be worshiped and glorified. So when we say God is the same, we are saying that Jesus Christ is the same and the Holy Ghost is the same. All that God ever was, God still is. All that God was and is, God will ever be. If you remember that, it will help you in the hour of trial. It will help you at the time of death, in the resurrection and in the world to come, to know that all that God ever was, God still is. All that God was and is, God ever will be. His nature and attributes are eternally unchanging. I have preached about the uncreated selfhood of God; I'll never have to change or edit it in any way. I go back over some of my old sermons and articles, and I wonder why I wrote them like that. I could improve them now. But I can't improve on the statement that God is always the same—He is self-sufficient, self-existent, eternal, omnipresent and immutable. There would be no reason to change that because God changes not. His nature, His attributes, are eternally unchanging.

Whatever God felt about anything, He still feels. Whatever He thought about anyone, He still thinks. Whatever He approved, He still approves. Whatever He condemned, He still condemns. Today we have what they call the relativity of morals. "Well, you can't be too tough on people," they say. "After all, right and wrong are relative terms. What's right in

Timbuktu may be wrong in New York. And what's wrong in New York may be entirely right in Buenos Aires." But remember this: God never changes. Holiness and righteousness are conformity to the will of God. And the will of God never changes for moral creatures.

God intends that moral creatures should always be like Him—righteous, holy, pure, true—always, forever and ever. However, God sometimes "winked at" sin in ancient days (Acts 17:30) because men were ignorant and the plan of salvation was not yet revealed. God also puts up with some things in us today, because we're still children and don't know and can't yet grasp His eternal purposes for us. He's not excusing it—He's simply patiently putting up with us until we come around to the truth. But God always hates sin.

If you want to know what God is like, read the story of Jesus Christ. "He that hath seen me hath seen the Father" (John 14:9). So that however Jesus felt about anything, God feels the same. When Jesus picked a baby up and put His hands on its head to bless it, that's the way God feels about babies. But when they brought their children to Him, the disciples said, "Take those kids away! This is a theological school, don't you know! We are busy talking theology. Get those babies away!" But the Lord said, "Suffer little children, and forbid them not, to come unto me: for of such is the kingdom of heaven" (Matthew 19:14).

In the city of Chicago there was a Sunday school among Italian immigrants. One little girl had memorized this verse. She lived on the streets, and her language wasn't the best. One Sunday they asked her to quote the passage she learned the Sunday before and she said, "let the little kids come to me, and don't you tell them they can't, because they belongs by me." She had it all right, even if she didn't have the King James Version!

The Lord loves little ones like that—He still does. And He still thinks the same of the penitent harlot that He always did. He still thinks the same of the tenderhearted man seeking eternal life. He did not, does not and cannot change.

We're in the middle of a world that's changing all the time. And I for one am glad it's changing. I'm glad the weather changes, aren't you? We're glad when the weather report says it's going to warm up a bit—unless it's August, and then we don't want to hear it! In the world of nature, I hardly need mention how a seed produces a plant, a plant produces a flower, a flower produces a seed and so on through the eternal cycle. Things are changing!

God allows things to change in order that He might establish that which cannot change. The book of Hebrews has this for its thesis. The altar changed from the temporary altar to the eternal altar; the priesthood changed from the temporary priesthood of Aaron to the eternal priesthood of Christ; the tabernacle changed from the temporary tabernacle in Jerusalem to the eternal tabernacle in the heavens; the blood sacrifice changed from the blood that was shed repeatedly to the blood that was shed once for all and does not need to be repeated. Things changed until they perfected themselves and then they changed no more. "And all things, as they change, proclaim the Lord eternally the same."

Now what does all this mean to you and me? It means that my poor, helpless, dependent self finds a home in God. God is our home! I look forward not so much to heaven as my home but as God is my home, in His heaven and the eternity of God. We poor victims of the passing moment, we have found the Timeless One. When I preach, I notice some people looking at their wristwatch. We're victims of time—counting our pulse beating, tearing off from the calendar the page that tells us that one more month has gone by.

But there is One who contains time in His bosom: the Timeless One, who stepped out of eternity into time, in the womb of the virgin Mary, who died and rose and lives at the right hand of God for us. He invites us into His bosom where time is no more. And instead of getting old, we stay young in Jesus Christ. Do you know that song, "Now rest, my long-divided heart; Fixed on this blissful center, rest!"[5] What did he mean? "If a house be divided against itself, that house cannot stand" (Mark 3:25), said our Lord. There is confusion, revolution and tumult until we find rest in Christ. What is that blissful center? It is none other than the Son of God made flesh, crucified and risen. And He invites us to rest in His bosom. There is a real sense in which nobody knows rest of mind or heart until they find it in Jesus Christ our Lord. "God has made us for Himself

and we find not rest till we find it in thee," said
Augustine. An old song we used to sing says:

> Come sinners, to the living One,
> He's just the same Jesus
> As when He raised the widow's son,
> The very same Jesus.

> Come feast upon the living bread,
> He's just the same Jesus.
> As when the multitudes He fed,
> The very same Jesus.

> Come tell him all your griefs and fears,
> He's just the same Jesus
> As when He shed those loving tears,
> The very same Jesus.

> Calm midst the waves of trouble be,
> He's just the same Jesus
> As when He calmed the raging sea,
> The very same Jesus.[6]

And you'll find Him yesterday and today and forever the same. He has not receded into history past.
He is the same today as before He went away. He's
the same Jesus Christ the Lord. And if you turn to
Him now, as Mary turned to Him, as the rich young
ruler turned to Him, as Jairus and many others
turned to Him, He will fill you. He's not visible to
our sight, but "lo, I am with you always, even unto
the end of the world" (Matthew 28:20).

If you turn to Him for clearer light, you'll find He is the same Jesus as when He gave the blind their sight—the very same Jesus. He'll feed you as He fed the multitude, He'll calm you as He calmed the sea. He'll bless you as He blessed the children. He'll forgive you as He forgave the woman that fell at His feet in her shame. He'll give you eternal life as He gave eternal life to His people. He'll wash you as He washed their feet, back there. He's the same! The God we preach is the same God, unchanging and unchangeable, forever and ever.

I recommend to you Jesus Christ, the unchanging One. I recommend to you God's answer to your questions, God's solution to your problems, God's life for your dying soul, God's cleansing for your sin-cursed spirit, God's rest for your restless mind and God's resurrection for your dying body. For your advocate above, I recommend Him to you. You will find Him to be all He ever was—the very same Jesus.

Jn 2 - 24, 25

Chapter 6

God's Omniscience

His understanding is infinite. (Psalm 147:5)

*Neither is there any creature that is not manifest
in his sight: but all things are naked and opened
unto the eyes of him with whom we have to do.
(Hebrews 4:13)*

These texts say that God's understanding is
limitless, that His knowledge is perfect, and
that there isn't a creature anywhere in the universe that isn't plainly visible to His sight. Nothing
is shut before the eyes of God. That is what is called
divine omniscience, one of the attributes of God. An
attribute, as I have said before, is something which
God has declared to be true about Himself.

God has declared by divine revelation that He is
omniscient, that He knows everything. The human
mind staggers under this truth when we consider
how much there is to know and how little we know.
Ralph Waldo Emerson said, for example, that if a

man were to start reading the books in the British Library on the day he was born and read day and night for seventy years, without taking time to eat or sleep, he would only be able to read a small section of the books in that collection.

Even those who know so very much, know so very little. Dr. Samuel Johnson, the great English lexicographer, was known as the most learned man in England. When he was compiling the first English dictionary, he defined a hock (the middle joint on a horse's rear leg) as a horse's knee (the middle joint on a horse's front leg). Some time afterward, at a party somewhere, a society lady turned to the great doctor and thought she would get a rise out of him.

She said, "Dr. Johnson, why did you define a hock as a horse's knee?"

He said, "Ignorance Madam, sheer ignorance."

He was the most learned man in all England, but he admitted that he was ignorant on some things. Will Rogers said, "Everybody is ignorant—only on different subjects."[1] And when it comes to knowing anything, I get very discouraged when I go to a library. I come out feeling as if I know absolutely nothing at all—which, if the truth were known, is a lot nearer to the facts than I would like to admit!

When I received one of the honorary degrees that have been bestowed on me, I said, "The only thing that is learned about me is this pair of glasses." If a man has his hair slicked back and a pair of learned-looking glasses, they call him a doctor. We don't know very much, really, and when we consider the great God who knows all there is to know with perfection of knowledge, we stagger under that. The weight of the truth is too much for our minds.

When Sir Isaac Newton, the great English scientist, was an old man, someone said to him, "Dr. Newton, you must have a tremendous store of knowledge."

He responded, "I remind myself of a little boy walking along the seashore picking up shells. The boy has a handful of shells in his little hand, but all around him is the vast seashore stretching all directions as far as the eye can see. All that I know is simply a handful of seashells, but the vast universe of God is filled with knowledge that I do not possess."

When we talk about God's knowledge of everything, we're talking about a rational approach to God. There are two ways to approach God: theologically and experientially. You can know God experientially and not know much theology, but it's good to know both. The more you know about God theologically the better you can know Him experientially.

A rational approach to God is what I can get into my head. You can't get too much into your head, really. And what I can get into my head about God isn't very much at all. But that's one way to approach God—through theology, through your intellect, through doctrine. But the purpose of doctrine is to lead you to see and to know God experientially, to know God for Himself, for yourself. But until we know God theologically, we're not likely to know God very well experientially.

Reason can best think of God in negatives. In

other words, as the old mystic devotional writers used to say, we can best conceive of God by conceiving of what He is not. We can always know what God is not, but we can never know quite what God is. The greatness of God's mind leaves all our soaring thoughts behind. God is ineffable (incapable of being expressed in words), inconceivable and unimaginable.

What's *unimaginable* mean? It just means that you can't think of what God is like. One man I heard about used to kneel down in front of a chair and say, "Jesus, You take the chair." And then he'd imagine Jesus on the chair. I've never cared for that sort of thing. I've never cared much for religious pictures, either. I'm always horrified when I see Michelangelo's picture of the creation. God Almighty is portrayed as an old, bald-headed man lying on a cloud, pointing His fiery finger down at Adam, as Adam comes to life. Can you imagine conceiving of God as a bald-headed old man? I think the artist would have done us a wonderful favor if he had reverently laid down his brushes and never tried to paint the figure of God.

We don't know what God is like. If you can think it, it isn't God. If you can think it, it is an idol of your own imagination. If you don't believe what I'm saying, read what the Holy Ghost said in 1Corinthians 2:7-11:

> But we speak the wisdom of God in a mystery, even the hidden wisdom, which God ordained before the world unto our glory: which

none of the princes of this world knew. . . . But as it is written, Eye hath not seen, nor ear heard, neither have entered into the heart of man, the things which God hath prepared for them that love him. But God hath revealed them unto us by his Spirit: for the Spirit searcheth all things, yea, the deep things of God. For what man knoweth the things of a man, save the spirit of man which is in him? even so the things of God knoweth no man, but the Spirit of God.

And you'll never know what I'm talking about without the illumination of the Holy Ghost. When we crowded the Holy Ghost out of the church and took in other things instead, we put out our own eyes. The church is filled with blind men who cannot see because the Holy Ghost has never opened their eyes. Lydia could not believe in Christ till the Lord had opened her eyes. Those disciples could not believe on Christ there on the Emmaus Road until He had opened their eyes. No one can see God nor believe in God until the Holy Ghost has opened their eyes. When we grieve and quench the Holy Ghost, when we neglect Him, crowd Him out and substitute other things for Him, we make blind men out of ourselves.

We must come to God reverently, on our knees. You always see God when you're on your knees. You never see God when you're standing boldly on your feet, in full confidence that you'll amount to something. God is unimaginable, inconceivable; you cannot get into your head what God is like, or visualize God's being. The rule is, if you can think it, God isn't like that.

God is not like anything you know, except the soul of a man. It was old Meister Eckhart, the German saint, who said that the soul of a man was more like God than anything in the universe. He made man in His own image; you can't see a man's soul and therefore you've never seen anything that is like God. You've never heard or touched anything that is like God, except within your own heart. God lies beyond our thoughts, towers above them, escapes them and confounds them in awful incomprehensible terror and majesty.

As I said, we are driven to the use of negative statements when speaking about God. When we speak of the self-existence of God, we say God has no origin. When we speak of God's eternity, we say God has no beginning. When we speak of the immutability of God, we say God has no change. When we speak of the infinity of God, we say that God has no limits. When we speak of the omniscience of God, we say that God has no teachers and cannot learn. All these are negative statements.

We would cut down the length of a lot of prayers if we recognized that God can't learn anything. The average church deacon may take up to twenty minutes every Sunday giving God lessons. But God can't learn because He already knows everything there is to know. He knows the thing that you're trying to tell Him and He knows it more perfectly than you do.

Well now, the Scripture takes this negative method too. Scripture says the Lord "fainteth not, neither is weary" (Isaiah 40:28) and that He "cannot lie" (Titus 1:2). It says, "I am the LORD, I change not" (Malachi 3:6). It says, "with God nothing shall be impossible" (Luke 1:37). And it says God "cannot deny himself" (2 Timothy 2:13). And all of those things are, of course, negative. Now in case somebody charges me with being negative in my outlook, let me read what our Lord Jesus Christ said here in the 11th chapter of Matthew:

> At that time Jesus answered and said, I thank thee, O Father, Lord of heaven and earth, because thou hast hid these things from the wise and prudent, and hast revealed them unto babes. Even so, Father: for so it seemed good in thy sight. All things are delivered unto me of my Father: and no man knoweth the Son, but the Father; neither knoweth any man the Father, save the Son, and he to whomsoever the Son will reveal him. (11:25-27)

I cannot know with my head but I can have it revealed to my spirit, by the Holy Spirit. My knowledge of God is not the knowledge Paul referred to when he said,

> And I, brethren, when I came to you, came not with excellency of speech or of wisdom, declaring unto you the testimony of God. For I determined not to know any thing among you,

save Jesus Christ, and him crucified. And I was with you in weakness, and in fear, and in much trembling. And my speech and my preaching was not with enticing words of man's wisdom, but in demonstration of the Spirit and of power: that your faith should not stand in the wisdom of men, but in the power of God. (1 Corinthians 2:1-5)

Remember, this was a Grecian city; they thought in the context of Greek philosophy. Paul was a thinker too, a philosopher. But he said, "When I came to you, I came not using big words; I came determined to know nothing except Jesus and Him crucified."

You see, if your faith stands in human argument, someone who is a better arguer can argue you out of it again. But when the Spirit of God reveals truth to your heart and God manifests that truth to your heart, nobody can argue you out of it. If you know God through Jesus Christ the Lord, nobody can argue you out of it.

When I was in my twenties, I used to read more philosophy than I did theology. I read books by psychologists and philosophers, yards and yards of them. I tried to make myself acquainted with what the great minds of the ages have thought. And sometimes I would run into somebody with an argument I couldn't answer, which made it look bad for the Bible and bad for me. Then I would get down on my knees and say with joy in my heart, "Lord Jesus, this man got to me too late. I have found Thee, and though I can't answer his arguments, I have Thee and I know Thee." And I would have a joyful time of worship on my knees. My head couldn't enter, but my heart was already in, on its knees saying, "Holy, holy, holy is the Lord God Almighty."

Since then I have learned that nobody knows enough to contradict the Word of God successfully. Some people think they do, but they don't. One man told me, "Sometimes I am troubled by the foundations of my faith. But when I'm worried about the foundations, I dive deep down into the Bible and examine the foundations. And I always come back out and shake the water out of my hair and sing, 'How firm a foundation, ye saints of the Lord, is laid for your faith in His excellent Word!' " You may be sure nobody knows enough to contradict the Word of God.

God Knows Himself

Divine omniscience, among other things, means that God knows Himself. According to Paul, "the things of God knoweth no man, but the Spirit of God" (1 Corinthians 2:11). God thus knows Himself. And since God is the source and author of all things and contains all things, it follows that God knows all things. In one effortless act, God knows instantly and perfectly all things that can be known.

It's good sometimes to be around people who can do things easily. They don't have to strain until the muscles stand out in their necks. For example, I like to hear someone take a high note and hold it. We have a record of a great Italian soprano; there seems to be no top to her voice at all! She goes way up over the staff, up over the top of the book, up to the ceiling and then threatens to soar away into the blue. And she never seems to strain one muscle at all.

It's nice to know somebody can do something without effort. Most of us have an awful time getting anything done. I've written some books and it's cost me sweat and blood. But when it comes to God, He does everything effortlessly. God never strains. He never says, "Oh, this is going to be a hard one!" Never! God is able to do it as easily as He is able to do anything else.

In the same way, God, in one effortless act, knows instantly (not a little at a time, but instantly and perfectly) all things that can be known. That's why I say that God cannot learn. As I said before, if we realized that God couldn't learn, we could shorten our prayers quite a bit and step up their power. There is no reason to tell God things that He knew before you were born!

God knows the end from the beginning and He knew it long before it happened. Long before your parents met, God knew what you would be doing at this very moment. Before your grandparents met, before England was a nation, or the Roman Empire dissolved, or the Roman Empire was formed, God knew all about us. He knew everything about us—every hair on our head, our weight, our name, our past. And He knew it before we were born.

He knew it before Adam was. And when Adam

walked in the garden with God, God knew all about Adam, all about Eve, all about their sons, all about the human race. God never gets astonished, astounded or surprised, because He already knows. You can walk down the street, turn the corner and get the surprise of your life. But God never turned the corner and got surprised, for the simple reason that God was already around that corner before He turned it. God already knew before He found out! God knows all things.

It's nice to sit down and talk things over with God. The Psalms are full of that, as well as the history of the saints. It's good to talk to God, even though we are talking to God about things He already knows. But this idea of giving God a lecture, I never did believe very much in it.

I love to hear people pray, but I don't like to hear them pray the same prayers, day in day out. That's why I don't always go to all the prayer meetings I might. I know what they're going to say anyhow, so why not just say as the cowboy did when he wrote his prayer on a card and stuck it on the head of his bed. When he got into bed, he said, "Lord, them's my sentiments," and went to sleep! I don't know why I should have to go and spend a half hour on my bony knees listening to some old deacon lecture God for three quarters of an hour. God already knows! He cannot learn.

If there was anything God could learn, it would mean that God didn't know it before. If He didn't know it before, then He didn't know everything. And if He didn't know everything, He wouldn't be perfect, and if He isn't perfect then He isn't God. The God who can learn anything is not God. God already knows all that can be learned, all there is to know, and He knows it instantly and perfectly and without strain or selfconsciousness. He knows it all. That's what Paul meant in Romans 11:33-36:

> O the depth of the riches both of the wisdom and knowledge of God! how unsearchable are his judgments, and his ways past finding out! For who hath known the mind of the Lord? or who hath been his counsellor? Or who hath first given to him, and it shall be recompensed unto him again? For of him, and through him, and to him, are all things: to whom be glory for ever. Amen.

It says God has no counselor—another negative expression. God had no teacher. He never went to school. Who could teach God? Could God call in an archangel and say to him, "Archangel, I'd like to get a little information about this"? We know the President of the United States has people all out over the country with their ears to the ground, providing him information. Politicians are always trying to find out what the public is saying. And as soon as a politician finds out what the public is saying, he gets up and boldly announces, "Them's my convictions." And he gets elected. But he got elected by finding out what the public wanted him to know. Can you imagine God calling in a seraphim and saying, "There's a galaxy out there so many billion light-years away that kind of got out of my range; I'd like to have you visit it and bring back information so I'll know how to run my universe"? I couldn't worship a God like that; I'd pity Him. I'd say, "What a wonderful big universe, but such a small god!" No, God never sends anybody out after information. God has it instantly, perfectly and effortlessly. God knows all that there is. He never discovers anything and He never finds out anything. He never wanders around seeking information.

One challenge to this that may come to mind is that passage back in Genesis, "I will go down now and see if these things be true, about that city of Sodom" (see 18:21). Do you know why God said that? God—who had made Sodom, who knew the end from the beginning—knew what was true, but He was dealing with people. Sometimes our Lord asked people questions, but He didn't ask for information, "because he knew all men . . . he knew what was in man" (John 2:24-25).

He just asked to draw the man out, the same as if you said to a five-year-old boy, "Johnny, who was the first President of the United States?" You're not asking him in order to gain information! Reminds me of the boy who started his first day of school. He came home and announced that he wasn't going back.

"Why?" asked his mother.

"Well," he said, "the teacher is the dumbest woman I've ever seen in my life. She knows absolutely nothing at all. She has to ask me everything!"

So God said, "I'll go down now and I'll see" and He asked a question. Jesus our Lord asked questions of His disciples, but He already knew the answers. So God knows!

It is a great consolation to me that God knows instantly, effortlessly and perfectly all matter and all matters, all law and all laws, all space and all spaces, all principles and every principle, all minds, all spirits and all souls. God knows all causes and all relations, all effects and all desires, all mysteries and all enigmas, all things unknown and hidden. There are no mysteries to God.

There are many things that are mysteries to you and me. "And without controversy great is the mystery of godliness: God was manifest in the flesh" (1 Timothy 3:16). Theologians throughout the centuries have reverently tried to discover how the infinite, inimitable God could condense Himself into the form of a man. It's a great mystery. We don't know, but God knows and God isn't worried about it. That's why I can live a good and peaceful Christian life, even though I am not a man that takes things very easy.

I'm not worried about these satellites they're shooting around the earth. I'm not worried about Kruschev (former leader of the Soviet Union) or any of the rest of those fellows over there with names you can't pronounce. Because God's running His world and He knows all about it. He knows where these men will die, He knows where they will be buried and He knows when they'll be buried. God knows all hidden things, "dwelling in the light which no man can approach unto" (6:16).

And He also knows His people. You who have fled for refuge to Him, Jesus Christ the Lord, He knows you, and you're never an orphan. A Christian is never lost, though he may think he is. He may be in the north woods hunting deer and lose his way, but he's not lost; the Lord knows where he is. The Lord knows all about him. The Lord knows about his health and knows about his business. Isn't it a consolation to you that our Father knows it all?

> He knows, He knows
>> The storms that would my way oppose
> He knows, He knows
>> And tempers every wind that blows.[2]

Is that a consolation to you? It is to me. It's a consolation to me to know that

> I know not where His islands lift
>> Their fronded palms in air;
> I only know I cannot drift
>> Beyond His love and care.[3]

Is your blood pressure running high? Are you worried? Maybe you don't know what to do and you think nobody else knows. Well, I have news for you. He that is perfect in knowledge is with you and He knows! If you'll trust Him He'll bring you out all right. He is perfect in knowledge and will lead you through. And when you come out you will know that everything God did was right.

"He hath done all things well" (Mark 7:37). Do you believe it? Do you believe that God's dealing with you is right? Maybe the person you married didn't turn out to be the angel that you thought. Well, God knows all about you. And He knows that even if it was a mistake, it is a mistake that God can overrule. God can take nothing and make something out of it. God can take your mistakes and polish those mistakes.

Have you heard the old story about the beautiful cathedral window that was vandalized? Some children threw pebbles at it and it was cracked all over. They sent for one of the finest artists in the land and asked, "What can you do?"

He said, "Leave it to me." And he went to work with his fine chisels and began cutting the glass. He made artistic lines wherever there was a break, turning each crack into a beautiful thing. When it was all over, the sun shone in on one of the most beautiful pieces of art glass in the world.

I remember that passage back in the book of Psalms that says, "Though ye have lien among the pots, yet shall ye be as the wings of a dove covered with silver, and her feathers with yellow gold" (68:13). Now what does that mean? It shows the picture of a poor dove that fell down among the old cans and broken pots, the place where old junk is thrown out. Perhaps someone shot an arrow, hit this little dove and she went tumbling down and landed there. She wasn't dead, but she was in bad shape. So she got some sunshine and pecked a few seeds here and there, waiting for nature to heal her wing. And one day the sun was bright and the other birds were up in the air, so she tried out her engines, revved up her motor and off she went.

As she circled around, someone said, "Oh, look at the beautiful dove, shining in the silver!"

"Yes," another said, "look at the gold along the edges of her wing."

She had just been down in the junk pile a little while before, but now she arose by the grace of God into the sunshine. That was David's way of saying that God can take nothing, can take the poor wrecks of you and me, and can change us and make us into doves with wings of silver and gold.

God Knows the Unsaved

God even knows the unblessed man, the man without God. If I were speaking to an unsaved man, the first thing that I would say to him is, God knows you by name. Isaiah 45:4 says, "I have even called thee by thy name . . . though thou hast not known me." God knows your name and He knows you fully. According to Psalm 139, He knows why you're rejecting His Son. He knows your secret sins.

You know, a person with a secret sin can get away with it for a long time. I read in the newspaper about men who for twenty years have been robbing banks. You can rob banks or juggle your books, but one person knows about it, and that's God. God knows your excuses and your real reasons, those that you hardly know yourself. He knows your checkered past and your future.

He knows the last place that you're going to lie

down. He knows the name of the driver of the hearse that's going to drive you out to that last place. He knows all about it. He knows and sees what you don't know or see. He knows why you're not a Christian, why you're not following His Son. So why not put yourself in His keeping now?

There's a great old Latin hymn in which the writer reminds Jesus Christ (I'll put this in my own words), "Lord Jesus, remember why You came this way. I'm the reason." That's your plea, no matter how bad you are, no matter how crooked, deceptive and deceitful, no matter how you've assimilated and dissimilated. You can always go to Jesus Christ and the Lord will take you and receive you to Himself. What wonderful news—"This man receiveth sinners, and eateth with them" (Luke 15:2).

We can't tell God anything He doesn't already know and we can't excuse ourselves for anything. Our reasons are paper-thin and God sees through them. But in spite of it, God loves you, God invites you and God will receive you. There is no reason why you shouldn't come.

Chapter 7

God's Wisdom

The L ORD by wisdom hath founded the earth; by understanding hath he established the heavens. (Proverbs 3:19)

He hath established the world by his wisdom, and hath stretched out the heavens by his discretion. (Jeremiah 10:12)

To God only wise, be glory through Jesus Christ for ever. (Romans 16:27)

With him is wisdom and strength, he hath counsel and understanding. (Job 12:13)

Wherein he hath abounded toward us in all wisdom and prudence. (Ephesians 1:8)

To the intent that now unto the principalities and powers in heavenly places might be known by the church the manifold wisdom of God. (Ephesians 3:10)

The English language, you will notice, has succeeded in creating new words by uniting one word to another. For instance, we take the word *science,* meaning "knowledge," and we unite it to the word *omni,* meaning "all" to create *omniscience.* We take the word *potent* and unite it to the word *omni* to create *omnipotence.* But when we come to the word wisdom, the word-makers never got around to making such a word. We haven't any such word as "omniwisdom." Webster's dictionary has something like 250,000 words, yet when we want a word we have to make one! So I will not make a new word, but I will simply say that God is wise! And if God is infinite, then God is infinitely wise.

It tells us in Proverbs 3:19 and Jeremiah 10:12 that the Lord founded the earth, established and stretched out the heavens by wisdom, understanding and discretion. Those are two of many verses in the Bible that tell us about the wisdom of God.

The wisdom of God is something to be taken on faith. Anselm tells us, as I have said before, that we do not reason in order that we might believe, but we reason because we already believe. If I have to reason myself into faith, then I can be reasoned back out of it again. But faith is an organ of knowledge; if I know something by faith, I will reason about it.

For this reason I make no attempt to prove God's wisdom. If I tried to prove that God is wise, the embittered soul would not believe it anyway, no matter how perfect and convincing the proofs I might bring. And the worshiping heart already knows that

God is wise and does not need to have it proved. So I will not attempt to prove anything, but simply begin with the statement that God is wise.

We also should not ask God to prove His wisdom. We believe God is wise because God is God. Any demand we might make on God for proof would be an affront to the perfection of His deity. If you were to come to me after a service and ask me for some proof of something I said, you would not insult me, because I am only a man and I can make mistakes. But if we ask God for proof, we are affronting the Majesty which is in the heavens. And to think low of God is the supreme degradation.

It is necessary to our humanity that we grant God two things at least: wisdom and goodness. The God who sits on high, who made the heaven and the earth, has got to be wise, or else you and I cannot be sure of anything. He's got to be good, or earth would be a hell and heaven a hell, and hell a heaven. We have to grant goodness and wisdom to God, or we have no place to go, no rock to stand on, no way to do any thinking or reasoning or believing. We must believe in the goodness and in the wisdom of God, or we betray that in us which differentiates us from the beasts—the image of God Himself.

So we begin with the assumption—not a guess, not a hope, but a knowledge—that God is wise. But someone will ask, "If God is good and wise, how do you explain polio, prison camps, mass executions, wars and all the other evils that are in the world? Many people lie in a bed of suffering, or go about with one leg, or are deaf or blind. And if God is good and wise," says the critic, "then will you explain how this could be?"

Let me answer by an allegory. Let us say that a man is very, very wise and is not only wise, but is rich to the point of having all the money in the world. And let us suppose he decides to build the most beautiful palace that has ever been built in the world. So in some little country, say in Europe, he gathers together the finest artists and architects, the finest designers that can be found anywhere. He combs the nations of the world and buys the top brains and the top talent of the world, and brings them there.

Then he says, "I have billions of dollars to put at your disposal. Money is no object. I want the most beautiful building in all the world. I want its floors to be gold, I want its walls to be jasper, I want its appointments to be carved ivory. I want it to be studded with diamonds and rubies. I want it to be the epitome of all that is beautiful, all that is gracious, all that genius can create. When it is finished, I want it to be the talk of all the world. I want everyone everywhere, from Broadway to Piccadilly Circus to the jungles of Africa and Borneo, to talk about that palace. Now go to work and give me the best that you can give."

And, pooling their wisdom and genius, they built a most beautiful building—a building that makes the Taj Mahal look like a barn. It was beyond all possible beauty, this palace.

Well then, let us suppose that, after a year or so,

the political fortunes change and a conquering army comes in and takes over that little country. The soldiers come in and take over the palace—great, tough, barbarian soldiers with hobnailed boots. They care nothing about beauty, about art, about the diamonds and gold. Let us suppose that they stable their horses in the palace, that they spit on the floor and throw beer cans all over the place and make a wallow out of it. Eventually, the beautiful palace is filled with dirt, old rags and filth of every kind; the man who owns it and the artists who built it have fled into exile.

While the heel of the barbarian treads down the little country, one passerby whispers to another, "There's the great palace, the greatest concentration of universal beauty known in the world."

And the other person says, "Why, it doesn't look like it to me—or smell like it! It's a pigpen! How can you say it's beautiful?"

"Just wait for a while," the first passerby replies. "There's been a war and this is an occupied country. The fortunes of war will change again and the oppressor will be driven out."

And let us suppose that these bestial and brutal men are driven out. Then the rich man comes back from some far away retreat and says to his artists, architects and sculptors, "Let's get to work and clean this up. We will begin at the bottom and work to the top, and put it back into shape again."

After a year or so of work, the palace stands once again, shining in the noonday sun—the epitome of all beauty and the essence of all that man can possibly do. And once again, all around the world, newspaper, TV and radio reporters talk about it. It is seen once more as the most beautiful thing in the world.

Once there was someone named God—God the Father Almighty, Maker of heaven and earth. He turned His mighty wisdom loose on the making of man. He said, "Let us make man in our image" (Genesis 1:26). Then he made a garden eastward in Eden and He put man in it. He said to man, "I will make him an help meet for him" (2:18). He put man asleep and from his side He took a rib and made a woman and said, "This will be your mate, your wife." And He called her name Eve.

Then Satan came into the garden and wound himself about the limbs of the tree of life. He began to whisper insinuations against God. And then the fortunes of moral war changed; Satan took over and man sinned, betraying the God who made him. That which used to be the most beautiful of all gardens and most lovely of all worlds, populated by the most radiant of all creatures, made in the image of God, now is turned into a pigpen and plunged into darkness.

And so the critic walks about as the passersby did by the palace. And he says, "Are you telling me that a wise God made this pigpen?"

But I say, "Wait just a minute. God in His great wisdom and in His providential dealings with this world has allowed foreign soldiers to occupy. And this epitome of all beauty, this flying ball we call the earth, this glorious home of the creature made in

the image of God, is now under a cloud, a shadow."
It tells us in Romans 8:19-22,

> For the earnest expectation of the creature
> waiteth for the manifestation of the sons of
> God. For the creature was made subject to van-
> ity, not willingly, but by reason of him who hath
> subjected the same in hope, because the crea-
> ture itself also shall be delivered from the
> bondage of corruption into the glorious liberty
> of the children of God. For we know that the
> whole creation groaneth and travaileth in pain
> together until now.

God's wise plans will be carried out, but God in
His wisdom has allowed, for a little time, this foreign
occupation. The world we live in, with its cyclones,
tornadoes, tempests, tidal waves and other forces of
destruction, is under occupation. The soldiers of the
devil march up and down in it with their hobnailed
boots, their ignorance and their lack of appreciation.
They catch God's beauty and destroy it.

The state of Pennsylvania, where I was born, has
rolling hills, flashing streams, waterfalls, meadows
and lovely forests. If you have ever driven through
it, you know how beautiful it is. Near where I lived
when I was a boy, money-loving men have done
what they call strip mining. Instead of digging into
the hill to get the coal, they strip the top off and get
the coal from above. And the result looks as though
nature were weeping, as though the whole world
were a graveyard. I have seen thousands of acres of

the lovely hillsides, green and beautiful, that I knew as a boy, lying wounded and bleeding. They have used the bulldozer, the plow and other great instruments to tear nature apart—just to get at a little bit of her treasure and make a little more money. Just so they can have a bigger swimming pool and a larger yacht.

But do you think that God Almighty has surrendered and gone away forever? No! God says, "I'm running creation, even though it is groaning under the plow and the bulldozer, under the heel of the foe." And one of these days the great God Almighty is going to send His Son "from heaven with a shout, with the voice of the archangel, and with the trump of God: and the dead in Christ shall rise first: then we which are alive and remain shall be caught up together with them in the clouds" (1 Thessalonians 4:16-17). We will be changed, raised, glorified and made into the image of God. He's going to clean house down here and there shall be peace from the river to the ends of the earth. Where the dragon lay, there shall be roses blooming and the fruit of paradise. Then we'll see that God was wise. But we're going to have to be patient and go along with God for a little while, because we're under occupation.

Wisdom Defined

What is wisdom? It is the skill to achieve the most perfect ends by the most perfect means. Both the means and the ends have to be worthy of God. Wisdom is the ability to see the end from the beginning, to see everything in proper relation and in full focus. It is to judge in view of final and ultimate ends and to work toward those ends with flawless precision.

God Almighty must be flawlessly precise. God doesn't bumble. The British used to say of themselves, "We muddled through," meaning they got through somehow, playing it by ear, hoping for the best and taking advantage of situations. They've done it well for the last thousand years. That's the way we have to do it, but God never works that way. If God worked that way it would prove that God didn't know any more than we did about things. But God works with flawless precision because God sees the end from the beginning and He never needs to back up.

Did you ever notice that our Lord Jesus Christ, when He walked the earth, never apologized? He never got up in the morning and said, "I'm sorry, boys. Yesterday when I was talking I misspoke Myself and I said this, but I meant that." Never! Because He was wisdom divinely incarnated in the voice of a man. And when He spoke, He said it right the first time. He never had to apologize.

I've had to get up and explain myself a few times. I've even had to get up publicly and tell the people I've made a donkey of myself a few times. I'm just a man, you know. But Jesus Christ never once said, "I'm sorry, but I said the wrong thing yesterday; I didn't mean to leave that impression." He always said it right, because He was God. He never apologized, never explained. He said, "This is the way it is," and they either got it or they didn't. And if they didn't get it, He told them a little more but He never backed out on anything that He said, because He is God.

Wisdom in the Bible is different from wisdom on earth, in that Bible wisdom has a moral connotation. It is high and holy, full of love and purity. The idea of shrewdness or cunning is never found in Scripture except when attributed to Satan or evil men. But wisdom, when attributed to God, to good men or to angels, always means the skill to achieve on a high, pure, loving level. There is never any shrewdness or craftiness in it.

God's Wisdom Is Infinite

Because God is wise, He has to be all-wise. He couldn't be a little bit wise. If I thought that God were only a little bit wise, or even ninety percent wise, I'd never get to sleep tonight. If I were to listen to the 10 o'clock news and hear what they're doing in the Congo and in Laos, if I heard that enemy soldiers had broken through the lines—if I knew those things and believed that God were only partly right, I'd never be able to sleep. I'd worry myself into a state of shock. But I believe that God is infinitely wise, altogether discreet. "The LORD by wisdom hath founded the earth; by understanding hath he established the heavens" (Proverbs 3:19). We don't have to worry about it, because God is wise—infinitely wise.

The wisdom of God is seen in His creation and in His redemption, in that God has planned the highest good for the highest number for the longest time. I hate the word *opportunist*. I don't hate people, I hate things. I don't hate a cringing, palm-licking opportunistic preacher. I couldn't hate him and be a Christian. But I hate the cringing, crawling, slimy way he lives. And I don't like opportunism, because it's an attitude that doesn't think about next year, let alone eternity; it's only about the next time—the next time they send in a report to headquarters, or the next time they're called somewhere else. Opportunists work only for the time being.

God, on the other hand, always thinks of the highest good, for the greatest number, for the longest time. God always thinks in terms of eternity. When God plans to bless a man, He takes that poor, little, time-cursed creature in His hand and says, "My son, I breathe into you eternity and immortality; I let you share in my endlessness." If you really knew how long you were privileged to live and to be with God, you would rejoice! God Almighty has planned that you shall not only enjoy Him now, but for all the eternities to come. And it's for the greatest number and the highest good.

Sometimes churches and governing boards do things to get a little more money or a few more members, but it's not for the highest good of the people. Every church should be run for the highest good of the greatest number of people, even if it appears to flop. That's the way God has planned it.

God's Wisdom Revealed

As we look at where the wisdom of God is revealed, remember that allegory of the beautiful palace; remember that it can be disputed by unbelieving men. They will walk by the beautiful palace that now is a pigpen and say, "You can't prove to me that the God who made this is wise and good—there's too much pain, crime, sin and filth." I repeat: God Almighty is running His world; the day will come when God will lift a cloud off the world and they shall gather in admiration from everywhere and say how wonderful God is:

> Thou art worthy, O Lord, to receive glory and honour and power: for thou hast created all things, and for thy pleasure they are and were created. . . . Thou art worthy . . . for thou wast slain, and hast redeemed us to God by thy blood out of every kindred, and tongue, and people, and nation; and hast made us unto our God kings and priests: and we shall reign on the earth. . . . Worthy is the Lamb that was slain to receive power, and riches, and wisdom, and strength, and honour, and glory, and blessing. (Revelation 4:11; 5:9-10, 12)

And we shall be admired and God shall be admired in us.

Notice that when God did His most awful, majestic works, He always did them in the darkness. In the creation, you may remember that it says, "In the beginning God created the heaven and the earth. And the earth was without form, and void; and darkness was upon the face of the deep. . . . And God said, Let there be light: and there was light"

(Genesis 1:1-3). Back there in the darkness, God was doing some wonderful, awful, terrible, glorious things—as much as to say, "I don't even want the angels, seraphim or archangels to see what I'm doing."

And when God incarnated His Son, bringing Him into the world as a man, He did not send Him down out of heaven, shining like a meteor to startle the world. He formed Him in the sweet darkness of the virgin's womb, unseen by mortal eye. The bones were formed in the womb of her that was with child. It was as if God were saying, "In My infinite wisdom, I am incarnating My eternal Word in the form of a Man, and no one will see My mystery." And they never did!

And when He was nailed on the cross, hanging there twisting and writhing in death for you and me, darkness settled down on the earth, like a cloud upon Him—as though God were saying, "You can't see Him; I won't even let you see Him die. I'm doing my wonders of the atonement in the darkness." And when the atonement was done and He said, "It is finished" (John 19:30), God lifted the night and they took Him down and put Him away in the tomb.

And when they came to see Him rise, He was already risen. They came a long while before day, when it was still dark, but He was not there; He was risen! Every great thing that God has done, He has done in the silence and the darkness because His wisdom is such that no man could understand it anyhow.

In redemption, Christ was crucified: "Christ the power of God, and the wisdom of God. . . . But we speak the wisdom of God in a mystery, even the hidden wisdom, which God ordained before the world unto our glory" (1 Corinthians 1:24; 2:7). In salvation, God requires us to repent and believe. This is done by the wise counsel of God: "For after that in the wisdom of God the world by wisdom knew not God, it pleased God by the foolishness of preaching to save them that believe" (1:21). And in the consummation, we also see God's wisdom: "To the intent that now unto the principalities and powers in heavenly places might be known by the church the manifold wisdom of God" (Ephesians 3:10). So in all of this, the all-wise wisdom of God is being revealed.

The crux of your life lies right there. It doesn't matter whether you know this little wisp of systematic theology or not; that isn't the point. The point is that it's either got to be God's wisdom or yours. It's either God's way or yours. All that you and I have lived for, hoped for and dreamed over in our heart of hearts—life, safety, happiness, heaven, immortality, the presence of God—hinges on whether you're going to accept the ultimate wisdom of the Triune God, as revealed in the Scriptures and in His providential working in mankind. Or are you going to go your own way?

The most perfect definition of sin that I know of is given by Isaiah in 53:6: "All we like sheep have gone astray; we have turned every one to his own way." Turning to our own way is the essence of sin. I turn to my way because I think it is wiser than God's way.

God may say to some businessman, "Tithe your income this year."

The businessman says, "Oh, God, I can't do it!" God says, "Tithe it, son."

And he says, "I can't do it, because if I do, I won't be able to pay my taxes."

God says, "Tithe it, son."

But he still says, "I can't do it, God," and he doesn't. And the next year, he doesn't make as much and his business peters out. Why? Because he's not obeying God.

A starry-eyed young lady looks at that big fellow that she loves and wants so much, but he's a sinner and has no intention of being anything else but a sinner, while she's a born-again Christian. So she throws herself down on her knees before God and cries, "Oh, God, what shall I do?"

The voice within her says, *You know what you need to do: "Be ye not unequally yoked together with unbelievers: for what fellowship hath righteousness with unrighteousness? and what communion hath light with darkness?"* (2 Corinthians 6:14).

But she leaps to her feet and says, "No, God. I can't pay that price; it's too much." So she compromises; she takes her wisdom against God's wisdom and marries the guy. Then he refuses to go to church at all and makes her life a hell from that hour on. Five years and two or three children later, her husband has left her. She comes to her pastor with a broken heart and says, "Pastor what can I do?"

Being a decent pastor and not wanting to hurt her feelings, he doesn't remind her that back when the wisdom of God said, "Don't marry him," she said, "I know better than You, God."

This is the crux of our life. This is the difference between revival and a dead church. This is the difference between a Spirit-filled life and a self-filled life. Who's running it? Who's the boss? Whose wisdom is prevailing—the wisdom of God or the wisdom of man?

In all the providential dealings of God with me, I must take my stand and decide that God's way is right. When things seem to go wrong with me, instead of believing they're going wrong, I believe they're going right. I take on faith Romans 8:28: "And we know that all things work together for good to them that love God, to them who are the called according to his purpose."

I've got to decide whether I shall go my way or trust blindly in the wisdom of God. If I trust blindly in God's wisdom, God promises, "I will bring the blind by a way that they knew not; I will lead them in paths that they have not known: I will make darkness light before them, and crooked things straight" (Isaiah 42:16). God will lead me through and "when he hath tried me, I shall come forth as gold" (Job 23:10). And God will lead me into a rich place and make me rich with treasures in heaven that can never die.

But if a man wants his own way, the Lord will let him go his own way. We have to decide as Christians whether we insist on our plans and ambitions, or whether we will take God's way. If we insist upon our plans and ambitions, we imperil everything we have, because we lack the wisdom to know how to do it. You dare not run your life.

Once I got on a flight out of New York and as we started off, it was terribly windy. A man sitting next to me had flown a lot, but he didn't like the turbulence. "Well," I said, "when we get over the city and gain altitude, it'll level off." And it did. But when we were in that turbulence, I didn't jump up and run into the cockpit and say to the pilots, "Now, listen boys, let me take over." Do you know where we'd have been if I'd have taken over? We'd have been nose down in Times Square. I didn't take over; I let the pilots have the controls.

I don't mind a little turbulence when we're landing or taking off, but when we're flying up there at 17,000 feet and the "fasten your seat belt" sign comes on, I say to myself, "Uh-oh— what are we in for now?" But I have always kept my head and I've never gone forward to the cockpit and said, "Now, you two fellows get out of here"—never.

And yet we're doing that to God all the time. We go to church and we pray to give our heart to the Lord; we sign a card and get converted; we join the church and get baptized. But then things get turbulent and we run and say, "Lord, let me run this thing!" That's why we're so messed up in our Christian lives. We're not ready to let God run our world for us—to run our family, our business, our home, our job, our everything.

The wise God always thinks of your highest good, for the longest time. He always does what he does with flawless precision, seeing the end from the beginning, never making any mistakes and never asking anything from you that you can't do or don't have. He never makes any unfair demands, but knows you're flesh and treats you with a heart of compassion. Whatever He commands, He gives you the power to obey the command—always. You can trust this kind of God. The difficulty with us is, we don't trust God. And that's why we're in the fix that we're in.

Are you going to turn everything over to the Infinite Love? I heard a great preacher one time tell about a man whose business had failed and someone else had bought him out. So on Friday they bought him out and Monday he was back sitting in the executive desk. And the man who bought him out came and said, "Who are you?"

He replied, "I'm the fellow who used to own this business." "Yes, you used to own it," the new owner said, "but you ran it into the ground and I've taken over." Then he chased him out of there and took over.

When God takes over a bankrupt human life He says, "You're in debt over your ears. I'll take over. I'll bail you out, I'll pay your debts, I'll fix you up. But I'll run your business." Then after we get blessed Sunday night, on Monday morning we're back at the desk again. And the Holy Ghost says to us, "I thought that last night in prayer you got out of that chair! Get out of there, let Me run it." God wants to run your business, your home, your wife, your husband, your children, your school and everything. He wants to do it and He will do it.

Three Classes of People

The average congregation is divided into three classes of people: the unblessed, the uncommitted and the committed. The unblessed are those who do not believe sufficiently in the wisdom of God to trust Him to take their life over. They have never given themselves to Jesus Christ, because they know it means a commitment that they are not willing to make. They may believe in God; they may believe that Christ died for their sins, but they are not ready to surrender themselves and let God run their world. They are out of the fold, not born again, unblessed.

Then there's the uncommitted. They are not rebels against God; they have "accepted Christ," as we say, and had some kind of spiritual experience, but they've never been willing to turn their lives over. They have not been willing to say before God, "Lord, You run my life from now on." They are hanging in the middle. They are the ones that are always spiritually up and down.

In the South, such people go to the altar every time a new evangelist comes around. They have a kind of a wry joke about it down there. They will say about a such a man, "The only way he'll get to heaven is if somebody hits him over the head with an ax just after he's converted!" He's sure to be backsliding, because he doesn't commit himself. He gets "conversion" whenever the evangelist comes around, which is two or three times a year, then he backslides in the meantime.

Of course, up North we've had better Bible teaching, so we don't do that. The uncommitted will say,

"I'm saved and that's it. I believe I'm saved and I'm kept." They've got all the answers, but they're uncommitted and miserable.

Many students are uncommitted to their education. They play their way through school and get fairly good grades by cramming for exams. And there are Christians who play their way through life, getting old while playing at Christianity.

Then there are the committed ones—they've committed themselves to the wisdom of God forever. They are satisfied that God shall have His way and that His wisdom will rule them from now on. They won't interfere and let their own heads get in the way. They begin to shine like the sun. You can always recognize them.

Down at Nyack College a generation ago, a man said to me, "You know, there are a few students who come here that are different. They seem to have something. The rest of us are just good folks. But these few seem to have something. You can always tell it." And you can—they're the committed ones, the ones who have gone to God and have said, in effect, "My Father, from this moment on take over my life. You run it; I will not interfere. I will not complain if it's hard, get discouraged if it seems to fail or take credit if it seems to succeed. Thine be the glory, Thine be the honor. I'm committed, Lord, to Thy eternal wisdom. I'm not going to dishonor Thee by doubting."

You can make that decision. It's just like getting married. Two people simply say "I do" and they are married. No matter which direction their emotions may run, they've settled something by a vow. In the same way, you can go before God and pull that ragged uncommitted life into full commitment. God says, "Wilt thou, from this day forward, forsake all others and take Me? Will you trust My Son to run your life and not try to run it yourself? If so, answer 'I do.'"

If you answer, "Oh, God, I do," it becomes to you what the vows of wedlock become. It changes the course and direction and relationships of your life.

Will you dare to trust His eternal wisdom? If so, then pray, *Oh, God the Father, forgive me for doubting. Thou art infinitely wise and I need infinite wisdom in my ignorance. Take over my life and be my wisdom, my righteousness, my sanctification. From here on, I acknowledge that Thou art eternally wise. Be my Anchor and Guiding Star.*

It will change your whole life.

Chapter 8

God's Sovereignty

*Know therefore this day, and consider it in thine heart, that the L*ORD *he is God in heaven above, and upon the earth beneath: there is none else. (Deuteronomy 4:39)*

See now that I, even I, am he, and there is no god with me: I kill, and I make alive; I wound, and I heal: neither is there any that can deliver out of my hand. For I lift up my hand to heaven, and say, I live for ever. (Deuteronomy 32:39-40)

*Who knoweth not in all these that the hand of the L*ORD *hath wrought this? In whose hand is the soul of every living thing, and the breath of all mankind. . . . With him is strength and wisdom: the deceived and the deceiver are his. He leadeth counsellers away spoiled, and maketh the judges fools. . . . Why dost thou strive against him? for he giveth not account of any of his matters. (Job 12:9-10, 16-17; 33:13)*

*O house of Israel, cannot I do with you as this pot-
ter? saith the LORD. Behold, as the clay is in the
potter's hand, so are ye in mine hand, O house of
Israel. (Jeremiah 18:6)*

*How great are his signs! and how mighty are his
wonders! his kingdom is an everlasting kingdom,
and his dominion is from generation to generation. . . . And all the inhabitants of the earth are
reputed as nothing: and he doeth according to his
will in the army of heaven, and among the inhabitants of the earth: and none can stay his hand, or
say unto him, What doest thou? (Daniel 4:3, 35)*

*The LORD is slow to anger, and great in power, and
will not at all acquit the wicked: the LORD hath
his way in the whirlwind and in the storm, and
the clouds are the dust of his feet. (Nahum 1:3)*

To say that God is sovereign is to say that He
is supreme over all things, that there is no
one above Him, that He is absolute Lord over
creation. It is to say that His Lordship over creation
means that there is nothing out of His control, nothing that God hasn't foreseen and planned. It means
that even the wrath of man must ultimately praise
God and the remainder of wrath God will restrain
(Psalm 76:10). It means that every creature on
earth, in heaven and in hell must ultimately bow
the knee and confess that Jesus Christ is Lord to the
glory of God the Father (Philippians 2:10).

God's sovereignty logically implies His absolute

freedom to do all that He wills to do. God's sovereignty does not mean that He can do anything, but it means He can do anything that He wills to do. The sovereignty of God and the will of God are bound up together. The sovereignty of God does not mean that God can lie, for God does not will to lie. God is truth and therefore God cannot lie, for He wills not to lie. God cannot break a promise, because to break a promise would be to violate His nature, and God does not will to violate His nature.

Therefore it is silly to say that God can do anything. But it is scriptural to say that God can do anything He wills to do. God is absolutely free—no one can compel Him, no one can hinder Him, no one can stop Him. God has freedom to do as He pleases—always, everywhere and forever.

God's sovereignty means that if there's anybody in this wide world of sinful men that should be restful and peaceful in an hour like this, it should be Christians. We should not be under the burden of apprehension and worry because we are the children of a God who is always free to do as He pleases. There is not one rope or chain or hindrance upon Him, because He is absolutely sovereign.

God is free to carry out His eternal purposes to their conclusions. I have believed this since I first became a Christian. I had good teachers who taught me this and I have believed it with increasing joy ever since. God does not play by ear, or doodle, or follow whatever happens to come into His mind or let one idea suggest another. God works according to the plans which He purposed in Christ Jesus before Adam walked in the garden, before the sun, moon and stars were made. God, who has lived all our tomorrows and carries time in His bosom, is carrying out His eternal purposes.

His eternal purposes will not change, however the prophetic teachers may change their minds or whatever contemporary theologians may decide is the right thing to believe. God Almighty has already given us His theology, and I don't give a snap of my finger for contemporary theology. I believe in theology, which is contemporary surely, but it is also as ancient as the throne of God and as eternal as the eternities to come. And we Christians are in this mighty river, being carried along by the sovereign purposes of God.

The sovereignty of God involves all authority and all power. I think you can see instantly that God could never be sovereign without the power to bring about His will or the authority to exercise His power. Kings, presidents and others who rule over men must have the authority to govern and the power to make good on that authority. A ruler cannot stand up and say, "Do this, please, if you feel like doing it." He says, "Do it," and then has an army and a police force behind him. He has authority to command and power to carry out his commands. And God has to have both of these.

I can't conceive of a God who has power and no authority. Samson was a man who had power but no authority, and didn't know what to do with it. There are men who have authority but no power. The United Nations is a pathetic example of authority without power. In the Congo, for example, the U.N. stands up and says, "We order you to do this and that," but the Congolese laugh and say, "You and who else?" and do as they please. Authority without the power to carry out that authority is a joke. Power without authority puts a man where he can't do anything. But God Almighty, to be sovereign, must have authority and power.

We've already discussed how God is infinite in His perfections, one of which is His absolute power. God is omnipotent—He has all the power there is. The next question is, does God have the authority? I think it is rather foolish even to discuss it. Can anyone imagine God having to ask permission? Can anybody imagine the great God Almighty, maker of heaven and earth, having to send out a memo to a higher authority and ask, "Might I please roll this star over there, or do something with this galaxy?" Can you imagine Him applying to a higher authority? To whom would God apply? Who is higher than the highest? Who was there before He was? Who is mightier than the Almighty? At whose throne would God kneel for authority? No, there is no one greater! "I am the first, and I am the last; and beside me there is no God" (Isaiah 44:6).

There is a religion, Zoroastrianism, which is to my mind the best of the non-Christian, non-revelational religions. It postulates a theological duality. That is, it says that there are two gods, a good one and a bad one. It's a neat way of getting around things, you know. Ahura Mazda is the good god, who made everything good. But then there was a rascal of a god named Ahriman. For everything good that Ahura Mazda made, Ahriman made something bad. Ahura Mazda made the sunshine, Ahriman made the snow. Ahura Mazda made love and Ahriman made hate. Ahura Mazda made life and Ahriman made death. There were two gods, both of them creating.

Now God Almighty declares this couldn't be so, because He is the sole Creator. The Bible tells us this about Jesus Christ our Lord:

> For by him were all things created, that are in heaven, and that are in earth, visible and invisible, whether they be thrones, or dominions, or principalities, or powers: all things were created by him, and for him: and he is before all things, and by him all things consist. (Colossians 1:16-17).

"In the beginning God created the heaven and the earth" (Genesis 1:1) and God made all things that are therein. There was no other creating god. That is one attribute that God did not give to anybody else. God can impart some of His attributes, such as love, mercy or kindness. But He can't impart the attribute that enables Him to create. God Almighty alone is the Creator; there are not two gods, only one.

But sin is loose in the universe and this I do not understand. It is called "the mystery of iniquity" (2 Thessalonians 2:7) and it is said that it already works. This mystery of iniquity I do not understand. I do not know why a Holy God could allow to let loose in His world this iniquitous thing. But I know that God contains it and I know that God's plans took it into account. And I know that when God laid His plans for heaven and earth and the creation of Adam, He knew about sin and knew about its wild, fugitive presence in the universe, so He took it into account. Though this outlaw called sin is now in the heavens, it can no more change the purposes of God or frustrate the plans of God than an outlaw hiding in the wilds of Canada can prevent the work of this nation.

God's Sovereignty and Free Will

But if God is sovereign, what about man's free will? Maybe you would rather not have your mind troubled about this. Maybe you'd rather just rest. But to quote someone else, the business of a prophet of God is to comfort the afflicted and afflict the comfortable. If you are comfortable, perhaps you need to be afflicted. And one of the best ways to afflict you is to get you thinking about divine things.

The matter of man's free will versus God's sovereignty can be explained in this way: God's sovereignty means that He is in control of everything, that He planned everything from the beginning. Man's free will means that he can, anytime he wants, make most any choice he pleases (within his human limitations, of course). Man's free will can apparently defy the purposes of God and will against the will of God. Now how do we resolve this seeming contradiction?

Down through the years, two divisions of the church have attempted to resolve this dilemma in different ways. One division emphasizes the sovereignty of God, believing that God planned everything from the beginning, that God ordered that some would be saved and some lost, that Christ died for those who would be saved, but He didn't die for the others who would not be saved. That is actually what followers of John Calvin believe. On the other side, there are those who say that Christ died for all and that man is free to make his choice. But those who teach the sovereignty of God in this exclusive way say that if man is free to make a choice, then God isn't sovereign. Because if a man can make a choice that God doesn't like, then God does not have His way.

I've thought this through and come to a way to resolve this dilemma. I don't know anyone else who has expressed this same theory in preaching or writing. The theologians can straighten me out on this if I'm wrong. (I preached this one time in the presence of Dr. Martin Lloyd Jones, one of the great English authorities in theology, and he didn't dispute it; he just smiled. He didn't say he believed it, but he didn't say that he didn't!) But I'd like to give it to you and see what you think of it.

God's sovereignty means absolute freedom, doesn't it? God is absolutely free to do anything He wants or wills to do—anywhere, anytime, forever. And man's free will means that man can make any choice he wants to make, even if he makes a choice against the will of God. There is where the theologians lock horns like two deer out in the woods and wallow around until they die. I refuse to get caught on either horn of that dilemma! Here is what I see: God Almighty is sovereign, free to do as He pleases. Among the things He is pleased to do is give me freedom to do what I please. And when I do what I please, I am fulfilling the will of God, not controverting it, for God in His sovereignty has sovereignly given me freedom to make a free choice.

Even if the choice I make is not the one God would have made for me, His sovereignty is fulfilled in my making the choice. And I can make the choice because the great sovereign God, who is completely free, said to me, "In my sovereign freedom I bestow a little bit of freedom on you. Now 'choose you this day whom ye will serve' (Joshua 24:15). Be good or be bad at your own pleasure. Follow Me or don't follow Me, come on or go back. Go to heaven or go to hell."

The sovereign God has put the decision in your lap and said, "This is yours; you must make that choice." And when I make a choice, I'm fulfilling His sovereignty, in that He sovereignly wills that I should be free to make a choice. If I choose to go to hell, it's not what His love would have chosen, but it does not controvert nor cancel out His sovereignty. Therefore I can take John Calvin in one hand and Jacob Arminius in the other and walk down the street. (Neither of them would walk with me, I'm sure, because Calvin would say I was too Arminian and Arminius would say I was too Calvinistic!)

But I'm happy in the middle. I believe in the

sovereignty of God and in the freedom of man. I believe that God is free to do as He pleases and I believe that, in a limited sense, He has made man free to do as he pleases—within a certain framework, but not a very big one. After all, you're not free to do very many things. You're free to make moral choices. You're free to decide the color of your necktie, what foods you'll have and whom you'll marry—if she agrees, of course. You're free to do a few things, but not that many. But the things you are free to do are gifts from the God who is utterly free. Therefore, anytime I make a choice, I'm fulfilling the freedom God gave me and therefore I'm fulfilling God's sovereignty and carrying it out.

To illustrate what I'm talking about, suppose a ship leaves New York City bound for Liverpool, England, with a thousand passengers on board. They're going to take a nice, easy journey and enjoy the trip. Someone on board—usually the captain— is an authority who carries papers that say, "You are to bring this ship into the harbor in Liverpool."

After they leave New York and wave to the people on shore, the next stop is Liverpool. That's it! They're out on the ocean. Soon they lose sight of the Statue of Liberty, but they haven't come yet in sight of the English coast. They are out floating around on the ocean. What do they do? Is everyone bound in chains, with the captain walking around with a stick to keep them in line? No. Over here is a shuffleboard court, over there is a tennis court and a swimming pool. Over here you can look at pictures; over there you can listen to music.

The passengers are perfectly free to roam around as they please on the deck of the ship. But they're not free to change the course of that ship. It's going to Liverpool no matter what they do. They can jump off if they want to, but if they stay on board, they're going to Liverpool—nobody can change that. And yet, they're perfectly free within the confines of that ship.

In the same way, you and I have our little lives. We are born and God says, "I have launched you onto the sea from the shore of birth. You're going to go into the little port we call death. In the meantime, you are free to romp around all you want— just remember that you are going to answer for what you've done when you get over there." So we throw our weight around and make demands, declaring that we can do as we please. We boast about our freedom. We've got a little freedom, all right, but remember, we can't change God Almighty's course. God has said that those who follow Jesus Christ and believe in Him shall be saved, and those who refuse shall be damned. That's settled—eternally, sovereignly settled. But you and I have freedom in the meantime, to do anything we want to do. And though most people think very little about it, we're going to answer for that someday, according to the sovereign will of God.

God has certain plans that He is going to carry out. "The LORD hath his way in the whirlwind and in the storm, and the clouds are the dust of his feet" (Nahum 1:3). When God is carrying on His plans, He is moving in a certain direction. When the enemy comes along (exercising the little freedom God has given him to be an enemy of God) and intersects the will and purpose of God, then there's trouble. As long as we move in the will of God, everything goes smoothly. But when we get out of the will of God, then we have trouble on our hands.

God made the heaven and the earth in Genesis 1:1, but then there was a mysterious gap between Genesis 1:1 and 1:2: "And darkness was upon the face of the deep. And the spirit of God moved upon the face of the waters." What had happened between verses 1 and 2? Perhaps this was when the great fall from the heavenly places occurred. Perhaps this was when Satan and his legions fell and brought darkness upon the world. Then God Almighty moved upon that darkness and the Spirit of God brooded upon the face of the waters. "And God said, Let there be light: and there was light" (1:3). God began a work of re-creation; He re-created the earth, put man upon it and started things all over again.

Then the fall came and it looked as if man was lost forever. I think Milton was right in *Paradise Lost* when he pictured Satan as saying, "I think that I can do God more harm by injuring His human race than I can by trying to injure Him." So he gave up the idea of taking heaven by military storm; instead, he came to the garden and tempted the woman. After the human race was fallen, it looked as if God's plans once more had been controverted and that God could not now carry on His plan to fill His world with a people made after His own image.

Once I heard a Southern preacher describe the first Adam as a wheel spinning on an axle. When the wheel flew off the axle, God put the last Adam on. That's a good way to describe it. When the first Adam was fouled, the second Adam stepped in. In fact, He's been in the plan of God from the beginning of creation. God had His way in the whirlwind and the storm, and made the clouds of history to be the dust of His feet.

When the Israelites were in Egypt, God wanted to take them back to the Promised Land. God said, "Let my people go" (Exodus 7:16). But Egypt, exercising its little authority which God had allowed it to have, refused to let them go. Then came the clouds that were the dust of God's feet: the ten terrible plagues which God sent out of heaven, to strike down the ten gods of Egypt. And when it was all over, there was a death in every home in Egypt, but Israel was free, singing the song in the fifteenth chapter of Exodus. They were free on the other side of the Red Sea, while the terrible armies of Egypt were all dead men.

When history goes along with God, all is well. When history goes contrary to the ways of God, then there is storm and flood and fire. But when it's over, God has His way in the whirlwind and the storm, and makes the clouds to be the dust of His feet.

When Jesus Christ our Lord was born, I would think He was an average baby boy who couldn't hold his head up, couldn't speak, had no teeth and, I suppose, very little hair— poor, helpless little lad!

If they left Him alone even for a little while, He'd have died. He had the true helplessness of a baby. And He hadn't been born very long when Herod issued the order that all the babies in Bethlehem should be slain (Matthew 2:16). Here God Almighty allowed, in the irony of history, that this tiny piece of humanity, so small He had to be nursed to sleep on His mother's bosom, would be arrayed against the whole Roman Empire.

But look who won! Before many decades had gone by, the Roman Empire went down into dust and disgrace, but the baby Jesus grew to manhood, was crucified and rose again from the dead. God raised Him up and seated Him up yonder, so that the baby that once stood opposed to the Roman Empire now looks down upon an empire that doesn't exist anymore.

I remember back in the days of Stalin [early leader of the Soviet Union], he was quoted as saying, "We will pull that bearded god out of the sky." But the God who looked down upon chaos and said, "Let there be light," who looked down upon Egypt and said, "Let my people go," who looked down upon the Roman Empire and said, "You can't slay My Son" but allowed that empire to slay itself—that God looked down quietly upon Stalin and heard him say, "We will pull that bearded god out of the sky." But that great God Almighty is still in His sky.

Stalin, on the other hand, is dead. They've pickled him and put him on display in the Kremlin—the one who was going to "pull the bearded god out of the sky." But the God who makes the whirlwinds of history to be the dust of His feet looks with a pitying smile upon one of the worst men that ever lived.

It says in the book of Revelation (how I love this passage; it is beautiful to me, though I don't have to know all that it means),

> After this I looked, and, behold, a door was opened in heaven: and the first voice which I heard was as it were of a trumpet talking with me; which said, Come up hither, and I will shew thee things which must be hereafter. And immediately I was in the spirit: and, behold, a throne was set in heaven, and one sat on the throne. And he that sat was to look upon like a jasper and a sardine stone: and there was a rainbow round about the throne, in sight like unto an emerald. (Revelation 4:1-3)

A rainbow is just a half-circle—it starts at the horizon, arches around and stops at the horizon. But this rainbow made a full circle—as though God were saying, "The green emerald rainbow, meaning immortality and endlessness, circles My throne." No one can destroy God.

Sovereignty in the Crucifixion

God's sovereignty was seen at Jesus' death. He had lived His life on earth among men. He was thirty-three years old and the time came when He should have been king over Israel, so the people thought. They even tried to make Him king by force (John

6:15), but He said no. So they took Him and nailed Him on the cross.

I heard a Welsh preacher say one time—and I think he's right—that the disciples never thought anybody could nail Jesus on the tree, that they never believed Jesus could die. They believed that this Man, this wondrous Man that could still the waves, heal the sick, cast out the devil and make the blind to see, could not die. Or if He died, they believed He would immediately rise again in majesty and be king over Israel. And yet, there He lay, hanging on a cross. They came and took Him down. With great sadness and tears they wrapped Him up in His burial robes. They used ointments to try to give Him some kind of embalming and laid Him in Joseph's new tomb.

A few days later, two men walked alone on the road to Emmaus. And as they walked, a Man arrived beside them, and said to them (I'm paraphrasing here), "Why do you look so sad? Why are your voices so low? Why do you seem so depressed?"

They replied, "You must be a stranger in Jerusalem. Don't you know that a great prophet arose and we believed He was the Son of God? And we didn't believe He could die, or, if He died, we believed He would rise. Now this is the third day and nothing has happened and all our hopes have caved in. There's nothing but bleak discouragement before us."

And He began to talk to them. As He talked, He acted as if He was going to continue on, so they invited Him to stay and eat. When He broke the bread, they saw the nail prints in His hands, so they looked at each other and He disappeared from their sight. They leaped to their feet and said, "Did not our heart burn?" (See Luke 24:13-32.)

God Almighty came down and did the wonderful miracle of all miracles: He raised from the grave a Man that had died and glorified Him. And so the Sovereign God had His way in the whirlwind and the storm again.

Today we are entering a period in history the likes of which there has never been since Jesus Christ and the Roman Empire stood opposed to one another. The God who lived back then lives now, so I have no fear and no doubt; I can sleep restfully because I believe that God has His plans and will carry them out.

What are the plans of God? For one thing, there are God's promises to Abraham and to Israel. God made them and God will carry them out. God said to Abraham that his descendents would have the land. And He said to Israel that he would reign over the house of Jacob forever. I believe that God will fulfill His promises to Abraham and Israel. I don't think that there is any possibility of stopping God from doing it.

God has also decreed that a ransomed company would be called and glorified. Right after the second World War, missionaries began to say that there were only so many more years left for missionary activity. Young people that felt called to the mission field didn't go because they said, "What's the use of getting ready for the mission field? It looks as if the doors are closing, one after another."

But you can be absolutely certain that the God who is perfectly free, anywhere, all the time, to do everything He wills to do, will carry out His purposes. And one of His purposes is to bring forth a ransomed people from every tongue, people, tribe, nation, color, race and ethnic origin around the world (Revelation 5:9). He will make them to be like His holy Son, and they will be the bride of His Son. Jesus Christ, the Son of God, will introduce them to the Father—ransomed, redeemed and purified—for they were virgins and they walked with the Lamb. I believe in this.

I don't believe that the divisions in the church or the false "isms" that are abroad everywhere will change or hinder the purpose of God. He will have His way in the whirlwind and in the storm, and the clouds will be the dust of His feet.

God has also declared that sinners shall be cleansed out of the earth (Psalm 104:35). The sinners are pretty deeply entrenched now. Organized crime in the United States is operating from coast to coast. The criminals are so well organized that the authorities, even the FBI, can't oppose them. If they arrest them, the Supreme Court turns them loose on insufficient evidence. Sin is pretty well entrenched in the world—organized like a cancer that's gone to work on the body of a man.

I've heard of cancer spreading throughout a person's body until its roots were everywhere, like an octopus. Of course, that patient didn't last long. If it were not for the Sovereign God running His world, the human race couldn't last long. The cancer of iniquity, like some vile disease, has its roots everywhere. But God says that He's going to cleanse sinners out of the earth. There will be "new heavens and a new earth, wherein dwelleth righteousness" (2 Peter 3:13). God has ordained that the earth shall be renovated and sinners shall be cleansed away.

Nothing and nobody can stop God. You may say, "God means well, and He has power and authority, but some unforeseen circumstance may derail His plans." But for God there are no unforeseen circumstances! When you start out on a walk down the block, a black cat may run in front of you; a policeman may call you aside; you may drop dead; a car may run up on the sidewalk and break your leg. You never can tell. Unforeseen circumstances are everywhere around you and me—but the Sovereign God knows nothing about unforeseen circumstances. He has seen the end from the beginning. He never needs to ask what is in a man; He knows every man. So there can be no unforeseen circumstances.

There are also no accidents in God's eyes, because God's wisdom prevents an accident. You may be driving down the highway at forty miles an hour. A tire blows and you turn over in the ditch. Somebody didn't make that tire quite right and it didn't hang together. (I used to make tires in a rubber factory in Akron, Ohio; with some of the workmanship we put into them, it's a wonder they didn't blow out before they got out of the factory!) But God Almighty's wisdom never has a blowout. God Almighty knows what He's doing; He's utterly wise and there can be no accident. Nobody can countermand an order.

They say that one of the greatest difficulties during World War II was countermanded orders. They had so many tough generals—Montgomery, Alexander, Eisenhower—and these men were busy. One would give an order and another would countermand it. You can read accounts of it here and there. One fellow starts doing something and somebody else says, "Just a minute! I got an order from so-and-so, canceling that." Then the other fellow would say, "I just got an order from somebody else telling me to do it." Round and round they ran in circles.

But I ask you, who can countermand an order given by the great God Almighty? When the Sovereign God says it shall be this way, it's that way and nobody can change it!

Some may wonder if God might fail because of weakness. But the omnipotent God couldn't be weak, because God has all the power there is. H-bombs, cobalt bombs, A-bombs and all the rest of them— they are nothing! They are the marbles God plays with. God, in His infinite strength, wisdom, authority and power, is having His way in the whirlwind and the storm. That's what sovereignty means.

What does all this mean to you and me? It means that if you walk out of church contrary to the will and way of God, God does not will that you should do it, but He wills that you should be free to do it. And when you freely choose to walk against the way of God, you choose freely to go on the road to perdition. That's one thing about heaven and hell—no one is in either place by accident. Hell is populated by people who chose to go there. They may not have chosen the destination, but they chose the highway. They are there because they love the way that leads to darkness. And they were free to take it because the Sovereign God had granted them that much freedom. Everyone in heaven above is there because he chose to go there. No one wakes up to find himself in heaven by accident, saying, "I never planned to come here." No! It says that the rich man died and in hell he lifted up his eyes; the poor, good man died and went to Abraham's bosom (Luke 16:22-23). Each of them went where he belonged. When Judas died he went "to his own place" (Acts 1:25). And when Lazarus died, he went to his place—places they had chosen. So remember this: Whoever is not on God's side is on the losing side.

All of this applies to the matter of consecration and the deeper life, of obedience to the Lord. We smile and shrug and make it look as if it was optional—something we could do or not do, as we please. But consecration to the will of God is an absolute necessity, if you're going to be on God's side. If you're on God's side, you can't lose; if you're on the other side, you can't win. It's as easy as that. No matter how nice we may be, how righteous, how much we give to missions, how moral we are, if we're opposing God we can't win. But if we surrender and come over to God's side, we can't lose.

A man who is with God can't lose, because God can't lose. God is the sovereign God who is having His way in the whirlwind and the storm. And when the storm is over and the whirlwind of history has blown itself out, the God who sat on the throne with the rainbow round about it will still be seated on that throne. Beside Him will be a ransomed company who chose to go His way; heaven will not be filled with slaves.

There will be no conscripts marching in the armies of heaven. Everyone will be there because he exercised his sovereign freedom to choose to believe in Jesus Christ and surrender to the will of God.

I talked to a young man last Sunday night who said something to this effect: "I can't say yes to God. I can't surrender." He's a very fine, likeable, intelligent young man. But he couldn't say yes to the winning side. So he was saying yes to the losing side. If you say yes to God you can't lose. And if you say no to God you can't win.

If that's your trouble, you're striving with God. You ask, "Why don't I get filled with the Holy Ghost?" It's because you're striving with God. God wants you to go this way, but you go part way and then veer off. There's always a controversy there between you and God.

Are you on God's side—completely, wholly, forever? Have you given Him everything—your home, your business, your school, your choice of a partner in life? Choose Christ's way, because Christ is Lord and the Lord is sovereign. It's foolish to choose any other way. It's folly to try to outsmart God, to try to fight against Him. "Why dost thou strive against him?" (Job 33:13).

Chapter 9

God's Faithfulness

I will sing of the mercies of the LORD for ever: with my mouth will I make known thy faithfulness to all generations. . . . thy faithfulness shalt thou establish in the very heavens. . . . thy faithfulness also in the congregation of the saints. . . . O LORD God of hosts, who is a strong LORD like unto thee? or to thy faithfulness round about thee? . . . But my faithfulness and my mercy shall be with him: and in my name shall his horn be exalted. (Psalm 89:1-2, 5, 8, 24)

If we confess our sins, he is faithful and just to forgive us our sins, and to cleanse us from all unrighteousness. (1 John 1:9)

If we believe not, yet he abideth faithful: he cannot deny himself. (2 Timothy 2:13)

Faithful is he that calleth you, who also will do it. (1 Thessalonians 5:24)

God is never out of date. Regardless of the season of the year, it's always proper to preach about God. The faithfulness of God is one of the attributes of the most High God, whose we are, and whom we claim to serve. The preceding verses are only a few of the texts that say that God is faithful. I intend to define faithfulness and then try to apply it and show what it means to us now.

Faithfulness is that in God which guarantees that He will never be or act inconsistent with Himself. You can put that down as an axiom. It is good for you now and good for you when you're dying. It will be good to remember as you rise from the dead and good for all the eons and millenniums to come. God will never cease to be what He is and who He is. Everything God says or does must be in accord with His faithfulness. He will always be true to Himself, to His works and to His creation.

God is His own standard. God imitates nobody and is influenced by nobody. That may be hard to take in this degenerate age, when we've introduced the idea of the V.I.P., the man of influence. And they say, crudely enough, "It isn't what you know, it's who you know." But you can't influence God one way or another. And God imitates nobody—He is never forced to act out of character. Nothing can force God to act otherwise than faithfully to Himself and to us—no person, no circumstance, nothing.

If I can imagine someone who can influence God strongly enough to change His mind or compel Him to do anything that He hadn't planned to do, or be anything that He isn't, then I am thinking of someone greater than God—which is obvious nonsense. Who can be greater than the Greatest, higher than the Highest or mightier than the Mightiest?

The faithfulness of God guarantees that God will never cease to be who and what He is, just as His immutability guarantees that. You may remember what I said about the immutability of God—that if God changed in any way, He'd have to change in one of three directions: from better to worse, from worse to better or from one kind of being to another. Because God is absolutely, perfectly holy, He couldn't be anything less than holy, so He couldn't change from better to worse. And God couldn't get any holier than He is, so He couldn't change from worse to better. Also, God, being God and not a creature, could not change the kind of being that He is. God's perfection secures this. God's faithfulness also secures it, because God can never cease to be who He is and what He is.

Now that may sound a little dry, but if you get that inside of you and build on it, you'll be glad you know it the next time you're in a tough circumstance. You can live on froth and bubbles and little wisps of badly understood theology—until the pressure is on. And when the pressure is on, you'll want to know what kind of God you're serving.

This is the kind of God you're serving: All that God says or does must accord with all of His attributes, including His attribute of faithfulness. Every thought that God thinks, every word that God speaks, every act of God must accord with His faithfulness, wisdom, goodness, justice, holiness, love, truth and all His other attributes.

To magnify one phase of God's unitary character and diminish another is always wrong. The man of God who stands in the pulpit ought always to correct this error, as far as he can. He ought to see to it that we see God full-rounded, in all of His perfection and glory. If we magnify one attribute to the diminishing of another, we have an asymmetrical concept of God, a lopsided God—that is, He is lopsided as we see Him.

If you look at a tree, standing straight and tall, through the wrong kind of lens, you'll see it crooked. And you can see God crooked, but the crookedness is in your eye, not in God. For instance, if we make our God to be all justice, then we have a god of terror and we flee from him in fright. There was a time when the church swung over to hell, judgment, sin and all that. We rather tremble when we think of how the church went through this period, when about all she talked about was the justice of God. God was looked upon as a tyrant and the universe as a kind of totalitarian state, with God at the top, ruling with a rod of iron. If we think only of the justice of God, that's the concept we'll have.

Then over on the other side, as a reaction from that, came the time when we only thought about God as being love. "God is love" (1 John 4:16) is our main text now. We no longer have a god of terror, but a sentimental, spineless god—the god of the Christian Scientist. God is love and love is god and all is love and all is god and god is all. Pretty soon we haven't got a thing left. It's like the cotton candy that you buy at the circus—all you have is sweetness and nothing but sweetness. We've magnified the love of God without remembering that God is just.

Or if we make God all good then we have the weak sentimentalist of the modernist and the liberal. The god of the liberal and the modernist is not the God of the Bible, because in order to get the god they get they have to get rid of almost everything God did in the Old Testament. God couldn't make the sun stand still and He couldn't send fire on Sodom and Gomorrah. They say that was just nature. God couldn't send a worldwide flood upon the ungodly. They say that was just a little flood, like they had in Texas some time back. So in order to make room for a god that's nothing but good, that just sits up there in a great glob of goodness, they had to get rid of almost everything God ever did by way of justice.

If we make Him a god of grace and nothing else, as gospel churches have over the past fifty years, we have a god who cannot see moral distinctions. This is why the church has been unable to see moral distinctions. Instead of a separated, holy church, we have a church that's so geared into the world, you can't tell one from the other. It was said of a certain great English preacher that he preached grace in such a manner as to lower the moral standards of England. It's entirely possible to preach grace in the church until we become as arrogant and brazen as can be, forgetting that grace is one of the attributes

of God, but not all. While God is a God of grace, He
is also a God of justice, holiness and truth. Our God
will always be true to His nature, because He is a
faithful God.

Faithlessness is one of the greatest sources of
heartache and misery in all the world. God will
never be faithless; He cannot be. Back in the book
of Genesis, it says,

> Noah builded an altar unto the LORD; and
> took of every clean beast, and of every clean
> fowl, and offered burnt offerings on the altar.
> And the LORD smelled a sweet savour; and the
> LORD said in his heart, I will not again curse the
> ground any more for man's sake; for the imag-
> ination of man's heart is evil from his youth;
> neither will I again smite any more every thing
> living, as I have done. While the earth re-
> maineth, seedtime and harvest, and cold and
> heat, and summer and winter, and day and
> night shall not cease. (Genesis 8:20-22)

Therefore, don't pay a bit of attention to these
people who are saying that the world is going to be
swept off the earth with an atom bomb or a hydro-
gen bomb. Pay no attention to warnings that the
human race is going to be annihilated. God says,
"While the earth remaineth, seedtime and harvest,
and cold and heat, and summer and winter, and day
and night shall not cease" (8:22). And, "I will not
again curse the ground any more for man's sake"
(8:21). God has said it here. Further along, it says,

And God spake unto Noah, and to his sons with him, saying, And I, behold, I establish my covenant with you, and with your seed after you; and with every living creature that is with you, of the fowl, of the cattle, and of every beast of the earth with you; from all that go out of the ark, to every beast of the earth. And I will establish my covenant with you; neither shall all flesh be cut off any more by the waters of a flood; neither shall there any more be a flood to destroy the earth. . . . And it shall come to pass, when I bring a cloud over the earth, that the bow shall be seen in the cloud: and I will remember my covenant, which is between me and you and every living creature of all flesh; and the waters shall no more become a flood to destroy all flesh. And the bow shall be in the cloud; and I will look upon it, that I may remember the everlasting covenant between God and every living creature of all flesh that is upon the earth. (9:8-11, 14-16)

God wrote that long before they made that little bomb over there at the University of Chicago. God made that covenant before man made science and I'm perfectly restful in that covenant. I do not expect my children, grandchildren, greatgrandchildren or great-great-grandchildren to cease to be. And I don't expect them to turn into green men with one eye in the middle of their forehead. I expect God to fulfill His promise, because God can't help but do it. God must be true to Himself, and when God makes a promise, He must keep that promise. God made this promise unconditionally and will see to it that it stands.

We will continue to have summer and winter. We won't have Florida weather all over the world. We will always have snow in the winter. God said that summer and winter, harvest and springtime will always be here, so you can expect that. God said it, and I believe it.

God says in the Psalms that "He hath remembered his covenant for ever, the word which he commanded to a thousand generations" (Psalm 105:8). And our Lord said, "Till heaven and earth pass, one jot or one tittle shall in no wise pass from the law, till all be fulfilled" (Matthew 5:18). You can count on that.

That is the fact before us: God is faithful! He will remain faithful because He cannot change. He is perfectly faithful, because God is never partly anything. God is perfectly all that He is and never partly what He is. You can be sure that God will always be faithful. This faithful God, who never broke a promise and never violated a covenant, who never said one thing and meant another, who never overlooked anything or forgot anything, is the Father of our Lord Jesus and the God of the gospel. This is the God we adore and the God we preach.

God's Faithfulness to Sinners

Let us now look at God's faithfulness in its application. As it applies to sinners, if you are lost and you know it, God has declared that He will banish from His presence all who love sin and reject His Son. God has promised that; He has declared that; He has warned and threatened, and it will be so. Let no one trust a desperate hope, for it is based on the belief that God threatens but doesn't fulfill. No, God waits that He may be gracious! And He will sometimes postpone in order to give us another thirty days, another sixty days, to make up our minds. But just as sure as the mills of God grind, the souls of men fall into them and are ground exceedingly small. God moves slowly and is very patient, but God has promised that He will banish from His presence all who love sin, who reject His Son and refuse to believe.

That is the message for the sinner who won't come, who loves his sin. But there's another kind of sinner that the old writers call the returning sinner. The ultimate example in the Bible of a returning sinner is, of course, the Prodigal Son. Do you remember what that boy said? "Father, give me the portion of goods that falleth to me" (Luke 15:12). He wanted his part of the will before the old man had died. And his father gave it to him! He took it and left, and when he came down to nothing, he started back.

Now there's a returning sinner! He's still a sinner —he still has his rags on him, he still smells of the swine pen, but he's a returning sinner. And our Lord calls returning sinners: "Come unto me" (Matthew 11:28). The promises and invitations of the Lord are as valid as the character of God.

D. L. Moody found that if he offered a poor child

a dollar, the child would often back off and refuse to take it. He didn't trust Moody strongly enough to believe that Moody expected the child to take it. When God promises anything, you may be sure that God expects to do it. But we in the church have gotten so we scarcely believe anything at all. Even Martha believed that her brother would rise again on the last day, although she didn't believe that the Lord would raise him right then (John 11:24). We, too, put off everything into the future—and then we call it eschatology! That's a big word for unbelief, you know. I suppose to be perfectly right about it, I ought to say that eschatology is a theological word for end-time things. But I have noticed that eschatology is a dustbin into which we sweep everything we don't want to believe.

We believe in miracles, but we believe in them eschatologically, that is, they'll happen way out there sometime. We believe that the Lord will heal the sick, but He'll do it way out there. We believe that the Lord will manifest Himself to men, but He'll do it tomorrow or the day after, or next millennium. And so we sweep it under the rug and go on about our business. That's eschatology!

We believe that God will bless the Jews in the days to come. (I have noticed that some Christians are getting away from that now; they don't believe in any future for Israel—but I do!) We believe that the Lord will bless the church sometime when He comes back again. But the idea of His blessing anybody now? We have a tough time believing that.

I said in a sermon one time that unbelief is one

of the slickest things in the world. Unbelief always says, "Somewhere else, but not here; some other time, but not now; some other people, but not us." That's unbelief. We fight for the miracles of the Old Testament, but won't believe in a miracle happening today. We believe in miracles tomorrow or yesterday, but we stand in a gap between miracles. I believe that if we had faith, we'd see miracles now—though I don't believe we ought to celebrate miracles by putting up big tents and advertising that we're going to have a miracle!

I don't believe in advertising miracles because God isn't going to allow Himself to be advertised. God doesn't have a going out of business sale. The Lord never gives cheap miracles. He never exposes His glorious, mysterious will to please the carnal saintlings. But the Lord is perfectly willing to do the impossible when His people dare to believe that He is a faithful God and meant what He said. Yet we don't take God at His word at all!

But if you are a returning sinner and you leave your old rags behind you and come to the Lord, you'll find that when the Lord said, "Come unto me . . . and I will give you rest" (Matthew 11:28), He meant exactly that! Frances Havergal said that she came to a spot where she believed that the Lord meant exactly what He said. When He said, "If we confess our sins, he is faithful and just to forgive us our sins, and to cleanse us from all unrighteousness" (1 John 1:9), she found out that the Lord meant exactly what He said.

Why don't you start reading your Bible with the

thought that God meant exactly what He said there? We're getting so many translations now, but I find they add up to about the same thing. It's one of the biggest fallacies, one of the biggest delusions possible, to imagine that if you get it said another way, it will mean more. People imagine that if they get a new translation that tells them a little better what it means, it will be wonderful. Actually, it will simply be a big disappointment. I know, because I am the prime sucker for a new translation. Every time one comes out, I run and get it. I hopped down to the bookstore the other day and bought the latest New Testament. It's all right, but it doesn't give me any more faith, it doesn't make God any more real and it doesn't bring heaven any closer.

When you read your Bible, instead of wondering about it, say to yourself, "God wrote this and God is faithful; God cannot lie." For example, read 1 John 1:7: "But if we walk in the light, as he is in the light, we have fellowship one with another, and the blood of Jesus Christ his Son cleanseth us from all sin." That's a heartening and wonderful truth, if you are a Christian who may have sinned.

I have heard people say, "I don't believe in sinning Christians." I don't either, but I meet a lot of them! I don't think Christians ought to sin and I don't think we ought to make light of it. I think that when a Christian sins, they're doing a deadly, dangerous and terrible thing. But I also know that the Holy Ghost said, "My little children, these things write I unto you, that ye sin not. And if any man sin, we have an advocate with the Father, Jesus Christ the righteous" (1 John 2:1). And He also said, "If we confess our sins, he is faithful and just to forgive us our sins and to cleanse us from all unrighteousness" (1:9).

Now here's something you may have never noticed: "He is faithful *and just* to forgive us our sins, and to cleanse us from all unrighteousness." God promised He would forgive and He is faithful to do so. But it says He is faithful *and just* to forgive. *Justice* is on our side now! Instead of justice being against us and grace being for us, the blood of Jesus Christ works such an amazing wonder before the throne of God and before the presence of man that now justice has come over on the side of the returning sinner. And when the sinner comes home, there isn't a thing standing between him and the very heart of God. It's all been swept away by the blood of the Lamb.

So if any old memories back in your mind, or the devil or some preacher tells you that justice is against you, remember that the Scriptures say, "He is faithful *and just* to forgive." Justice has come over on the side of the Christian, because Jesus Christ is on the side of the Christian. So if you confess your sins, God will put them away and you will be delivered.

God's Faithfulness to the Tempted

God is also faithful to the tempted. First Corinthians 10:13 tells us, "There hath no temptation taken you but such as is common to man: but God is faithful, who will not suffer you to be tempted above that ye are able; but will with the temptation also make a way to escape, that ye may be able to bear it." The faithfulness of God is operating to deliver us also from the temptations that bother us.

Some poor, suffering Christians say, "I feel all boxed in, as if there was a wall all around me." Someone has pointed out that when you can't escape to the right, the left, forward or backward, you can always go up. God's faithfulness is the way out, because it's the way up, you can be sure of that. Your temptation is common to everybody. If you're on the borderline of the victorious life and you say, "Under the circumstances in which I live, I just can't make it," remember God says your temptation is common to all.

My father was a tough English farmer. I was proud of the strength of my father. But when he got a cold, he became the biggest baby in the world. He would say that nobody ever had a cold like his. My poor, little, old German mother could get so sick that she would go limping around, pale and tired out, yet she had to keep going. But when my big, tough father got sick, he laid down and called for her, and she had to wait on him. He thought that the kind of cold he got was unique, but it was a just a cold in his nose.

Likewise, we think we're tempted above all others. We should remember, however, that there have been saints that have crossed the briar patch where we are now, and they got out all right. If we believe God, we'll make it too.

Some men have wives that are wildcats—difficult to get along with—and they think they are tempted above all others. John Wesley was married to a wild-cat, and she didn't even have her claws trimmed. But God got John Wesley through all right. He used to kneel down and pray in Latin so his wife wouldn't be able to know what he was saying. And while he prayed, she threw old shoes at his head! Not a very nice family affair, but that's the way they got on.

The time came when Wesley said good-bye to his wife and went off preaching, even though she didn't want him to. And they never did get together much after that, though he saw to it that she was taken care of. She stayed home and grumbled as he went out everywhere preaching the gospel and trans-forming England. Then one day he was riding along on his horse, meditating or praying, looking up in the sky. Someone rode up alongside him and said, "Mr. Wesley, your wife is dead." And he looked down and said, "Oh, she died, did she?" And he went back to looking up. Wesley got along all right, in spite of the wife he had.

There are also some dear women who love God with all their heart, but are married to slobs—men who refuse to be anything else but carnal, vulgar and more or less not what their wives had hoped for. These women think, *There's nobody stuck the way I am.*

I knew a godly, praying woman whose husband, God bless him, was a drunkard. His stomach wouldn't hold down his food, so he used to come home with his clothes dirty clear to his feet. I'm afraid I know what I would have done to him, but she didn't. She prayed, cleaned him off and put him to bed. When he woke up the next morning with a hangover, he'd promise her anything, but then he'd go out again with the boys and come home swaying from side to side, covered with filth. And she'd go through the same thing all over again. She prayed for years for that man. I don't know how the poor woman ever endured it. But she prayed on. She was one of those happy Christians, a little wisp of a woman.

One day her drunken husband came to church, came down front, got down on his knees and bawled like a drunkard bawls—half self-pity, half something else. But God saved him. He became a model Christian and lived for God for some years afterward. And she walked around just as proud of him as an eagle that had hatched another. She'd brought him to God—hatched that fellow out by prayer and patience.

I suppose there were times when she heard him snoring in the corner in his drunken sleep and wished she'd never met him. And I suppose there were times when she used to pity herself and say, "God, how do You expect me to hang on?" But God whispered in her heart, *Temptations are common to all, but I'm faithful, I won't let you down.* The result was that not only did he get converted, but also a lot of the members of the family. And they'll be in heaven with their parents one of these days. It just shows that when God says that He is faithful and will not suffer you to be tempted beyond what you can bear, He means exactly that.

God's Faithfulness to Strugglers

Are you an anxious and fearful person, who just can't believe that everything is all right between you and God? Listen to what God has to say to you:

> For a small moment have I forsaken thee; but with great mercies will I gather thee. In a little wrath I hid my face from thee for a moment; but with everlasting kindness will I have mercy on thee, saith the LORD thy Redeemer. For this is as the waters of Noah unto me: for as I have sworn that the waters of Noah should no more go over the earth; so have I sworn that I would not be wroth with thee, nor rebuke thee. (Isaiah 54:7-9)

It was a great day in my life when I believed God about this. I believe that though God may have to correct me and chasten me, He will never be angry with me again, for Jesus Christ's sake, for His promises' sake and for His faithfulness' sake. He has sworn that He will not be wroth with me, nor rebuke me. "For the mountains shall depart, and the hills be removed; but my kindness shall not depart from thee, neither shall the covenant of my peace be removed, saith the LORD that hath mercy on thee" (54:10). That is His word to the anxious.

Then there's the Christian who may have been unfaithful to the Lord through the years. "If we believe not, yet he abideth faithful: he cannot deny himself" (2 Timothy 2:13).

Then there's the discouraged person. "Faithful is

he that calleth you, who also will do it" (1 Thessalonians 5:24). You may have been serving God quite a while, but instead of getting better, you feel you're getting worse. You know what's happening to you? You're getting to know yourself better! There was a time when you didn't know who you were and you thought you were pretty fine. Then, by the good grace of God, He showed you yourself—and it was shocking and disappointing to you. But don't be discouraged, because He is faithful that calls you and He will also do it. God will finish the job.

I've often wondered how a hen must feel about sitting for three weeks on an egg. My mother always put thirteen eggs under a hen and the old girl would sit right there. She might take a little coffee break once in awhile, but back she'd come again to the nest. For the first week, it was a novelty. Two weeks of it she might endure, but that last week must have been torture—just sitting there with nothing happening.

Then about noon of the twenty-first day, the first little experimental peep is heard under her wings. And she smiles as only a hen can smile and says, "Thank God, they're here." After that it is just a question of time. One after the other, the chicks peck themselves out of their shells. I used to get down on my hands and knees as a boy and watch them picking themselves out. They're messy when they first appear, but give them about ten minutes in the sunshine and they're fluffy as can be, and lovely to look at. But they only come after twenty-one long days of waiting.

God sometimes makes us wait. He made the disciples wait in Jerusalem for the Holy Spirit (Acts 1:4) and He may make you wait. But remember, God is faithful who called you, and He also will do it. This is our faithful God. I recommend to you that you withdraw your hope from a changing, treacherous and false world and put your trust in Jesus Christ. He is faithful, who also will do it.

Father, help us to believe. Forgive us for doubting. Take away our unbelief, our diffidence, our slowness to believe. Help us now to put our trust in Thee and throw ourselves upon Thee with all the trust of a child in the hands of his father. May we now trust Thee. We pray now for the discouraged, for the sinner, for the Christian who has failed Thee, for those who are on the borderline of despair and who are living under circumstances that are very hard to bear. Thou, O God, art faithful and will not allow us to fail. Thou wilt keep us and hold us up and bless us. Now greatly lift us and help us, through Christ our Lord. Amen.

Chapter 10

God's Love

Beloved, let us love one another: for love is of God; and every one that loveth is born of God, and knoweth God. He that loveth not knoweth not God; for God is love. In this was manifested the love of God toward us, because that God sent his only begotten Son into the world, that we might live through him. Herein is love, not that we loved God, but that he loved us, and sent his Son to be the propitiation for our sins. Beloved, if God so loved us, we ought also to love one another. No man hath seen God at any time. If we love one another, God dwelleth in us, and his love is perfected in us. Hereby know we that we dwell in him, and he in us, because he hath given us of his Spirit. And we have seen and do testify that the Father sent the Son to be the Saviour of the world. Whosoever shall confess that Jesus is the Son of God, God dwelleth in him, and he in God. And we have known and believed the love that God hath to us. God is love; and he that dwelleth in love dwelleth

in God, and God in him. Herein is our love made
perfect, that we may have boldness in the day of
judgment: because as he is, so are we in this world.
There is no fear in love; but perfect love casteth out
fear: because fear hath torment. He that feareth is
not made perfect in love. We love him, because he
first loved us. If a man say, I love God, and hateth
his brother, he is a liar: for he that loveth not his
brother whom he hath seen, how can he love God
whom he hath not seen? And this commandment
have we from him, That he who loveth God love
his brother also. (1 John 4:7-21)

The love of God is the hardest of all His attributes to speak about. You may not understand
God's love for us. I don't know that I do myself. We are trying to comprehend the incomprehensible. It is like trying to take the ocean in your
arms, or embrace the atmosphere, or rise to the
stars. No one can do it, so I suppose I must do the
best I can and trust the Holy Spirit to make up for
human lack.

The text above says, "God is love," but this is not
a definition of God. It is most important to understand this. There are a great many crackpot poets
and religious people that are saying that God is love,
so love is God and therefore all is love, and all is
God. These people are busy and happy for the time
being. But they're also very, very confused in their
theology.

When the Scripture says, "God is love," it is not
defining God. It does not tell us what God is in His

metaphysical being. In the first place, the Bible never tells us what God is in His deep, essential being. No one can conceive what God is (except God), because God is inconceivable. Even if anyone could conceive it, it couldn't be expressed because God is ineffable. And if it could be expressed, it couldn't be understood because God is incomprehensible.

Therefore, to equate love with God is to go way off in your theology. If God is love in His metaphysical being, then God and love are equal to each other—identical. We could worship love as God! Thus, we would be worshiping an attribute of personality and not the Person Himself, thereby destroying the concept of personality in God and denying in one sweep all the other attributes of the deity. Don't forget that it also says, "God is light" (1 John 1:5) and "This is the true God, and eternal life" (5:20), but we don't try to limit His nature to just light or life!

When it says, "God is love," it means that love is an essential attribute of God's being. It means that in God is the summation of all love, so that all love comes from God. And it means that God's love, we might say, conditions all of His other attributes, so that God can do nothing except He does it in love.

I believe that at the end of time, when we know as we are known (see 1 Corinthians 13:12), it will be found that even the damning of a man is an expression of the love of God as certainly as the redeeming of a man. God cannot separate Himself into parts and do with one attribute one thing, and with another, another. All that God is determines all that God does. So when God redeems a man in love, or damns another man in justice, He's not contradicting Himself, but justice and love are working together in the unitary Being of God.

What we mean when we say, "God is love," is what we mean when we say of a man, "He is kindness itself." We don't mean that kindness and the man are equated and identical, but we mean the man is so kind that kindness is all over him and conditions everything he does. So when we say, "God is love," we mean that God's love is such that it permeates His essential being and conditions all that He does. Nothing God ever does, or ever did, or ever will do, is done separate from the love of God.

When I look at what love is, it reminds me of something my dear friend Max Reich (the son of a rabbi, an Oxford graduate and a great saint) said. I said to him one time, "Dr. Reich, what do you think of Rottherham's work on the Psalms?"

"Brother Tozer," he said, "Rottherham 'botanizes' the Psalms. A botanist takes a flower and pulls it apart to analyze and name the parts. When he is through, you do not have a flower, you have botany. Rottherham takes the Psalms and analyzes, classifies, breaks down and pulls apart. When he's through, you do not have David's Psalms anymore, you have theology!"

I thought that was pretty good, but now I feel a little self-conscious when I try to preach on the love of God. I'm concerned that I may be "botanizing"—tearing the petals off to find out what they are. But

I'll be careful to put them back together, so that you won't go away with a petal and think you have the whole garden.

Love Is Good Will

First of all, love is the principle of good will. The angels sang, "good will toward men" (Luke 2:14). Love always wills the good of its object and never wills any harm to its object. If you love somebody, really love him, you'll want to be good to him and to do good to him. You'll never want any harm to come to him if you can help it. That's why John says, "There is no fear in love; but perfect love casteth out fear" (1 John 4:18). If I know a man loves me, I'm not afraid of him. If I'm not sure he does, I may be a bit cagey around him. Love casts out fear, for when we know we are loved, we are not afraid. Whoever has God's perfect love, fear is gone out of the universe for him.

All real fear goes when we know that God loves us, because fear comes when we're in the hands of someone who does not will our good. A little boy lost in a department store will stand in a paroxysm of hysterical fear; people's faces are strange, even those who want to be kind. The child is afraid that he may be in the hands of somebody who wills him harm. But when he sees the familiar face of his mother, he runs sobbing to her and climbs into her arms. He's never afraid in the hands of his mother, because experience has taught him that Mother wills his good. Perfect love casts out his fear. When the mother is not there, fear fills the little child's heart, but Mother's kind, smiling, eager face drives out fear.

We are born into a world where there are a great many things against us: sin, Satan, accidents and many other things. If we're in the hands of accidents, of the devil, of sin, we have something to be afraid of. People have written books on how to conquer fear; I think they're as ridiculous as can be. They advise you to sit down and tell yourself, "Now, there's nothing to be afraid of. The sky smiles upon you. The wind is yours and also the sun." And about that time, you tumble over with a heart attack, or you're stricken with some disease, or you get a telegram that your son was killed in an auto accident or somebody declares war on somebody else. It's ridiculous simply to say, "Don't be afraid."

A man sitting on a railroad track can tell himself there is nothing to be afraid of, but five minutes later they will be picking him up in a basket. Of course there's something to be afraid of! If you believe you're in the hands of chance, of course there's something to be afraid of, and you're a fool if you're not afraid. If you're an unrepentant sinner and it seems as if a sword hangs over your head, of course there's something to be afraid of. If you've sinned against God and not repented, there's "a certain fearful looking for of judgment" (Hebrews 10:27) and it is right and natural that there should be.

But when, through the open door of the cross and the name and power of Jesus Christ, I commend myself to the Father's heart, then God cancels all my past, accepts all my present, swears His holy name for all my future and the love of God takes me over. Then fear goes out of my heart, because love has come in. I am no longer in the hands of men.

I said years ago at a denominational convention, "I am not in the hands of these delegates. They can't elect me and they can't kick me down; they can't put me in and they can't put me out." Later, another pastor came up to me and said, "You'd be surprised how fast they could."

But the truth is, they can't! I'm in the hands of God. And I appeal, not to delegates or any other human, but to the most high God. God is my friend through Jesus Christ and He wants me to prosper. Therefore, I'm not afraid; I put myself in His hands without fear. Love casts out fear. Love is the principle of good will and God wants to be our friend.

Love Is Emotional

Love is also an emotional fixation. That is, it identifies itself emotionally with its object. This may sound a little silly, but have you ever noticed that if you truly love somebody, you even love their clothes? The poet Ben Johnson wrote verses about a sash that his sweetheart wore. If you're a dignified old man, you may laugh at that. But the fact is, there was a day when you, too, had butterflies in your heart and just the sight of her handwriting was enough to set you off for the day!

We also love our children and we will their good. I think about our young daughter—she'll be twenty-two this summer, but she's still our little girl. If she had some deadly disease and I could save her with a blood transfusion—a blood transfusion that would kill me—I wouldn't even hesitate a second. I'm no hero; I'm just a father, that's all! Love emotionally identifies itself with its object. If I knew that she lay at the point of death in a hospital and that giving her my blood would make her live many years and let me die, I'd do it in a second. I'd lie down there with a smile. Any father who loves his children would. Love always identifies emotionally with its object.

Have you ever seen a thin wisp of a young mother staggering around with a big, fat baby? The mother is literally being nursed to death; the baby's getting fat and happy, while the mother is really suffering under it. And yet, does that mother complain? Not at all! She looks down into that little face and loves it and would give twice that, ten times that, because she has already identified herself emotionally with that baby.

Why was it that, between Calvary and the resurrection, Peter, John, Bartholomew and the disciples were walking around eating, drinking and sleeping, alive and healthy, while Jesus was dead and in the tomb? Because He had identified Himself emotionally with those disciples and with those He called the world. Dying for them was not a hard task. That's why I never care for mournful songs that portray Jesus weeping on His own shoulder and saying, "Oh, what a hero I was and you don't appreciate it! Too bad for Me!" Songs like that are not healthy. They're written by men who need psychiatric treatment.

Jesus Christ never went to His disciples and said,

"Now look, I died for you. Won't you remember My sufferings and My tears, and My groans and My blood?" Never! He said, "Mary," and Mary turned and said "Rabboni" (John 20:16). He never said, "I died for you." He simply said, "Mary." That's the difference between the New Testament and a lot of religious books. Religious books are often unhealthy, and in an effort to become spiritual they become more unhealthy still.

I want to be a healthy Christian. I believe it is the will of God that we should be healthy minded. The healthiest man was Jesus Christ and the healthiest disciple was Paul. We ought to be healthy men and women. That's why I don't go in much for Good Friday services where they sit around moaning and groaning, trying to follow Jesus through the stations of the cross. It is like trying to follow one's mother through the long hours of labor. It's enough to say, "Thank you, Mother, I'm here!"

A woman giving birth, Jesus said, "remembereth no more the anguish, for joy that a man is born into the world" (16:21)—if she's healthy minded. If she isn't, she writes poetry and cries on her own shoulder. She has to go to a doctor and have her head examined. But if she's healthy, she emotionally identifies with her child. Whatever prospers her child, prospers her; whatever hurts her child, hurts her. God was so emotionally identified with the human race that the devil knew the only way he could get at God was through the human race.

Milton understood this when he wrote *Paradise Lost*. This classic is not inspired Scripture and there's much of it that isn't scriptural at all. But at its center it is quite scriptural and Milton was theologian enough to know it. In *Paradise Lost,* Milton pictured the devil plotting with his horrible demons how they could get at God.

"We've been licked outright and there's nothing we can do," the demons said (I'm paraphrasing here, of course). "God's mighty engines have thundered and we're done for. We can never hope to take God's throne by storm. What will we do?"

Well, the devil, being the devil, said, "I think I've got it. There's some talk about how God is going to create a people that will be after His image and like Him. He loves them more than anything else in His universe. If I can get to them and ruin them, I will hurt God worse than if I'd overthrown His very dominion."

So he hunted down Adam and Eve and began to tempt them. And when he brought about the fall of the human race, he caused injury to the heart of God, because God loved the human race, made in His own image. Our sins are an emotional wound in the heart of God.

It says in Hebrews 2:6, quoting from Psalm 8:4, "What is man, that thou art mindful of him?" The Greek word for *mindful* means "fixture in the mind."[1] We're a fixture in God's mind. And the only wonderful, strange eccentricity of the great free God is that He allows Himself to be emotionally identified with me, so whatever hurts me, hurts Him. Whenever I'm in pain, God is in pain; whenever I suffer, He suffers. Scripture says, "The LORD . . . wilt make all [our] bed[s] in [our] sickness" (Psalm 41:3). God sits beside us and grieves when we grieve.

Love also feels pleasure in its object. God is happy in His love. When people love each other, they're very happy. When he was President of the U.S., Woodrow Wilson fell in love with a widow, Mrs. Galt. Wilson, you may remember, was a dignified old fellow, with a long face and a pair of thick glasses. He had been a professor and a college president, and he looked the part. He was so dignified that it was a production just to clear his throat. But one summer he met Mrs. Galt and she bowled him over. And he said, "Well, I'm going to get married." And then he jumped up and did a little dance around the presidential floor.

Imagine a president doing a thing like that! What had happened to the old man? Love had come. He thought that the snow on his roof meant the fire had gone out in the furnace, but there was still some emotion there. And he was happy to find it. Love always makes people happy.

A young mother is always happy over her baby. I've never seen one that wasn't. Sometimes a mother may get a little angry when the child gets big enough to push things over, but for the most part, love is a pleasurable thing. And God is happy in His love toward all that He has made.

I've just been reading again the early chapters of Genesis and there's no escaping the fact that God felt pleasure in His creation. God made the light, shook His head and said, "That's good!" He liked that!

Then He made the dry land to appear and put the seas in one place, and said, "That's good!" Then He made the sun, the stars and moon to rule the night and day, and said, "That's good!" Then He made man and said, "That's very good!" (See Genesis 1.)

God was an artist and every time He finished a painting, He shook His head and said, "That's good!" God loved it; He was pleased with what He was doing. And that's the kind of God I preach— not a faraway, dehydrated, sour, sulky God, hiding in some imperial palace. I preach a friendly God, who is happy in His work. It is only sin that has brought the curse, the pain and the grief—and He has sent His Son to deal with that sin business, too.

God makes delightful reference to His works and to everything that He has made. It says in Psalm 104:31, "the LORD shall rejoice in his works." And in Zephaniah 3:17 (I don't think anybody believes this wonderful passage of Scripture; if we did, we'd act like President Wilson and do a little two-step out of sheer joy), it says, "The LORD thy God in the midst of thee is mighty; he will save, he will rejoice over thee with joy; he will rest in his love, he will joy over thee with singing."

God Almighty is in the midst of us! He will save and rejoice over us with joy! God is happy if nobody else is and He will rest in His love. "He will joy over thee with singing"—the eternal God is singing! That's why I want our congregations to sing. I don't require that they sing on pitch—just that they sing with joy and enthusiasm.

I don't mind if the piano is out of tune, or if one

fellow is singing a little step behind the next fellow
—that doesn't bother me. But the lack of warmth
and enthusiasm makes me question the experiential
life of Christians. The Christian Church has God in
it and wherever God is, God will joy over His people
with singing. The singing of the church reflects the
great God singing among His people.

I notice that Jesus Christ our Lord said about His
church in Song of Solomon 4:9, "Thou hast rav-
ished my heart, my sister, my spouse; thou hast rav-
ished my heart with one [glance] of thine eyes."
When the Lord says this about His church, it can
only mean one thing: He feels toward His church as
a bridegroom toward his bride, as a mother toward
her child, as a lover toward the object of his affection. And there's a highly satisfying love content in
true Christianity if you go deep enough. The trouble
is, we don't go deep enough!

D. L. Moody told about a man who had never
slept on a feather bed. He found a feather, lay down
on it all night, and said, "If one feather is that hard
I can't imagine what a whole bed of them would be
like!" Moody was joking, but it illustrates something. We get just enough religion to make us miserable. If we would go on, we'd find God's love.

All that some people know about Christianity is
that it won't let you do things. A man once told
Spurgeon, "I don't drink, I don't use tobacco, I don't
swear, I don't attend theater."

Spurgeon replied, "Do you eat hay?"

He said, "No, I don't. What do you mean?"

And Spurgeon said, "I hoped you did something.

Up to now you've been doing nothing."

And to some people, Christianity is only what you don't do. That's not Christianity! The monks don't do much; the man in India that goes naked and sleeps on spikes doesn't do much either. He just lies around and rots. But that's not Christianity.

There's a love content in Christianity. And discounting all the irresponsible things people do, there is nevertheless a deep, healing, emotional content in the Christian life. That's why the Bible calls the church the Bride and Christ the Bridegroom. He means that His people should know His love and that we should feel it and sense it. I'm trying to analyze love, yet you can't describe love; you've got to feel it. You can see how it works, but you can't describe it. And you don't know it until you've felt it. So it is with the love of God.

It says in Hosea 2:16 that the time would come when they would no more call God *Baali* [a rejected name for God], but *Ishi,* meaning "husband." That means that God wants to be to us what a husband is to a new wife. He wants to shelter and care for and love and cherish us.

I've often wondered why women were willing to change their name when they get married. When Marcia Smith marries Mortimer Jones, one of the first things he'll say to her as they ride away with their hair full of rice is, "Well, Mrs. Jones, how are you?" And she giggles—she's delighted to take his name. I know many a newlywed husband who has had his wife paged at the hotel—"Paging Mrs. Mortimer Jones"—and she says, "Oh, this is wonderful!" She's taken the name of the man she loves and doesn't mind it at all.

Well, your maiden name was Adam, don't forget that. But the Lord wanted to give you a new name. He said, "I'll be your husband and you'll be called Christian." The love of God has made us Christians and has joined us to Him in the warmth of affection.

What a mechanical business marriage would be if there was no love in it! What a mechanical business rearing children would be! Wouldn't it be awful getting up five times a night to give them a glass of water they don't need, fixing bumps they never should have had, looking at those awful report cards? Raising a family would be terrible, except for one thing: the lubrication of love.

Whenever love is there, everything is all right. There is a little story about a very young girl who was carrying around a great big lug of a baby on her back. A man came by and said to her, "Well honey, that's quite a burden you have there." And she said, "That's not a burden, that's my little brother!" Whatever you love isn't a burden. God is not having any burdens. That's why I never join in with people that are pitying the Lord. Never! God is happy to do what He did! He is love and love is joyful.

If I were to try to talk about the greatness of love I would only run in circles, because I can't speak of that which cannot be spoken of. But to break it down a little, this love of God is an attribute of God, which means it is eternal, immutable and infinite. It never began to be and it can never end; it can never change and there is no boundary to it.

For the love of God is broader
    Than the measures of man's mind,
And the heart of the Eternal
    Is most wonderfully kind.[2]

Every time God thinks about you, He thinks about you lovingly. Even if He must chastise you, or allow hardships to come to you, it is love that allows it to come and love that sends it. And we never should be afraid of love, because love casts out fear.

We talk about love, but God proved His love. "But God commendeth [that is, proves] his love toward us, in that, while we were yet sinners, Christ died for us" (Romans 5:8). In Hebrews 7:25 it says, "Wherefore he is able also to save them to the uttermost that come unto God by him, seeing he ever liveth to make intercession for them." The same love that created us is the love that redeemed us and now keeps us.

The best preservative in the world is the love of God. Some people believe in the security of the saints from theological grounds. They take it from a text somewhere. I believe in the security of the saints because God is love and God always keeps that which He loves. We always keep what we love—always.

I hate to take the other side, but I just have to say this: The soul that can scorn such infinite, emotional, eager love as this, the soul that can trample it down, turn away from it and despise it, will never enter God's heaven—never. That soul would never be happy in God's heaven. The soul that loves hate and hates love, the soul that cultivates hate and despises the love of God, would never be happy in heaven above. Sometimes when a wicked old scoundrel dies, the preacher gets up and tries to preach them right into heaven—not knowing that the worst thing that could happen to them would be to go to heaven.

I once read the story of a very rich man who found a little urchin sleeping in an old, empty barrel down by the waterfront. The child was dressed in rags and picked up what he could get around the alleys and wherever anybody would give him a handout. The rich man decided to take the little fellow to his home. He took him to a mansion where one room led to another, each one grander and more luxurious than the last. The trembling, timid, little fellow was given clothes the likes of which he had never seen. His adopted father took him to his room. There were silk sheets and coverlets, a nightlight and all the beauties that wealth could bring to a boy's bedroom. The next morning the maid took him down to breakfast. There he ate food that he never knew existed, off beautiful plates with exquisite silverware.

One morning the boy had taken all he could and when they went up to get him, they found nothing there but his good clothes. They looked for the old rags they'd taken from him and they were gone. He'd taken off the rich wealthy clothes that made him miserable and got back into his old rags. He was psychologically conditioned to dirt and rags; he was used to eating banana peels and crusts of bread.

He wasn't conditioned to silk beds, fine clothes and a rich luxurious home. He was miserable there! In the same way, heaven would not be heaven to the man who does not have heaven in his heart.

Heaven will not be heaven to the man who does not have the love of God in his heart. Heaven will be a place where God's love fills it as the atmosphere fills a room and covers it in rich, life-giving air. Heaven is filled with love and whoever does not know the love of God on earth will not be happy in heaven. Certainly he will not be happy in hell, either. That's the horror of it—he won't be happy anywhere.

I heard a great Canadian preacher years ago preach on the text, "And it came to pass, that the beggar [Lazarus] died, and was carried by the angels into Abraham's bosom: the rich man also died, and was buried; and in hell he lift up his eyes" (Luke 16:22-23). He asked why this was so and finally arrived at this conclusion: The poor man didn't go to Abraham's bosom because he was poor, and the rich man didn't go to hell because he was rich. Each man went to the place that he had been conditioned for. Abraham's bosom was the place Lazarus belonged, because Lazarus had the love of God in his heart. When he died, the love took him where he belonged. The rich man didn't go to hell because he ate sumptuously and lived in a good home. He went to hell because he did not have the love of God in his heart. When he died, he went to his place. There's a place for everybody.

And love has opened the door for sinners to enter heaven. But wait a minute—am I contradicting my-

self? Didn't I just say that sinful people, people of
the world that don't have God's love, wouldn't be
happy in heaven? Of course they wouldn't. But
when you are saved, God changes your heart.

The Scripture says, "old things are passed away;
behold, all things are become new" (2 Corinthians
5:17). God puts the seed of God in us and we become
children of God. We are baptized into the kingdom
of God and thus become acclimated and psychologically conditioned to the kingdom of God. You love
great hymns, you love to sing, you love to pray, you
love to talk reverently about God, you love the sound
of anthems and the sound of Scripture being read.
And nothing pleases you more than to get up in the
morning and read your Bible. Nothing pleases you
more than to have time with God in prayer, all you
can get. If you live in the face of God then you'll be
happy in heaven, because you're conditioned for it.
God has already made heaven your natural habitat.

Bernard of Cluny's great hymn, "The Celestial
Country," in speaking of pilgrims that fought their
way through to heaven, says that they will go to
heaven because heaven demands them.[3] Heaven demands them because they belong in heaven. Hell is
a place where people go because they belong there.
God doesn't get mad and say, "Get out of here and
go to hell!" No, they go where they belong by nature. The gravitational tug of their moral lives is toward hell. Those who die and go to heaven go there
because the gravitational tug of their moral lives is
toward heaven, by the blood of Jesus, the blood of
the everlasting covenant.

Talking about the love of God is like going around the globe, visiting every country in the world, then spending five minutes telling your friends about it. You can't do it! The love of God is so great that even preachers such as Spurgeon and Chrysostom cannot hope to rise in the oratory of the pulpit to do it justice.

Julian of Norwich explained it this way:

For our soul is so specially loved of Him that is highest, that it overpasseth the knowing of all creatures: that is to say, there is no creature that is made that may [fully] know how much and how sweetly and how tenderly our Maker loveth us. And therefore we may with grace and His help stand in spiritual beholding, with everlasting marvel of this high, overpassing, in-estimable Love that Almighty God hath to us of His Goodness.[4]

Then she adds this little sentence, "And therefore we may ask of our Lover with reverence all that we will." He loves us so that no creature—neither seraphim nor cherubim nor archangel nor principality nor power nor all of them added together in all the vast universe of God—can ever hope to know how overpassingly great is the love of God, and how tenderly, how sweetly and how much He loves us.

What can the world do to a man or woman who is grounded in the love of God, who swims in the ocean of His love as a fish in the mighty ocean?

What can the devil do to a person like that? What can sin do? What can the world do? What can accident do?

Oh, love of God, how little we know about it, and how little we do about what we know! May God help us. If you've been away from Him, if you're backslidden or unsaved or unbelieving, dare to believe that God loves you. Dare to believe that He sent His only begotten Son to give His life as a ransom for you. And dare to believe that if you'll trust in Him, you shall have everlasting life.

If you've been a wanderer from God, dare to come home. Don't add to your sins that you won't come home. A teenage girl gets an impulse to run away from home, so she takes off and gets a job somewhere in a restaurant. Then she reads in the paper or hears over the radio how her grieving mother wants her home. But she is so ashamed of herself that she feels it wouldn't be right to go home after doing what she did. Why should she add this one more crushing blow to her mother, to refuse to come home, when her mother wants her to come?

And why should you add this one more blow at the heart of God? Of course, you don't deserve to come. And yes, it looks cheap and little, and it's a humbling thing. But are you going to add one more sin to your account by refusing to believe that God loves you?

God never took the lamp out of the window when you went away; it's still there. Every night He puts fresh oil in it, trims it and says, "Maybe she'll come back tonight! Maybe he'll be home tonight!"

It was said of the prodigal, "And he arose, and came to his father" (Luke 15:20). Will you arise and come, whatever the need might be?

Notes

Introduction: God's Character

1. Alfred Lord Tennyson, *Morte d'Arthur.*

2. John Milton, *Paradise Lost,* First Book.

3. Ibid.

4. Frederick William Faber, "Majesty Divine!" in A. W. Tozer, compiler, *The Christian Book of Mystical Verse* (Camp Hill, PA: WingSpread Publishers, 1963, 1991), p. 7.

5. Ibid.

Chapter 1: God's Self-Existence

1. Faber, pp. 7-8.

2. Isaac Watts, "O God, Our Help in Ages Past," *Hymns of the Christian Life,* 7th ed. (1978), #13.

3. Faber, p. 37.

Chapter 2: God's Transcendence

1. "Te Deum Laudamus," *Christian Book of Mystical Verse,* pp. 87-89.

2. Isaac Watts, "God Is the Name My Soul Adores."

3. Jessie B. Pounds, "The Way of the Cross Leads Home," *Hymns of the Christian Life,* #514.

4. Frederick William Faber, "The Eternal Father," *Christian Book of Mystical Verse,* p. 22.

Chapter 3: God's Eternalness

1. Augustine, *Confessions*, Book 1, Chapter 4, Section 4; Book 1, Chapter 6, Section 9.

2. Frederick William Faber, "The Eternity of God," *Christian Book of Mystical Verse*, p. 17.

3. Isaac Watts, "O God, Our Help in Ages Past" (stanza 4), *Church Service Hymns*, comp. H. Rodeheaver and G.W. Sanville (Winona Lake, IN: Rodeheaver Hall-Mack, 1948), #97.

4. Ibid.

Chapter 4: God's Omnipotence

1. Joseph Addison, "The Spacious Firmament on High," *Church Service Hymns*, #9.

Chapter 5: God's Immutability

1. Frederick William Faber, "The Eternity of God," *Christian Book of Mystical Verse*, p. 16.

2. John Wesley, "Psalm 114," *A Collection of Hymns, for the Use of the People Called Methodists* (London: Wesleyan Methodist Book-Room, 1889), #223.

3. Anselm of Canterbury, *Proslogium*, ch. 1.

4. Frederick William Faber, "Majesty Divine!," *Christian Book of Mystical Verse*, p. 7.

5. Philip Doddridge, "O Happy Day, That Fixed My Choice," *Hymns of the Christian Life*, #422.

6. L.H. Edmunds, "The Very Same Jesus," *Hymns of the Christian Life*, 5th ed. (1936), #437.

Chapter 6: God's Omniscience

1. Will Rogers, quoted in *Quote, Unquote*, comp. Lloyd Cory (Wheaton, IL: Victor Books, 1977), p. 161.

2. "My Father Knows" (hymn), S.M.I. Henry, 1897.

3. John Greenleaf Whittier (1807–1892), *The Eternal Goodness*.

Chapter 10: God's Love

1. James Strong, *Strong's Exhaustive Concordance of the Bible*, Greek #3403, referencing Greek #3415.

2. Frederick W. Faber, "There's a Wideness in God's Mercy," *Hymns of the Christian Life*, 1978 ed., #152.

3. Bernard of Cluny, "The Celestial Country," *The Christian Book of Mystical Verse*, pp. 128-140.

4. Julian of Norwich, *Revelations of Divine Love*, Chapter 7.

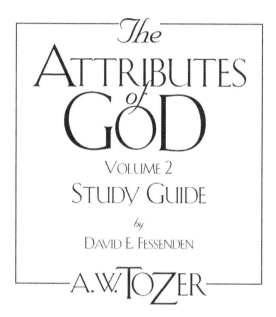

The

ATTRIBUTES of GOD

VOLUME 2
STUDY GUIDE

by

DAVID E. FESSENDEN

A.W.TOZER

MOODY PUBLISHERS
CHICAGO

Contents

Acknowledgments

I want to thank Jon Graf, who paved the way for Tozer study guides through his *Study Guide for The Pursuit of God*—from which I shamelessly copied the format for this study guide.

Janet Paull, Sunday school superintendent, teacher Dan Boreman and the class at Immanuel Alliance for trying this out.

My wife, who bravely gave up many hours together for this.

How to Use This Guide

This study guide has been developed to help you get the most out of A. W. Tozer's *The Attributes of God Volume Two*. It should enable you to understand more clearly what Tozer is saying and to apply to your own life the truths he sets forth.

The study guide is designed for both personal and group use. The personal study section (the material that comes first in each session of this guide) should be read after you read the corresponding chapter in *The Attributes of God Volume Two*. Let its comments and questions help you reflect on the major points Tozer is making. It will also provide you with additional Scripture to read and study. The group study section offers a lesson plan and discussion questions for those wishing to use *The Attributes of God Volume Two* as the text for an adult Sunday school class or a small group study.

Personal Study

Whether you are studying personally or as the leader of a class or small group, you will want to begin by reading the introduction from *The Attributes of God Volume Two*. Then go through the personal study section for the introduction. From then on, after you finish each chapter in the book, go through the personal study corresponding to that chapter. Unless you are a group leader, you need not read the "LESSON PLAN—Group Study" section.

Group Study—Leader's Instructions

As you prepare for each session of your class or group, you will want to read the entire section of this guide that coincides with the chapter of *The Attributes of God Volume Two* that your group is studying. In other words, you need to read both the personal study section and the group lesson plans.

The group lesson plans are set up with the same subtitles used for the personal study. This is to help you find information quickly. When the activity recommends that you read a quotation from *The Attributes of God Volume Two,* the page numbers from the text of the book are usually provided, or the quotation is in the personal study section of this guide under the correlating subtitle. The personal study section will also suggest to you things of significance that you will wish to stress.

Naturally, all members should have a copy of *The Attributes of God Volume Two* and keep up with the reading assignments. These lessons, however, are designed so that members who do not keep up with the reading assignments can still get some benefit from the class.

Introduction:
God's Character

Personal Study

Supplementary Materials: David J. Fant, Jr., *A. W. Tozer: A Twentieth-Century Prophet* (Moody); James L. Snyder, *The Life of A. W. Tozer: In Pursuit of God* (Bethany); A. W. Tozer, *Knowledge of the Holy* (HarperOne).

Welcome to *The Attributes of God Volume Two.* As you read the introduction, it may be helpful to learn a little about the author of this book and about how this volume came to be.

A. W. Tozer was born on a small farm in rural Pennsylvania. He came to Christ as a young man and began the pastoral ministry without any college or seminary training. He served only a few churches in his forty-four years of ministry, thirty-one of those years in a modest congregation in Chicago. Nothing in his background would indicate the profound impact he would have on the lives of millions of believers around the globe.

While he enjoyed a healthy reputation as a preacher, if it were not for his writing ability, he might never have gained the worldwide prominence he did. His two most popular books—*The Pursuit of God* and *The Knowledge of the Holy*—are considered classics in the genres of Christian living and popular theology.

The two volumes of *The Attributes of God* are something of a combination of these two bestsellers, in that they cover the same topic as *The Knowledge of the Holy* (God's attributes) but they have the devotional flavor of *The Pursuit of God*. Each attribute of God that is discussed in these two books is presented in the light of the believer's personal relationship with God.

Both volumes of *The Attributes of God* began as a series of taped messages—which might be a drawback if it were a preacher other than Tozer. The transcripts of most sermons, even many very good ones, can make for dull reading, because there is a definite loss in the power of expression when the message moves from the medium of live speech to the printed page. Not so with Tozer. It is said that he wrote his sermons in the format of a magazine article, which could explain why they retain so much of their dynamism on paper.

In addition, I have carefully but lightly edited the material to trim out the almost unavoidable redundancies and confusing phraseology inherent in any spoken message. I strove to maintain Tozer's "voice" while smoothing out the text to the high quality of his other written works. The result is a quite readable series of chapters on God's attributes, compiled in a format I think Tozer would have found acceptable.

As you begin this study, one question may come to your mind: Why was Tozer drawn to preach on God's attributes in the first place? The answer to that is wrapped up in the consuming ambition to which he dedicated his life.

Tozer was a man driven by a desire to know God in His fullness. Jon Graf, in his study guide to *The Pursuit of God,* said that Tozer once confessed to his lifelong friend Robert Battles, "I want to love God more than anyone in my generation." Graf goes on to say, "To some of us that may sound selfish and arrogant, but for Tozer it wasn't. It simply came out of an honest desire to enrich his relationship with the Lord."

The desire to know God deeper and more intimately naturally led Tozer to study God's attributes. As he himself said in *The Attributes of God Volume One,*

> Christianity at any given time is strong or weak depending upon her concept of God. And I insist upon this and I have said it many times, that the basic trouble with the Church today is her unworthy conception of God. (p. 41)

Reasons to Study God's Attributes

A worthy concept of God is crucial, because He is the cause behind all things and the only One who can give meaning to our existence. This is the first reason Tozer gives for studying God's attributes. "God gives to human life its only significance," Tozer declares in the introduction; "there isn't any other apart from Him. If you take the concept of God out of the human mind there is no other reason for being among the living" (p. 1). It follows, then, that learning a proper concept of God is absolutely essential if we want to have any real purpose to our lives.

But the importance of this task is, ironically, matched by its difficulty. Like "an insect trying to carry a bale of cotton" (p. 2), Tozer confessed his weakness and unworthiness in covering such a profound topic.

A second reason to study God's attributes is for our own spiritual protection. We must know what God is like, because mankind fell as soon as we lost a right concept of God. Tozer quotes Romans 1:21-28 to prove his point. Reread that passage and see what he means.

A third reason to study God's attributes is to develop faith and trust in Him. Tozer began the introduction with Psalm 9:10; it is worth reading again. In that verse, the word name means "character, plus reputation." If we know God's character, His reputation, what kind of a God He really is, we can't help but have faith in Him!

Another reason to study the attributes, Tozer says, is because we have lost the dignity and inwardness of true Christianity, and we are desperately in need of revival. Tozer, of course, was speaking those words fifty years ago. It is up to you and me to determine if his assessment is out of date or not. I would like to think that things have improved somewhat since his time, but as he lists the faults he finds in the church of his day, they seem eerily familiar to me. I'll just review them here and let you decide:

- "Our Christianity is thin and anemic, without thoughtful content, frivolous in tone and worldly in spirit" (p. 8).
- Our preaching has lost its lofty outlook and is lacking in substance. "We in the gospel churches think that we've got to entertain the people or they won't come back. We have lost the seriousness out of our preaching and have become silly" (p. 8).
- Our reading material lacks depth; it has become "religious fodder" which should be thrown out (p. 10).
- Our songs are lacking in theological content and tend to be frivolous (pp. 10-11).

While I wince at such a critique of contemporary Christianity, and want to respond that I see some positive signs as well, I have to admit that at least some of this rings true in my era, in my own church and in my own heart. Tozer says this is a result of a loss of a vision of "the Majesty on high" (p. 12)—a failure to see God as He really is, in all His greatness.

Tozer says that, for many of us, our failure to recognize God for who He is has grieved the Holy Spirit until He has "withdrawn in hurt silence" (p. 12). If this is true for you, there is a cure for this loss of

God's presence. Growing in the knowledge of God and His attributes will elevate our concept of God and provide an atmosphere where His presence can feel at home. "I want a vision of the majesty of God," Tozer says. "I want to live where the face of God shines every day" (p. 13). If this is your desire as well, this study of the attributes of God should be just what the doctor ordered.

LESSON PLAN—Group Study

AIM: To inspire in my students a desire to learn about God's attributes.

Introduction

1. Open with prayer.
2. If the books were handed out to the students prior to this meeting (recommended), ask who was able to read the introduction. Invite the students to share any concepts that especially intrigued them. Otherwise, simply go on to the rest of this study.

Reasons to Study God's Attributes

1. Ask the students to find the four reasons Tozer gives for studying God's attributes. (Help them out if necessary by writing a brief summary of the four reasons on a whiteboard.) Then ask the following questions:

   Are there other possible reasons besides these for studying God's attributes?

   What relationship does Tozer draw between our

concept of God and our Christian walk?
    Is this a valid claim? Why or why not?

2. Read the following definition of the word *attribute*: "a characteristic or quality of a person or thing" (*Webster's New World Dictionary,* Third College Edition, Simon & Schuster, 1988). Discuss with the class how learning about God's attributes can improve our concept of God.

3. If you have not already passed out copies of this book, do so now. Spend a few minutes looking over the various attributes mentioned in the table of contents. Ask, "What attributes especially intrigue you? Why?"

4. From the personal study, explain a little about the life of A. W. Tozer and how this book came to be. You will want to say everything you can to convince your class members that they should read the book chapter by chapter, in its entirety. (The lesson plans are designed so that a student who has not read the assigned chapter can get *something* out of each session, but those who thoughtfully, prayerfully read all that Tozer has to say will derive maximum benefit.)

Closing

1. Assign the reading of chapter 1 in the book. To whet the appetite of your group, you may want to read a short, incisive quote from the chapter.

2. Close in prayer.

Chapter 1:
God's Self-Existence

Personal Study

Supplementary Materials: A.B. Simpson, "Himself" in *The Best of A.B. Simpson* (Moody); A. W. Tozer, *Man, the Dwelling Place of God* (Moody).

Exodus 3:11-15 is a wonderful passage, and an excellent choice for Tozer to discuss God's self-existence, since it includes the phrase "I AM THAT I AM," which in essence defines this attribute of God. But Tozer could have simply quoted verse 14 as a proof-text. Why does he quote five full verses?

This is a great example of how much we can learn from reading the context of a verse. Look at the interaction between Moses and God and you will get a clue as to where Tozer intends to go with this message. Moses asks, "Who am I, that I should go to deliver Israel from slavery?" And God responds, in effect, "It's not a question of who you are, but who I AM." Tozer includes this conversation between Moses and God because he wants to emphasize how God's attributes affect our relationship with Him—a recurring theme throughout the book.

But before he discusses God's attribute of self-existence, Tozer wisely begins by defining the word *attribute*: "It is something which God has declared to be true of Himself. . . . An attribute of God is something we can know about God" (p. 17). He adds four important points:

1. An attribute is something God *is*, not something He is "made of." If God were "made" or "composed" of parts, it would imply that He was created.

2. Since we shouldn't think of God as being "made" of His attributes, we also shouldn't think of Him as ten percent mercy, seven percent grace, etc. He is *all* mercy, *all* grace and *all* of whatever else He is.

3. If an attribute is something God has told us about Himself, and something we can know about God, it stands to reason that there are things about God which He has *not* revealed, and things we are incapable of knowing. Only a rationalist has the arrogance to believe that he can know all about God. "God rises transcendently above all that we can understand. The human mind must kneel before the great God Almighty. What God is can never quite be grasped by the mind; it can only be revealed by the Holy Spirit" (p. 18).

4. God's attributes apply to all three persons of the Trinity. What is true of the Father is true of the Son and the Holy Spirit as well. To show that this point is a well-established doctrine, Tozer quotes the Athanasian Creed (circa fourth century), a beautiful

declaration of truth that is well worth reading.

Self-Existent Selfhood

Self-existence, in the words of the church father Novatian, means "God has no origin." How is this concept derived from "I AM THAT I AM"? The phrase means that God exists because He exists; in other words, His existence is not dependent upon anything else but Himself. While everything else originated from something else, "when you come back to God, you come back to the One who has no origin. He is the Cause of all things, the uncaused Cause" (p. 22).

This puts our relationship to Him in perspective. As Tozer says in *Man: the Dwelling Place of God,*

The I AM which is God is underived and self-existent; the "I am" which is man is derived from God and dependent every moment upon His creative fiat for its continued existence. One is the Creator, high over all, ancient of days, dwelling in light, unapproachable. The other is a creature and, though privileged beyond all others, is still but a creature, a pensioner on God's bounty and a suppliant before His throne.

God's Selfhood and Prayer

An understanding of God's self-existence should give us a fresh view of prayer. When we realize He is the origin of all things, we may stop coming to God with a "shopping list," treating Him like a grocery store. As the originator of all, He is clearly capable of giving us anything we ask, and He desires to provide for His people. But if we can get away from the idea of prayer being an impersonal transaction, we will actually get more than we ask, Tozer says: "He gives, but in giving He gives us Himself too. And the best gift God ever gives us is Himself" (p. 25).

This is reminiscent of the discovery that A.B. Simpson found later in his ministry—a discovery he put into verse:

> Once it was the blessing,
> Now it is the Lord;
> Once it was the feeling,
> Now it is His Word.
> Once His gift I wanted,
> Now the Giver own;
> Once I sought for healing,
> Now Himself alone.

Tozer touches on this same idea in *The Root of the Righteous,* where he speaks of "three degrees of love," the deepest of which is this: "There is a place in the religious experience where we love God for Himself alone, with never a thought of His benefits."

The next point Tozer makes is not easy to grasp, and may even seem heretical if we fail to think it through: *God loves Himself.* We have been taught—and rightly so—to deny ourselves, to die to self. But that is because the human self is fallen and sinful. God, the great Original Self, is holy and good, so there is nothing wrong with His love for Himself. God created love, and back before time began, love existed between the Father, Son and Holy Spirit.

This is crucial to a discussion of God's self-existence, because the very words "I am" are an expression of self. God is the "I AM" in all capital letters —the great Original Self. We can say "I am" in lowercase letters, because we are made in God's image— it's "a little echo of God" (p. 27), as Tozer says, and there is nothing wrong with that. What makes it sin is when we try to be the "I AM"—when we try to be little gods. "The definition of sin is fallen selfhood" (p. 28).

As I said earlier, a recurring theme in Tozer's study of God's attributes is how they affect our relationship to Him. The most fundamental aspect of our relationship with God is this fact: We are sinners! God, the great Originator, created us to revolve around Him, like planets around the sun. "Then one day," Tozer explains, "the little planet said, 'I'll be my own sun. Away with this God.' And man fell" (p. 28).

Tozer makes an important observation about Galatians 5:19-21, which lists various "works of the flesh," such as adultery, idolatry, hatred, strife and murder. We call such things sin, but in truth they are only manifestations, symptoms of the underlying disease. "No matter how many manifestations sin may have, remember that the liquid essence in the bottle is always self" (p. 30). Tozer notes that this was the reason why Lucifer was cast down from heaven (Isaiah 14:12-14).

That's why being moral will never bring us to salvation—it's only treating the symptoms, not the disease. We have usurped God's throne—that's the real problem. Being born again means getting off the throne and returning to the purpose for which we were made: to worship, glorify and love God, and to be objects of His love.

Tozer ends with what might seem like a prayer for salvation, but even if you've been saved for many years, it would be worth it to read and meditate on this. We need to remind ourselves that if Christ is on the throne of our lives, He is the One in charge.

LESSON PLAN—Group Study

AIM: To help my students understand God's attribute of self-existence and how it applies to their relationship with Him.

Introduction

1. Open with prayer.
2. Discuss the four aspects of an attribute, as identified in the personal study (p. 12).
3. If possible, get a copy of the Athanasian Creed (available from a number of websites) and read it aloud to the group. Ask them what phrases of the creed stand out to them.
4. Read Exodus 3:11-15. Discuss the interaction between God and Moses.

Self-Existent Selfhood

Continuing with Exodus 3:11-15, discuss the meaning of "I AM THAT I AM."

Ask the group this question: How does the fact

that "God has no origin" affect how we relate to Him? If they need help with this question, read the passage from *Man: the Dwelling Place of God* (p. 13).

God's Selfhood and Prayer

Have the group reflect on the content of their prayers in the light of Tozer's comments toward the end of page 24. They can write down their thoughts and then share them, perhaps in groups of two or three. Then discuss how we can make our prayers more than just a "shopping list."

Read the poem by A. B. Simpson in the personal study (p. 14). Invite comments on its meaning.

Ask the group these questions: What does Tozer mean when he states, "The essence of sin is independent self" (p. 28)? How are we supposed to deal with its presence in our lives? (For help with this question, see Luke 9:23; Romans 6:11; 1 Corinthians 15:31; 2 Corinthians 5:14-15; Galatians 2:20.)

Read Galatians 5:19-21 and discuss the distinction Tozer makes between sin's manifestations and its root cause—self. How does this relate to salvation— being born again? (If you think there are any in your group who have not come to salvation by faith in Christ, this is a good time to invite anyone with questions to stay after the meeting and discuss this further. Be prepared to share the gospel with a biblical presentation such as the "Four Spiritual Laws" or the "Romans Road.")

Closing

1. Slowly read aloud the prayer at the end of chapter 1 (p. 33), asking the group to meditate on their own relationship with God.
2. Assign reading of chapter 2 for next week's class.
3. Close in prayer.

Chapter 2:
God's Transcendence

Personal Study

Supplementary Material: A. W. Tozer, *The Root of the Righteous* (Moody)

As with most of these chapters, this one begins with multiple selected Scripture passages that help illustrate the attribute. Take another look at these verses and write down the key words and phrases in them. Then as we review the chapter, watch how Tozer touches on the various facets of transcendence suggested in Scripture.

The word *transcendent* means "to rise above," and it means that God and His ways are infinitely far above us. Tozer notes that this may seem contradictory to other attributes of God, such as omnipresence and immanence, "but as with many apparent contradictions, it's not at all contradictory; the two thoughts are entirely in accord with each other" (p. 36).

A crucial point that Tozer reminds us of is that "far above" is an analogy; transcendence does not mean that God is far above us in distance (though He is—but He is also right here as well!). His comparison of the little girl lost on a mountain and the desperate search for her (because she is transcendently of far more value than the mountain) is good, but then he puts the issue into divine perspective by saying, "God is just as far above an archangel as He is above a caterpillar" (p. 39). It is important to recognize that any comparison falls vastly short of God's infinite transcendence. No analogy between one creature (a mountain) and another creature (a little girl) is adequate to explain God, because *He is not a creature!* "God is of a substance wholly unique" (p. 40), Tozer concludes.

One is tempted to simply give up speaking about God, Tozer adds, since He is so far above the capacity of the human mind to know Him or of human speech to describe Him. But as Augustine said, "somebody must speak." And Tozer says that God is pleased with our attempts to speak of Him, as crude as they may be.

Tozer argues that if a seraph from heaven could come down and speak to us about God, we would lose interest in "timely" sermons and want to hear about God alone. This makes me wonder: When was the last time I heard a sermon about God alone? It's been a while. Much of what we hear from the pulpit, in Sunday school or at a Bible study is human-centered. And can we blame the preachers and teachers if that's what we ask for? It saddens me when Tozer quotes a beautiful anthem to God such as "Te Deum Laudamus" and then says we are not familiar with poetry such as this "because we're not spiritually capable of understanding it" (pp. 42-43).

At this point, I suppose many of us would argue with Tozer. We realize that God is not a creature, that He is infinitely far above us; that's basic theology. Why accuse us of being spiritually incapable of understanding something that everyone accepts as a matter of fact?

That is the very problem: We think we understand God, that we've got Him down pat. This is what Tozer means when he says that our Christianity is *programmed*. We think we've got it all figured out. But Job breaks down all our formulas when he declares, "Lo, these are parts of his ways: but how little a portion is heard of him?" (26:14). God is infinitely beyond our finite minds.

I took a philosophy class in college in which the professor defined God as "that beyond which nothing greater can be conceived." This definition is flawed, however; it limits God to our ability to conceive Him. I suggested an alternative: "He who is beyond all that we can conceive." When the professor replied that the definition was not "rational," I agreed. It wasn't irrational—opposed to reason—either, but it was *beyond* reason. To put it another way, it was a definition of God that had to be taken on faith. If rationality is defined as that which can be conceived by the human mind, then God is obviously above all rationality, just as He is above the physical realm.

The last chapter described an attribute as "something we can know about God" (p. 17), which implies that there are things we cannot know. Tozer reminds us that no matter how many attributes of God we study, we barely scratch the surface of His infinite being. "I point with a reverent finger to the tall mountain peak which is God, which rises infinitely above my power to comprehend. But that is only a little portion. The paths of His ways cannot be known; the rest is super-rational" (p. 43).

Tozer is calling for a return to Christian mysticism —a spirituality that is not irrational, but (to use his term) super-rational. It is a Christian walk which acknowledges God's transcendence and lives in a moment-by-moment, inner fellowship with Him—"to walk and talk with God, to live in the presence of God" (p. 43).

When we fail to live in the knowledge of God's transcendent presence, our Christianity becomes "programmed." In his book *The Root of the Righteous,* Tozer elaborates on this idea:

> In our times the program has been substituted for the Presence. The program rather than the Lord of glory is the center of attraction. So the most popular gospel church in any city is likely to be the one that offers the most interesting program; that is, the church that can present the most and best features for the enjoyment of the public. These features are programmed so as to keep everything moving and everybody expectant.

The problem, of course, is that we enter into worship with a focus on "putting on a good show" rather than on seeking to know God. It may "tickle our fancy, . . . satisfy our morbid curiosity or our longing after romance" (p. 44), as Tozer puts it, but it will never bring us into the intimate, mystical fellowship that we are privileged to have with our transcendent God.

Instead of seeking this intimate fellowship, we live darkened, closed lives which are centered around our own narrow interests and give little or no thought to God at all. Tozer compares this kind of living to a blind man who cannot see the sun rise, or to a worm in a cave. God desires to burst into our lives, breaking down every wall, every defense we have put up against Him.

And the day will come when He will do just that. Philippians 2:10-11 promises that one day every knee will bow before Him and every tongue will confess that He is Lord. You can meet God now or meet Him later—take your choice!

This invasion of God into our lives, Tozer says, is part of what conversion is. But many people go through their whole religious life without ever experiencing this. You can join the church, sing in the choir, teach a Sunday school class, "and yet never have an experience of the great God breaking in upon your consciousness, but living always once removed from God" (p. 46).

The Dread of God

So what happens when we encounter the transcendent God in our lives in this way? One thing we experience is *dread.* When Jacob encountered God, he said, "How dreadful is this place" (Genesis 28:17). When Peter had this experience, he fell to his knees and said, "Depart from me; for I am a sinful man" (Luke 5:8). This was not a fear of physical danger, but of what Tozer calls "creature consciousness" (p. 47). The fear of the Lord is a knowledge of our sinfulness in the presence of the Holy of Holies—"that sense of abasement, of being overwhelmed in the presence of that which is above all creatures" (p. 48). Is this something that Christians should experience? After all, we have been washed in the blood, right? I have to say yes. Remember, it is not a fear of danger, not a dread of judgment, but simply a knowledge of our unworthiness.

"Another thing that comes to us when we meet God," Tozer continues, "is a feeling of awful ignorance" (p. 48). Again, it is a recognition of how infinitely small our knowledge is in the presence of the all-knowing One, so that "the closer we come to God, the less we know—and the more we know we don't know" (p. 48).

The flippancy that Tozer complains about is our pride and arrogance, expressed on our lips. When Jesus was transfigured on the mountain, what did Peter do—fall on his knees in speechless awe? No, he opened his big mouth with what may have seemed like a great plan: "Master, it is good for us to be here: and let us make three tabernacles" (Luke 9:33). But when we meet God face to face, all our big plans fall by the wayside, and our words seem inadequate.

Still another thing we experience when we come into God's presence is a sense of weakness. When we see God high and lifted up, we see how weak we are in the midst of His great strength. After quoting Paul's declaration, "When I am weak, then am I strong" (2 Corinthians 12:10), Tozer points out very wisely that the reverse is true as well—when we are strong (or at least, when we *think* we are), then we are truly weak in spiritual power.

One moment in the presence of God will cure us forever of thinking we have it all together! As Paul says earlier in that second letter to the Corinthians, "Not that we are sufficient of ourselves to think any thing as of ourselves; but our sufficiency is of God" (3:5). Tozer himself admits to shaking inside when he entered the pulpit, overwhelmed by the responsibility of speaking about God to His people. Perhaps, like Tozer, we would see more of the power of God in our ministries if we trusted less in our own power.

Finally, Tozer makes a statement which may be the most profound in the entire chapter: "You may say, 'Must I live all of my life in a state of dread, of ignorance, of weakness, of impurity?' No. But you must arrive at that conviction about yourself and not just be told that by someone else" (p. 50). Then he admits that after he was saved, even after he became a preacher, he would preach to others that "all our righteousnesses are as filthy rags" (Isaiah 64:6), and yet, "I thought their filthy rags were filthier than mine" (p. 50). He needed a glimpse of the transcendent God to give him a proper view of himself.

I remember the day, years after I became a Christian, that I asked God to show me what I was really like. I had no idea what I was asking, but He was faithful to answer my request—and I caught a vision of just how proud and vain I really was. Like Tozer, I thought I was better than others, smarter than others, closer to God than others. What a blind fool I was!

And this is what Tozer is calling us to—a vision of the transcendent God, and through that, a vision of ourselves. But if God is so infinitely far above us, how can we meet Him? We meet Him where every blessing comes to us—by the way of the cross. We could never reach God, so God came down to us. Ironically, at the cross—the lowest point in Christ's life—is where we can reach the transcendent God. And just as ironically, we can't meet the One who rises above everything until we come down—until we humble ourselves before His cross. "I point you to God the Transcendent One!" cries Tozer. "And then I point you to the cross" (p. 54).

LESSON PLAN—Group Study

AIM: To help my students catch a vision of God's transcendence and how it puts everything else in perspective.

Introduction

1. Have volunteers read the six Scripture passages that begin the chapter (1 Chronicles 29:11; Job 11:7-8; 26:14; Psalm 145:3; Isaiah 55:8-9; 1 Timothy 6:16). Ask the group to identify the various words used to describe God in these passages, and list them on a board or overhead.

2. Remind the group that transcendence means "to rise above." Then ask this question: What does Tozer mean when he calls this definition an analogy?

3. Discuss Tozer's statement that "God is just as far above an archangel as He is above a caterpillar" (p. 39).

4. Read the portion of the "Te Deum Laudamus" on p. 42 of the book, or even the entire hymn (available on various websites). Discuss Tozer's comment that "we're not spiritually capable of understanding it" (pp. 42-43).

5. Ask the group to define "programmed Christianity." How do we avoid slipping into that? How do we avoid living "once removed from God"?

The Dread of God

Ask the group to name the things we experience when we come to a true encounter with God. Are these experienced only at salvation, or also post-salvation? If there are mature believers in the group, you may want to ask them prior to the meeting if they would be willing to share their experiences in encountering God, discussing especially its lasting effects.

Closing

1. Discuss how the cross bridges the chasm between us and the transcendent God. If the group is having trouble discussing this, seed the conversation with a few selections from pages 49-51 of the book.
2. Assign reading of chapter 3 for next week's class.
3. Lead the group in a moment of silent meditation, reflecting on the cross and asking God to reveal Himself. After a few moments, close in prayer.

Chapter 3:
God's Eternalness

Personal Study

Supplementary Materials: A. W. Tozer, *Jesus, Our Man in Glory* (Moody); Augustine, *Confessions*.

Tozer sounds a slightly different note in this chapter, telling us that God's eternalness is something that "everyone believes, but often without sufficient clarity and emphasis to make it worth their while" (p. 57). I think the point he is making is that we all believe God is eternal, but most of us have never meditated on that truth, thinking through the logical conclusions of that doctrine. Tozer believes that such an activity would substantially raise our level of spirituality. Why would meditating on God's eternalness make such a significant difference?

I think that phrases from two Scripture verses indicate the answer to this question. God is "the high and lofty One that inhabiteth eternity" (Isaiah 57:15) —which seems to imply that God's eternalness is directly connected to His high and lofty status. And the phrase "from everlasting to everlasting, thou art God" (Psalm 90:2) states that the very nature of deity is eternal—it's what makes Him God.

Tozer clarifies the situation by looking at it from the opposite viewpoint: What if God were *not* eternal? Could you worship a God who came into being at some time in the past—even the distant past—and may cease to exist in the future? Or, as Tozer puts it, could you worship a "pro tem" (means "for the time being") God (p. 58)? How could a temporal God be the creator of everything? (If He came into being at some time, aren't we tempted to ask, "Then who made God?")

But we *can* worship an eternal God, the One who inhabits eternity, who is from everlasting to everlasting. The Greek and Hebrew words—despite all attempts to qualify them—mean nothing less than infinite, time immeasurable, eternal. And if we catch a vision of His eternalness, we will begin to see God as He really is—and that is bound to affect our lives significantly.

God Is Not Dependent

Tozer challenges us to imagine America before the Europeans came, before the Indians were here. Then to expand our vision to imagine before mankind was created, before the earth was created, before *anything* was here. God was still here! As Augustine said, God was "before all that can be called 'before'."

If we understand God from this perspective, we see that God is not dependent upon anything else—

upon any part of His creation. I've heard it said that God created man because He was lonely, but that's bad theology. It would imply that God *needed* man, and God has never needed any part of His creation. He existed before it all, and He got along just fine without it.

God Has No Beginning

Just as God is not dependent, God never *began* to be. The word "began" is used to describe created things, because if something began, something else had to begin it. As was said before, if God came into being at some point in time, we are tempted to ask, "Then who made God?"

God Is Not in Time

The illustration that Tozer borrows from C. S. Lewis—of God as a sheet of paper extending infinitely in all directions, and all of time as a one-inch mark on that paper—is mind-boggling, and for some people it is impossible to comprehend. Lewis tells his readers that if the illustration is not helpful, then they shouldn't worry about it. Tozer also admits that since we live in time, we cannot conceive of "non-time." If this thought is beyond you, then drop it and go on. The important thing to know is that God is in control of everything—even time itself. "Time began in God and will end in God. And it doesn't affect God at all. God dwells in an everlasting now" (p. 63).

While we may be caught in time—having to meet deadlines, catching planes, living by a schedule—

God is not limited by time. He is never in a hurry, never too busy to talk to us. For those of us who are slaves to a clock, this is encouraging news.

God Has No Past or Future

Another encouraging aspect of God's eternalness is that "past" and "future" do not exist for Him, because He lives in the eternal "now." These terms are only used by creatures like us, who live in the flow of time: "God sits above time, dwelling in eternity: 'from everlasting to everlasting, Thou art God' " (p. 64).

This means that "God has already lived all of our tomorrows" (p. 64). I can endure anything that the future brings if I know that God has already walked that path before me. And if Jesus Christ is "the same yesterday, and to day, and for ever" (Hebrews 13:8), I know it will be the same Jesus walking that path with me.

The concept that God dwells in eternity, outside of time, would also explain why prophets, who are anointed with the Spirit of God, can foretell the future: "Declaring the end from the beginning, and from ancient times the things that are not yet done" (Isaiah 46:10).

Some theologians today believe that God does not know the future any more than we do. As a result, they have to rethink all they know of God, until they deny many of the traditional attributes of God. How can He be all-knowing if He doesn't know the future? How can He be unchanging if He dwells in time and is subject to the flow of time and change? And if God does not know the future, Isaiah 46:10, quoted above, becomes meaningless!

But thank God, He *does* know the end from the beginning! And if our life is "hid with Christ in God" (Colossians 3:3), we can share with Him (by faith, if not by sight) that eternal perspective that is above time. Tozer compares it to flying in an airplane: you may take off on a gloomy, overcast day, but when you rise above the clouds, everything is bathed in sunshine. So no matter how gloomy our present, temporal circumstances may be, we need to take God's perspective, and keep looking *down*—for we are seated with Christ in the heavenly places (Ephesians 2:6)!

On the other hand, Tozer reminds us, *we* are subject to time, even if our God is not. So we must learn "to number our days" (Psalm 90:12). This is why we can learn so much from the life of Christ. As both God and man, He lived with both eternal and temporal perspectives. Which one ruled His heart? Though He walked the roads of Israel in time and space, He never seemed to be in a rush or a panic. He was living by His Father's agenda.

We panic, and sometimes pray as if God has to panic along with us, Tozer says with good-natured humor. But God doesn't look at the clock; He does things when He chooses, and it's always just the right time. He sent His Son "when the fulness of the time was come" (Galatians 4:4), and yet—note the eternal perspective—He was the Lamb, "slain from the foundation of the world" (Revelation 13:8). Jesus Christ entered human history at a specific time designated by His Father, but from God's perspective, He had already lived and died for the sins of the world.

Time Marches On

Time is "like an ever-rolling stream," Tozer reminds us, carrying us away in its flow (p. 67). Our time on this earth is short, and we will all die someday, with one generation rising up to replace another. And just as the giant sequoia trees in California have stood for hundreds, perhaps thousands of years, looking down on the parade of one short generation after another, so God looks down on us—one generation after another.

Why does Tozer treat us to this sobering, even somewhat morbid, illustration? He wants to remind us of our mortality in preparation for his next point.

We Need God

"God is to you a necessity," Tozer concludes (p. 70). We need God—of course we do! Why is it that we need to be reminded of this obvious fact so often? When a preacher calls us to come to God, he's doing us a favor—we need God! And when it comes to the issue of our mortality, there is no place where we need God more. Humans are strange creatures. We are mortal, but we have eternity in our hearts (Ecclesiastes 3:11), so we cannot be satisfied with a few short decades of life on earth. (The word in this verse translated "world" in the KJV is translated "everlasting" in other verses. Therefore, it is suggested that the verse should read, "he hath set everlastingness [eternity] in their heart.")

Our immortality is in God, nowhere else. God is "our help in ages past"—our ages, not God's. He must guide us, for we can't do it alone. We are fragile; we can be killed by a microscopic bug. Only in God is immortality and eternity—only through Christ. Christ has conquered death and sits at God's right hand.

I could relate to Tozer's experience of seeing mummies in a museum and becoming depressed over the fact that "men made in the image of God had to die and turn to dust" (p. 71). In *Jesus, Our Man in Glory,* Tozer elaborates on this tragic theme:

> We are creatures of time—time in our hands, our feet, our bodies—that causes us to grow old and to die. Yet all the while we have eternity in our hearts!
>
> One of our great woes as fallen people living in a fallen world is the constant warfare between the eternity in our hearts and the time in our bodies. This is why we can never be satisfied without God.

But the good news is, we *can* be satisfied in God. Only He who is "from everlasting to everlasting" can fill that longing for eternity in our hearts. "He that believeth in me, though he were dead, yet shall he live: And whosoever liveth and believeth in me shall never die" (John 11:25-26).

"Why can we believe in our own immortality?" Tozer asks. "Because God is eternal. . . . We can look forward with calm restfulness to the time that shall be" (p. 74).

LESSON PLAN—Group Study

AIM: To help my students grasp, in some small way, God's eternalness, and how it gives us hope for our eternal future.

Introduction

Read the two Scripture passages at the beginning of the chapter (Isaiah 57:15; Psalm 90:1-2), emphasizing the phrases, "the high and lofty One that inhabiteth eternity" and "from everlasting to everlasting, thou art God." Discuss how these verses show the relationship between God's eternalness and His divine nature. What does it mean that God "inhabiteth eternity" and is "from everlasting to everlasting"?

God Is Not Dependent

Read the quote from Augustine's *Confessions* on pages 60-61 and ask what Augustine's words tell us about God's eternalness. How does it affect our relationship with God to know that He is not dependent on us or anything else—that He does not "need" us?

God Has No Beginning

Tozer tells us that "God never began to be" (p. 61). Ask the group, "Is there anything else that has no beginning?" (No.) Discuss the difficulty of thinking about God, because He is a unique being—eternal, uncreated, unchanging.

God Is Not in Time

Ask if anyone has a hard time understanding the concept of God as above time, dwelling "in an everlasting now" (p. 63). Read the illustration from C. S. Lewis on pages 62-63 and assure the class that the important thing to remember is that God is in control of all things—even time.

God Has No Past or Future

Anyone who cannot conceive of God as "above time" will also be confused by "God has no past or future." The idea that "God has already lived all of our tomorrows" (p. 64) may be even more confusing! Discuss these issues, trying to keep the tone positive. Ask the group how knowing that God is in control of time helps us to avoid worry and panic in our lives.

Be prepared for the possibility that someone will ask how we can have free will if God knows what we are going to do in the future. Emphasize to the group that if we could fully understand God, He wouldn't be God!

Time Marches On

Tozer seeks to get us thinking about the fact that our life is short and death is inevitable. Ask the group what causes them to be reminded of the brevity of life. Remind your group that Tozer points out this seemingly morbid and dark thought to emphasize the fact that we need God.

We Need God

Read Ecclesiastes 3:11 (see note in personal study if using the KJV) and 1 Corinthians 15:51-55. Ask how these Scriptures relate to God's eternalness, our need for God and our attitude toward death.

Closing

1. Invite the group to share anything they have learned this week about God's eternalness.
2. Assign reading of chapter 4 for next week's class.
3. Close in prayer.

Chapter 4:
God's Omnipotence

Personal Study

Supplementary Materials: A hymnal or worship song-book; A. W. Tozer, *Who Put Jesus on the Cross?* (Moody); A. W. Tozer, *Rut, Rot or Revival* (Moody).

The selected Bible passages at the beginning of this chapter give us a clue as to what direction Tozer plans to take this study of God's omnipotence. Spend a moment meditating on how God's unlimited power means that all things are possible.

Tozer defines omnipotence as "having an infinite and absolute plenitude (abundance) of power" (p. 76). The root meaning of both *omnipotent* and *almighty* are exactly that: God has all the power there is. The Bible never uses these words to refer to anyone but God. And since God is the only One who is infinite, these words can only refer to Him.

Tozer further defines God's omnipotence through three propositions:

God Has Power

Psalm 62:11 tells us that power belongs to God. In fact, God's power displayed in creation is one of the main evidences for His existence (Romans 1:20). "You look up at the starry heavens above and see the eternal power of God there. God's power and Godhead are found there" (p. 77). Read again the hymn by Joseph Addison on page 78. Does it remind you of any other hymns or songs of worship that extol God's power in creation? Open a hymnal or worship songbook and review the lyrics of several of these musical works of praise to God our Creator.

God Is the Source of All Power

"There isn't any power anywhere that doesn't have God as its source. . . . And the source of anything has to be greater than that which flows out of it" (p. 79). Tozer's humble illustration of a milk can is used to highlight a very apt point: you can't pour more out of something than that something can hold. So God, the Source of all power in the universe, must be equal or greater than all the power in the universe.

God Gives Power, But Still Retains It

God is absolute and perfect power. So if He gives some of that power to His creation, is He less powerful? Not at all! God isn't like a battery that runs down, says Tozer (pp. 79-80). He can delegate power to His creation and still retain it. God has no more or less power than He had before the universe was created. I suppose that means that, in a very literal sense, all the power that you and I have is "borrowed" from the hand of God. We don't own it; He can take it back any time He wants.

That thought, however, is not on Tozer's mind. He's thinking more about God and His ability to "keep" us—to sustain us in our Christian life, to help us make it in this world. I love the illustration Tozer uses of the fly perched on a seat in an airplane, worrying about whether the plane will be able to carry its weight! Isn't that like us so often? We actually worry that the Almighty God of the universe might not be able to handle our problems! But God sustains all things by His power (Hebrews 1:3).

Scientists refer to "the laws of nature," and sometimes we think of them as if they overruled God's power. But Tozer defines "the laws of nature" as "the path God's power and wisdom take through creation." In *Who Put Jesus on the Cross?* Tozer explains it this way:

> Why doesn't the sky fall down? Why is it that stars and planets do not go tearing apart and ripping off into chaos?
>
> Because there is a Presence that makes all things consist—and it is the Presence of that One who upholdeth all things by the word of His power. This is basically a spiritual explanation, for this universe can only be explained by spiritual and eternal laws.

Tozer says that science is mostly observing the "uniformity of phenomena"—recognizing that God works the same way all the time. Because His ways are predictable, we can navigate the ocean or build a skyscraper. We can trust that God will not change the laws of nature on a lark, but that He will always act the same way.

The same is true, Tozer reminds us, in the spiritual realm. God can be depended upon to fulfill His promises in Scripture—as long as we meet the conditions He has laid down. We also observe the "uniformity of phenomena" in the spiritual realm. But unlike the scientist, we go beyond the creation to the Creator Himself—the Source of it all.

Powerful, Yet Personal

It is amazing to think that what philosophers call the *mysterium tremendum*—that mysterious wonder that fills the universe—is also the God whom we are privileged to call "our Father in heaven." Just as a king is called "your majesty" by everyone but his children, who call him "Daddy," we can be intimate with God, "and God loves it," Tozer assures us. And God takes care of us in our every need (Psalm 41:3).

John 17:3 states that we can know God—the Almighty God of the universe! Tozer gets us to see the wonder of that fact by comparing it to knowing Beethoven or Michaelangelo—what would it have been like to have been their close friend? Would some of their genius have rubbed off on us? Would people have been impressed that we were friends with a great composer or sculptor? But instead of a symphony or sculpture, we can look at the sun, the moon, the stars in the Milky Way, and we can dare to say, "I know the One who made this."

And yet we settle for far less than the wonderful relationship that we can enjoy. Though we know God for Himself, Tozer says, we often act like the "children in the markets" that Jesus spoke of in Matthew 11:16-17. Comparing the "children in the markets" with Christians who go around "playing church" was a fresh interpretation of that passage for me! Instead of being spiritually childish, we need to be mature and serious in our search to know God.

Is Anything Too Hard for God?

Tozer makes an important point here: "hard" and "easy" don't mean anything to God, since His power is unlimited. A task that takes five percent of my power will not tire me out like a task that takes *ninety-five* percent of my power. But since there is no limit to God's power, no task takes any percentage of His power, because His power is immeasurable.

If I pick up an ant on my finger, it is really no harder for me to move that ant twelve inches than it is to move it three inches. In the same way (or even more so, since God's power has no limit), it is no harder for God to make a galaxy than to lift a robin's egg off a nest, to use Tozer's words.

Why is this point so important? Because if we really believed it, Tozer says, we wouldn't hesitate in our prayers to ask God for "hard" things—because there aren't any "hard" things for God! Remember Genesis 18:14—"Is any thing too hard for the LORD?" God must have had a bit of a chuckle behind that question, since "hard" isn't even in His vocabulary!

This applies to all our prayers, but especially to our prayers for healing. Sometimes we pray for God to heal a serious disease, but don't have faith to believe Him for a chronic disease—"I've had it too long; even God can't heal that." In response, Tozer tells the story of A. B. Simpson, who dared to believe God for healing of a chronic illness he had had all his life. Let's look at how Tozer tells the story in *Rut, Rot or Revival*:

> At thirty-six, Simpson was a Presbyterian preacher so sick that he said, "I feel I could fall into the grave when I have a funeral." He could not preach for months at a time because of his sickness. He went to a little camp meeting in the woods and heard a quartet sing, "No man can work like Jesus/ No man can work like Him." Simpson went off among the pine trees with that ringing in his heart: "Nobody can work like Jesus; nothing is too hard for Jesus. No man can work like Him." The learned, stiff-necked Presbyterian threw himself down upon the pine needles and said, "If Jesus Christ is what they said He was in the song, heal me." The Lord healed him, and he lived to be seventy-six years old. Simpson founded a society that is now one of the largest evangelical denominations in the world, The Christian and Missionary Alliance.
>
> We are his descendants and we sing his songs. But are we going to allow ourselves to listen to that which

will modify our faith, practices and beliefs, water down our gospel and dilute the power of the Holy Spirit? I, for one, am not!

Here is where the practical nature of studying God's attributes comes in. As Tozer puts it, this is "not ivory-tower theology" but "truths for you and me." It causes me to ask myself: am I living as if God were *not* omnipotent? We should be able to trust Him for *anything;* if we serve an *almighty* God, we need to start praying *large* prayers!

God's power, Tozer reiterates, is effortless, because effort means I'm *expending* energy; I'm working hard. We stand in awe of the Incarnation—but it wasn't hard for God. The Atonement wasn't hard for God. The Resurrection wasn't hard for God. So even that "hanging-on" sin that's been plaguing you isn't too hard for God. Nothing is impossible for Him, if we dare to trust Him.

LESSON PLAN—Group Study

AIM: To help my students understand God's omnipotence, and to have the faith to trust Him for great things.

Introduction

Read aloud and discuss the four passages at the beginning of the chapter. Ask the group to identify the distinction between the related truths of Matthew 19:26 and Luke 1:37.

Ask someone to define omnipotence; discuss why it is an attribute that only God can have.

1. God Has Power

Read Psalm 62:11 and Romans 1:20. Discuss how these two Scripture passages are related. If you have a hymnal available that includes "The Spacious Firmament on High" by Joseph Addison, read the words to the class.

2. God Is the Source of All Power

Introduce this statement to the group: "The source is always greater than what flows out of it." Discuss how this relates to God's power as displayed in His creation.

3. God Gives Power, But Still Retains It

Discuss the concept of God delegating power but still retaining it. If all power is ultimately God's, how should that affect the way we exercise our power?

Read Hebrews 1:3. What does it say about God's ability to protect and sustain us?

What does Tozer mean by the phrase "uniformity of phenomena"? How does it apply in the spiritual realm?

Powerful, Yet Personal

Ask the group to describe the paradox between God's being powerful, yet personal. If necessary, seed the discussion by reading the story on page 85 of Queen Elizabeth as a child. Also read Psalm 41:3 to the group.

Ask the group if they have ever become personally acquainted with someone who enjoyed a certain amount of fame. Invite them to share what it was like. Read John 17:3 and ask what promise is expressed in this verse.

Read Matthew 11:16-17. How does Tozer interpret the "children in the markets"? Is this a problem in today's church?

Is Anything Too Hard for God?

Discuss what Tozer means when he says that "hard" and "easy" have no meaning for God. Do we ever hesitate to ask for something because we think it's too hard for God?

Closing

1. Invite members of the group to share their "hard" prayer requests, and agree to trust God to see them come to pass.
2. Assign reading of chapter 5 for next week's class.
3. Close in prayer.

Chapter 5:
God's Immutability

Personal Study

Supplementary Materials: A. W. Tozer, *The Attributes of God Volume One* with Study Guide (Moody); *The Athanasian Creed.*

Immutability is one of those long words that scare people away from theology. Tozer admits that it may seem rather dull and imposing, "but when it's explained you'll find you've struck gold and diamonds, milk and honey" (p. 96).

It is silly, however, to be put off by the word *immutable,* which simply means "not subject to change." It means "not mutable." God, in other words, does not mutate. For instance, the vapor that is a cloud one day may be rain the next day and fog the day after, but not so with God. He is unchanging.

Review the four passages at the beginning of the chapter (Malachi 3:6; Hebrews 6:17-18; James 1:17; Hebrews 13:8) and meditate on their meaning. Tozer notes that these passages are without a trace of metaphor; they cannot be "interpreted" away. God simply never changes. Change is not even possible with God. "God never differs from Himself," Tozer says in summary (p. 97).

People, however, are changeable. The close friend you once had is now distant and cold. That little baby you once cuddled in your arms now wants to borrow the car. Only God remains the same. Tozer quotes a Wesley hymn to make his point: "And all things, as they change, proclaim the Lord eternally the same" (p. 98).

The theological fact of God's immutability is *revealed* truth—truth that we could not have known by our own reasoning unless God revealed it to us. At this point, Tozer applies the principle expressed by Anselm: "I do not seek to understand so that I may believe, but I believe in order to understand" (p. 98). In other words, some things cannot be reasoned out; you have to take them on faith before you can understand them.

But once you have taken a truth on faith, he adds, the act of reasoning it out can be a profitable exercise. So Tozer begins by answering the question, "Why can't God change?" He says that when something changes, one of three things happens: it gets better, it gets worse or it gets different (it changes from one kind of thing to another).

But God can't get better. How can a perfect being get better, or an infinite being get greater? And God certainly can't get worse. How can a holy and righteous God become worse? (By sinning? But how can God sin?) God also can't change from one kind of being to another, because as the infinite, holy God, He is unique—how could God change to "not God"?

God does not change, but we should be thankful that people can indeed change. In fact, changing is something we will probably continue to do even in heaven, suggests Tozer. As we move toward the perfect likeness of God, we "will become holier and wiser and better while the ages roll" (p. 100). But God cannot get better, because He is the standard by which all things are measured. Tozer covers this in the first volume of *The Attributes of God* when he discusses God's perfection:

> God is not at the top of the heap in an everascending perfection of being, from the worm on up until finally we reach God. On the contrary, God is completely different and separate, so that there are no degrees in God. God is simply God, an infinite perfection of fullness, and we cannot say God is a little more or a little less. "More" and "less" are creaturewords. We can say that a man has a little more strength today than yesterday. We can say the child is a little taller this year; he's growing. But you can't apply more or less to God, for God is the perfect One; He's just God.

Change, Tozer says, means nothing to God, because He is perfect and does not change, in the same way direction means nothing to God, because He is omnipresent and doesn't "go" anywhere—He's already there! "So these words—greater, lesser, back, forward, down, up—can't apply to God. God the eternal God remains unchanged and unchanging—that is, He is immutable" (p. 102).

If God cannot get better or worse (the first two ways of changing), can He then become different (the third way of changing)? Like a caterpillar to a butterfly, can He change from one kind of being to another?

People certainly can; they can change in their moral nature from good to bad, or (praise the Lord!) from bad to good. Tozer gives three examples of people who changed: John Newton, a wicked slave trader who later became a preacher and author of the hymn "Amazing Grace"; John Bunyan, by his own confession "one of the vilest men who ever lived" before he was converted and became the author of the classic *Pilgrim's Progress;* and of course, the apostle Paul, formerly a persecutor of the church and the "chief" of sinners (1 Timothy 1:15). They all changed morally from one kind of creature to another.

God, however, "cannot become anything else but what He is" (p. 103). That makes sense, because as the absolute, perfect, infinite God, He is already *everything* good and righteous and holy. He cannot change into something different, because anything different would be a step down from better to worse—and we've already argued the impossibility of that kind of change.

But what about the Incarnation? Didn't God "become" a Man? Didn't He "change" into something "different"? No, Tozer says, and he appeals to the ancient Athanasian Creed to show that this view of the

Incarnation was held by the early church. Part of the creed which refers to Christ reads as follows: "Who, although He is God and man, yet He is not two, but one Christ. One, not by conversion of the Godhead into flesh, but by taking of that manhood into God."

The exact nature of the Incarnation is a mystery, but Tozer is being faithful to Scripture and Bible-believing theologians of all ages when he says, "He took a tabernacle on Himself but His deity did not become humanity. His deity was joined to His humanity in one person forever. But God the eternal and uncreated can never become created" (p. 104).

Tozer also addresses another very important distinction: the Bible speaks of Christ living in us, of being filled with the Holy Spirit, but this is not the same as *pantheism,* in which God is considered identical to His creation. Unlike Buddhism, that teaches that after death "we pass away into Nirvana, into the eternal sea of deity and cease to be, like a drop of water into the ocean" (p. 104), Christianity asserts that we will keep our individual personalities throughout eternity in heaven. That's the wonder of salvation—God does not destroy His sinful creatures, but makes us new creatures in Christ!

Always the Same

All the attributes of God apply equally to all three Persons of the Trinity, including immutability. Again, Tozer quotes a line from the Athanasian Creed: "Such as the Father is, such is the Son, and such is the Holy Spirit" (p. 105). God is always the same—

Father, Son and Holy Spirit, forever and ever, world without end, Amen.

God's immutability also means there is no relativity of morals. What God approved and condemned, He still does. "Holiness and righteousness are conformity to the will of God. And the will of God never changes for moral creatures" (p. 107). The idea of right and wrong being relative terms is nothing less than a lie from the pit of hell.

It is true that in the past God has "winked" at sin (Acts 17:30), and that He still puts up with a lot of things in us because of our ignorance; He's waiting for us to grow up, to come to the truth. But God hates sin, and that will never change. His ultimate desire is that, in the moral arena at least, we become like Him in all we do.

So how can we know what God is like? Look at Jesus Christ (John 14:9). Just as Jesus welcomed little children (Matthew 19:14), He still welcomes the penitent heart that comes to Him for forgiveness.

The world is continually changing—which, for the most part, is a good thing. We wouldn't want to have the same weather all the time, or the same seasons all the time. Tozer notes that the thesis of the book of Hebrews is, "God allows things to change in order that He might establish that which cannot change" (p. 108). Hebrews shows how things moved from temporary to permanent in the altar, the priesthood and the tabernacle. Change occurs until something reaches perfection, then it changes no more.

Our permanent home is in God. We are victims of

time until we come home to the Timeless One—not heaven, but God. We are "a house . . . divided" (Mark 3:25) within ourselves until we find rest in Christ, our "blissful center" (p. 109). As Augustine said, we are made for God and we are restless until we find Him.

When we turn to Him in our need, isn't it wonderful to know that He never changes? He is with us always (Matthew 28:20), ready to take us in. Whatever our need—answers to your questions, life for your soul, forgiveness for your sins, rest for your labors—He is still "the very same Jesus" (p. 110).

LESSON PLAN—Group Study

AIM: To help my students understand the immutability of God and what it means for our relationship with Him.

Introduction

Have someone in the group read the four Scripture passages that begin the chapter (Malachi 3:6; Hebrews 6:17-18; James 1:17; Hebrews 13:8). These passages all discuss God's immutability, of course; ask what other theme is common to these verses (God's mercy and grace to His children).

Tozer says that God's immutability is *revealed* truth rather than *reasoned* truth. Ask the group if they agree with this statement. Discuss the difference between revelation and reason.

What, according to Tozer, are the three ways something can change? (It can get better, get worse or become different.) Discuss why God is not capable of any one of these kinds of change.

Discuss how to reconcile the Incarnation with God's immutability. If you have the text of The Athanasian Creed, make copies for each person in the group and read it together, especially the portion related to the Incarnation. (The creed is readily available on several Web sites.)

Discuss how the idea of Christ living in us and of being filled with the Holy Spirit is different from the pantheism of Buddhism and the New Age movement.

Always the Same

Tozer contends that all three Persons in the Trinity are unchangeable. Has your relationship to the Father, or Christ or the Holy Spirit appeared to change at any time in your Christian life? Who, then, is responsible for that change?

Choose two or three events in the Gospels (including Jesus and the children in Matthew 19) and observe Jesus' actions and words. Have the group divide into twos or threes and make a list of things that can be learned about God from these events in the life of Christ.

Closing

1. Have each person choose one or two of these truths about God from the life of Christ that relate to a specific need in his life. Spend some time in

silent prayer and meditation about God's sufficiency to meet that need.

2. Assign reading of chapter 6 for next week's class.

3. Close in prayer.

Chapter 6:
God's Omniscience

Personal Study

Supplementary Materials: A. W. Tozer, *That Incredible Christian* (Moody); A. W. Tozer, *The Christian Book of Mystical Verse* (Moody).

As you read the two Scripture passages that begin this chapter, notice that they emphasize two different aspects of God's omniscience. Psalm 147:5 is more information-oriented; it tells us that God understands all data, knowledge and facts. Hebrews 4:13, however, is more relational; no creature—including us—is hidden from His eyes. He sees right through us. As we look through this chapter, you will notice that Tozer deals with both of these aspects of God's omniscience.

Tozer confesses to being overwhelmed by the thought of "how much there is to know and how little we know" (p. 113). Emerson's comment that no one in his whole lifetime could read more than a small fraction of the books in the British Library is especially amazing when you consider that much of the information in those books is now obsolete! There is also the popular claim that the world's collective body of scientific knowledge doubles every seven years, five years or two years (depending on whom you ask). While that statistic is questionable, it is true that we are making unprecedented leaps in scientific understanding.

And yet God knows all this and far more. We truly are like Sir Isaac Newton, who humbly admitted he was like a small boy with just a handful of shells on the vast seashore of knowledge. We know so little in comparison to the God who has "perfection of knowledge" (p. 115).

Tozer is not dismissing human knowledge or reason, however—not even the use of reason to approach God. As long as we recognize the limits and fallibility of human reason, it can be useful. We can approach God both theologically (rationally) and experientially. "You can know God experientially and not know much theology, but . . . the more you know about God theologically the better you can know Him experientially" (p. 115).

Reason, however, is limited; God is ultimately ineffable (inexpressible in words), inconceivable and unimaginable. That's why Tozer says it is easier to think of God in terms of what He *is not* rather than what He *is*. It is also why Tozer doesn't seem to think much of "visualization" in prayer, and why he is "horrified" by Michaelangelo's depiction of God (on the ceiling of the Sistine Chapel) as an old, bearded man.

We might not all be as bothered by this as Tozer,

but he does have a point. God warned us in the Ten Commandments not to make "any likeness of any thing that is in heaven above, or that is in the earth beneath, or that is in the water under the earth" (Exodus 20:4). The infinite, invisible, incomprehensible God wants no finite image to represent Him, for He cannot be represented. As Tozer puts it, "If you can think it, it isn't God. If you can think it, it is an idol of your own imagination" (p. 116).

Reread 1 Corinthians 2:7-11, and focus on what the passage says man knows versus what God knows. One of the strongest messages of this verse is that we can't know the things of God without His illumination— He has to reveal it to us. In *That Incredible Christian,* Tozer summarizes the need for such illumination:

> The sum of what I am saying is that there is an illumination, divinely bestowed, without which theological truth is information and nothing more. While this illumination is never given apart from theology, it is entirely possible to have theology without the illumination. This results in what has been called "dead orthodoxy," and while there may be some who deny that it is possible to be both orthodox and dead at the same time I am afraid experience proves that it is.

This is what Tozer is warning about when he says, "When we crowded the Holy Ghost out of the church and took in other things instead, we put out our own eyes" (p. 117). By quenching and grieving the Holy Spirit, we pushed away the One who could guide us into all truth.

Tozer is calling us to return to a deep reverence for God, so that He can again illumine us and open our eyes to see wondrous things in His Word (Psalm 119:18). "You always see God when you're on your knees," he says (p. 117).

As beings made in His image, we are more like God than any other part of His creation, yet we really know so little of the divine nature. "God lies beyond our thoughts, towers above them, escapes them and confounds them in awful, incomprehensible terror and majesty" (p. 118). That's why it's easier to describe God by what He is *not* than by what He *is*: self-existence—*no* origin; eternity—*no* beginning or end; immutability—*no* change; infinity—*no* boundaries or limits.

How, then, do we discuss God's omniscience in this same negative way? Well, God has no teacher; He *cannot* learn. If God knows everything, He can't learn anything new! Tozer's dry humor is in evidence as he points out that our prayers would be a lot shorter if we remembered that we can't tell God anything He doesn't already know.

Ultimately, God is incomprehensible; we can't know Him with our heads. But Christ promises to reveal Him to us (Matthew 11:27). This is entirely different from the human knowledge that Paul determined *not* to have (1 Corinthians 2:1-5). True Christianity has an element to it that goes beyond human reasoning, because, as Tozer says, "if your faith stands in human argument . . . a better arguer can argue you out of it again" (p. 120). But when revealed by the Spirit, "nobody can argue you out of it" (p. 120). Even if we cannot answer a particular argument against our faith, we will still have the knowledge of God revealed to us in our hearts.

God Knows Himself

God contains all things and knows all things; He even knows Himself—as no one else does (1 Corinthians 2:11). As in the chapter on omnipotence, Tozer emphasizes that it takes no effort on God's part to be omniscient. He knows everything instantly and perfectly; He cannot learn. He knows the end from the beginning, long before it happens; He is never surprised. If we don't understand how this can be, it's only because we are finite human beings. We have to learn to not think of God as if He were a mere human being; others have been rebuked for that (see Psalm 50:21).

Tozer said before that we could shorten our prayers if we remembered that God already knows everything. But at this point in the chapter Tozer qualifies that statement, assuring us that it is good to sit down and talk with God, even though we are telling Him things He already knows. We should never be afraid to pour out our hearts to God in prayer.

What Tozer is criticizing is "lecturing" God, which usually occurs during corporate prayer and is probably for the purpose of impressing the speaker's human listeners. We all know the type of person he's talking about—a person like the Pharisee Jesus spoke about, who went to the temple and "prayed thus *with himself*" (Luke 18:11, emphasis added). He prayed "with himself" because God had stopped listening; He already knew all the Pharisee was bragging about!

Prayer is for *our* benefit. God already knows everything—He can't learn anything from us. So when we pray, we should feel free to share with Him all that is in our hearts, all the while recognizing that none of this information is new to the Lord; it doesn't hurt to remember the biblical admonition to "let thy words be few" (Ecclesiastes 5:2).

Romans 11:33-36 is worth meditating upon whenever we are tempted to think about how wise and important we are. Even someone as important as the President of the United States needs dozens of people to advise him and keep him informed as to what is going on around the world. But we are very wrong if we think God needs his angels to travel around the universe and keep Him up-to-date! God never has to "find out" anything; He already knows.

When we read passages like Genesis 18:21, where it indicates that God is "going to" Sodom to learn what it is like, we have to realize that God is dealing with humans and is accommodating His language to their finite minds. God didn't have to "go to" Sodom—He was already there. He didn't have to learn what it was like—He already knew. And when Jesus asked questions, He already knew the answers —He simply did that to draw people out.

We should see it as a great comfort that God already knows it all—matter, space, time, causes and effects. There are no mysteries with God. With you and me, well, that's another story. We are confronted with many mysteries, including, for example, the Incarnation: How did God condense Himself into human form (1 Timothy 3:16)? We don't know, but God does, so we don't have to worry about it.

Tozer lived in an era where worry was in plentiful supply. The Soviet Union was an aggressive world power; thermonuclear war seemed to be a continuously imminent possibility. Tozer didn't know what the future held—but God did, so Tozer wasn't worried. Today we face other seemingly imminent threats, but like Tozer, we can trust that God knows all about it and nothing will take us from the palm of His hand. God knows His people, so we are never orphans, never lost—isn't that a great comfort?

If you are worried, remember that God knows it all, and you cannot "drift beyond His love and care" (p. 127). All we have to do is trust Him, and God will make all the right choices, because "He hath done all things well" (Mark 7:37). If you need a reminder of God's care for you, take a tip from Tozer and read the words to some of the great hymns of the church, or look through a poetry collection such as *The Christian Book of Mystical Verse*.

Even if you make a mistake, God can overrule it. Tozer's illustrations of the cracked cathedral window and the dove in the scrap heap (based on Psalm 68:13) are worth meditating on if you need to be reminded of this fact.

God Knows the Unsaved

Isaiah 45:4 is a wonderful promise to the unsaved: God knows everything about them as well, and is still calling them by name. Even if we don't know God, He knows us, according to Psalm 139. Even to the atheist, God can say, "You may not believe in Me, but I believe in you." God still receives sinners (Luke 15:2).

And even if we know Him, we have to learn that He knows us far better than we know ourselves. Nothing we can tell Him will shock Him, for He knows it all already. He sees right through us, but loves us anyway. We should be always ready to confess our sins, our doubts and our fears to Him; there's nothing we can hide from Him, anyway!

LESSON PLAN—Group Study

AIM: To help my students become consciously aware of God's omniscience, and be inspired to live transparent lives before their Lord.

Introduction

Have two people in the group read aloud the two passages at the beginning of the chapter (Psalm 147:5 and Hebrews 4:13). Discuss the difference between the two kinds of knowledge described in these passages.

List (on a board or overhead) various subjects in which members of the group would be considered knowledgeable—law, science, art, education, etc.

Then quote Will Rogers underneath the list: "Everybody is ignorant—only on different subjects." Point out that although we are "ignorant," God has "perfection of knowledge" and would know everything there is to know on all these subjects.

Ask the group what Tozer means by approaching God theologically and experientially. If God is ultimately ineffable (incapable of being expressed in words), inconceivable and unimaginable, what is the purpose of theology?

Read 1 Corinthians 2:7-11. What does this passage say that man knows? What does it say that God knows? Is this informational knowledge or relational knowledge (see the beginning of the personal study)—or both?

Discuss what Tozer means when he says that in crowding out the Holy Spirit, "we put out our own eyes." Is this situation still a problem in today's church?

Have volunteers read Matthew 11:25-27 and 1 Corinthians 2:1-5. Discuss what these two passages teach us about God's omniscience and our own knowledge.

God Knows Himself

Have volunteers read 1 Corinthians 2:11 and Psalm 50:21. What do these verses say about how we are to relate to the omniscient God?

Pose this question to the group: If God already knows everything we are going to ask for, why should we pray?

Discuss Tozer's statement, "God cannot learn." Read Romans 11:33-36 as input into the discussion.

Using a hymnal or a book of Christian poetry, read some passages that discuss God's love and care for us. Ask the group how an understanding of God's omniscience helps us to keep from worrying.

God Knows the Unsaved

Discuss what we might say to an unbeliever about the omniscience of God that would draw them to repentance.

Closing

1. Ask each person in the group to think about a personal secret that they might not want anyone else to know. Remind them that, as with everything else, God knows about this, and loves them anyway. Encourage them to discuss their secret with God in prayer.
2. Assign reading of chapter 7 for next week's class.
3. Close in prayer.

Chapter 7:
God's Wisdom

Personal Study

Supplementary Material: C. S. Lewis, *The Problem of Pain* (Macmillan).

My first thought on beginning this chapter was, *How is God's wisdom different from the subject of the previous chapter, God's omniscience?* Certainly wisdom and knowledge are closely related, but wisdom involves more than knowing information or knowing a person; it is knowing the right thing to do in a given situation. The most crucial place we see God's wisdom exercised is in His will and plans for our lives, which is the thrust of this chapter.

Look over the six Scripture passages at the beginning of the chapter. Meditate on what they mean for your personal relationship with God.

While there is no such word as "omniwisdom," we know that God is infinitely wise, since every aspect of Him is infinite. This is one attribute of God which we do not try to prove; instead, we take it on faith. "If I tried to prove that God is wise, the embittered soul would not believe it anyway. . . . And the worshiping heart already knows that God is wise and does not need to have it proved" (pp. 132-33). Tozer makes a good point that asking for proof of God's wisdom is an insult to His deity, since to question His wisdom is to assert our own—to say we are wiser than He is. It also casts doubt on our wisdom, since if He created us, and He is not wise, then how could we be wise?

> It is necessary to our humanity that we grant God two things at least: wisdom and goodness. The God who sits on high, who made the heaven and the earth, has got to be wise, or else you and I cannot be sure of anything. He's got to be good, or earth would be a hell and heaven a hell, and hell a heaven. (p. 133)

Probably the most common challenge to God's wisdom (and His goodness and power, for that matter) is what C. S. Lewis calls "the problem of pain"— if God is so wise, why is there so much cruelty, war, famine and disease in the world? Tozer answers the critic with the allegory of a wise man who built a beautiful palace, but an invading army captured it and used it as a horse stable, so that its beauty was marred and hidden under filth and grime.

Interestingly, the allegory Tozer describes is much like what happened to Monticello, the home of Thomas Jefferson. During the Civil War, his home— an architectural masterpiece designed by Jefferson himself—was captured by Confederate soldiers, sold and used for storage. Eventually, the house was acquired by admirers of Jefferson and restored to its original beauty. But certainly, back when it housed bales of hay, there must have been many who doubted that the dirty old building was once the pride and joy of the great Thomas Jefferson.

That is our world. Romans 8:19-22 says "the whole creation groaneth," waiting for Christ to return. The world is under the foreign occupation of Satan and his hordes, but one day God will restore His palace to its former beauty.

Tozer illustrates this also with his description of how coal companies, using strip-mining techniques, have devastated the beautiful hills and streams around his boyhood home in Pennsylvania. In the interest of making a fast buck, they tore the top off a mountain to get at the coal beneath. "And the result looks as though nature were weeping, as though the whole world were a graveyard" (p. 137).

But God has not surrendered His creation; He is running it, even if it is "groaning under the plow and the bulldozer, under the heel of the foe" (p. 138). Someday God will send His Son to get us (1 Thessalonians 4:16-17). We will be changed and glorified into the image of God. "He's going to clean house down here" (p. 129). Peace will prevail, and beauty. But for now, we "have to be patient and go along with God for a little while, because we're under occupation" (p. 138).

Wisdom Defined

Tozer defines wisdom as "the skill to achieve the most perfect ends by the most perfect means" (p. 138).

Both the means and ends are worthy of God. God sees the end from the beginning and judges in view of final ends. His wisdom is flawlessly precise. God doesn't "muddle through"; He never needs to back up and correct anything. Jesus never apologized— He never had to. We, on the other hand, often have to apologize; Tozer tells of having to apologize for saying the wrong thing. But Jesus always said it right the first time. Bible wisdom is different from wisdom of the earth, because it has a "moral connotation" (p. 140). It is high, holy, pure and lovely—never shrewd or cunning or crafty.

God's Wisdom Is Infinite

God is all-wise; His wisdom is perfect and complete. No problem is too much for Him. With the conflicts that rage throughout the world, it is comforting to know that God is infinitely wise and we don't have to worry. "If I thought that God were only a little bit wise, or even ninety percent wise, I'd never get to sleep tonight" (p. 140).

His perfect wisdom plans for "the highest good, for the greatest number, for the longest time" (p. 141). God is not a mere opportunist, looking for short-term results and quick successes. "God always thinks in terms of eternity" (p. 141). For example, our salvation is not only for the present; God has breathed into us His eternity and immortality. "God Almighty has planned that you shall not only enjoy Him now, but for all the eternities to come" (p. 141). If we intend to reflect God's wisdom, we should operate our ministries and churches this way. They "should be run for the highest good of the greatest number of people, even if it appears to flop" (p. 141), instead of aiming for short-term success that can run roughshod over people.

God's Wisdom Revealed

Tozer admits that God's wisdom can be disputed by unbelieving men. They say the beautiful palace that is now a pigpen could not have been made by a wise and good God. But he reiterates, "God Almighty is running His world; the day will come when God will lift a cloud off the world and they shall gather in admiration from everywhere and say how wonderful God is" (p. 142). Read Revelation 4:11; 5:9-10, 12 for a description of that day.

Since men of limited wisdom and unmitigated gall will always question God, many of His greatest works are hidden from our eyes and done in the darkness. The creation of the world began in the dark (Genesis 1:1-3); the Incarnation began in the darkness of a virgin's womb, so no one could see His mystery. And when Jesus was nailed to the cross the sky went dark, so they could not see him die. The resurrection was also done in the dark; when they went to the tomb early in the morning, he had already risen. "Every great thing that God has done, He has done in the silence and darkness because His wisdom is such that no man could understand it anyhow" (p. 143).

Redemption was accomplished in His wisdom (1 Corinthians 1:24; 2:7); salvation through faith was by His wisdom (1 Corinthians 1:21); and in the consummation, His wisdom is also revealed (Ephesians 3:10).

That's the crux of our lives—it's either God's wisdom or ours. Will we accept God's wisdom or go our own way? According to Isaiah 53:6, the essence of sin is the human idea that "I turn to my way because I think it is wiser than God's way."

Whether it's a question of how we spend our money or who we marry, our lack of obedience will make us miserable, because we reject God's wisdom and say, "I know better than you, God." This is the difference between revival and a dead church, between a Spirit-filled and a self-filled life. Whose wisdom is being followed—God's or yours?

We have to take a stand and decide that God's way is right. Even when things seem to go wrong we have to trust God and ride out the storm, by taking on faith Romans 8:28: "All things work together for good to them that love God . . ." Make a decision: either go your own way or trust blindly in the wisdom of God. If you trust blindly, He promises to lead the blind (Isaiah 42:16); after you are tried, you will "come forth as gold" (Job 23:10).

If we want to go our own way, God will let us go. We have to give up our plans and ambitions, because we don't have the wisdom to make them succeed. "You dare not run your life" (p. 147).

Tozer makes a humorous point when he says that when we're on an airplane and hit a little turbulence, we don't run to the cockpit and try to take over;

we've got to trust the pilot. "And yet," he adds, "we're doing that to God all the time. We go to church and we pray to give our heart to the Lord. . . . But then things get turbulent and we run and say, 'Lord, let me run this thing!' " (p. 147). Our lives are messed up because we won't let God run it all—family, business, home, job.

God is only after your highest good; He never makes mistakes, never demands more than you can handle, always gives you the power to do anything He calls you to. Isn't this the kind of God we can trust? "The difficulty with us is, we don't trust God. And that's why we're in the fix that we're in" (p. 148).

Tozer tells the story of the man who went bankrupt and tried to go to his old office after someone else bought out his business. The new owner came in and kicked him out! When God takes over our bankrupt lives, we can't get back into the owner's chair— that's God's chair now. He has to run the whole show.

Three Classes of People

Tozer identifies three classes of people in the average congregation:

1. The unblessed, who don't believe in God's wisdom enough to trust Him with their lives, "because they know it means a commitment that they are not willing to make" (p. 149); they are not born again.

2. The uncommitted, who have "accepted Christ" and had some kind of spiritual experience, but are unwilling to turn their lives over, so they are always spiritually up and down. Tozer says these people are

playing at Christianity, and he appears to doubt that they are truly saved.

3. Those who are committed to God's wisdom for their lives. They let God have His way and let His wisdom rule them; they don't interfere.

The committed ones have given their lives to God to run. They don't complain if it gets hard, they don't doubt or get discouraged and they don't take credit when it succeeds, but give all the glory to Him. This kind of decision is like getting married. It's a simple "I do" that will stand through conflicting emotions, because it's settled by a vow.

Tozer concludes with a prayer of commitment that is worth reading over again. In fact, it wouldn't be a bad practice to pray this prayer regularly.

LESSON PLAN—Group Study

AIM: To help my students catch a vision of God's wisdom and inspire them to trust Him more fully with their lives.

Introduction

Have different members of the group read the six Scripture passages at the beginning of the chapter (Proverbs 3:19; Jeremiah 10:12; Romans 16:27; Job 12:13; Ephesians 1:8; 3:10), then discuss how the subject of God's wisdom differs from the subject of the previous chapter, God's omniscience.

Tozer declares that if we doubt God's wisdom,

we have no foundation for our own thinking, reasoning or believing. Why is this?

Ask the group what they think of Tozer's allegory about the beautiful palace (read it from pp. 134-35, if necessary). Is this allegory a viable answer to the question of pain, suffering and evil in the world?

Wisdom Defined

How does Tozer define wisdom? What does he mean when he says God is "perfect" in wisdom?

God's Wisdom Is Infinite

Tozer refers to God's wisdom as seeking "the highest good, for the greatest number [of people]" (p. 141), as opposed to short-term solutions. What acts of God could be seen as examples of this?

God's Wisdom Revealed

Read Revelation 4:11; 5:9-10, 12. How do these passages vindicate the wisdom of God?

What does Tozer mean when he says that our belief in the wisdom of God is the crux of our life?

How is trusting God like riding in an airplane?

Three Classes of People

Review the three classes of people that Tozer describes (pp. 149-50). What distinguishes each group?

Discuss Tozer's comment that trusting in God's wisdom is like getting married.

Closing

1. Ask the group to bow their heads as you read the prayer of commitment (p. 151).
2. Assign reading of chapter 8 for next week's class.
3. Close in prayer.

Chapter 8:
God's Sovereignty

Personal Study

Supplementary Material: A. W. Tozer, *The Early Tozer: A Word in Season* (Moody).

Sovereignty, Tozer says, means God is "supreme over all things, that there is no one above Him, that He is absolute Lord over creation" (p. 154). There is nothing out of His control, nothing unseen or unplanned. The concept of sovereignty implies His absolute freedom to do anything He wills to do. Reread the various Scripture passages at the beginning of the chapter and think about the connection between God's sovereignty and the attributes discussed in previous chapters, such as His omniscience, wisdom and omnipotence.

Can God do absolutely anything? Surprisingly, Tozer says "no" to this question! And that is an entirely scriptural answer. God's sovereignty does not mean that He can do anything at all; for example, God cannot lie (Titus 1:2). What does this mean? It means God can do anything *He wills to do.* He would never will to do anything that violates His nature, so He "cannot" do it.

This may seem like a silly game of semantics, but it is a common method of arguing against belief in God, or at least belief in a sovereign God. In my college philosophy class, they presented us with this supposedly unanswerable question: "Can God make a rock so heavy He can't lift it?" (The correct answer, though a philosopher might object to it, is: "No, because He does not will to do it.")

God has absolute freedom. As children of a God who is completely free to do as He pleases, we should be restful and peaceful, free of worry and care. We can trust the sovereignty of God, because He doesn't "play by ear" or do anything on the spur of the moment. He has planned out everything since before the world began and, in His time and by His will, He is carrying out His eternal purposes.

Tozer refers to God's sovereignty as a "mighty river," and we Christians as being "carried along" in its current (p. 156). At this point, I am sure some Arminian/Wesleyan believers are beginning to fidget in their seats, but Tozer addresses that issue a bit later in the chapter. For now, they may have to put up with being a little uncomfortable.

How is God's sovereignty fulfilled in this world? He exercises His complete authority and power. A ruler must have both the authority to make commands and the power to carry them out. Samson is a good example of power with no authority; no one would listen to him, even though he had the strength of ten men. The United Nations is an example of authority with no power. The member nations may agree that a regional conflict should be settled peacefully; but how do they enforce it? A ruler must have both authority and power.

We discussed in a previous chapter that God has all power, but does He have all authority? Tozer has a simple answer for that: just who would have authority over God that He would have to ask permission? The Almighty, maker of heaven and earth, answers to no one else. He has all authority (Isaiah 44:6; Colossians 1:16-17). God is the only true Creator; that ability is given to no one else.

So where did sin come from? Did God create sin? How could a holy God create sin? Tozer has no answer for this, and contends that this is what Paul means when he refers to "the mystery of iniquity" (2 Thessalonians 2:7). But we don't have to know how sin came to be; all we need to know is that God knew about it beforehand and planned for it, so that it can never frustrate the purposes of God.

God's Sovereignty and Free Will

Sovereignty brings up a lot of thorny questions, including this age-old one: If God is sovereign, what about man's free will? Many preachers, writers and even theologians avoid this issue, because it can become a briar patch of argument. But Tozer fearlessly addresses it head-on. He feels the problematic nature of the question is good if it forces us to think about divine things.

Here's how Tozer explains it:

God's sovereignty means that He is in control of everything, that He planned everything from the beginning. Man's free will means that he can, anytime he wants, make most any choice he pleases (within his human limitations, of course). Man's free will can apparently defy the purposes of God and will against the will of God. Now how do we resolve this seeming contradiction? (p. 159)

Calvinists teach that if man is free to make a choice, then God is not sovereign. What Tozer contends is that God can do anything He pleases. And one thing He pleases to do is to give us freedom of choice. When I exercise my freedom of choice, *even if I make it against God,* I am fulfilling the will of God, because I am acting the way God created me. Joshua 24:15 ("Choose you this day whom ye will serve") proves it. Tozer is probably too Calvinist for the Arminians, and too Arminian for the Calvinists. "But I'm happy in the middle," he says. "I believe in the sovereignty of God and in the freedom of man" (pp. 161-62).

His idea is that the small circle of man's freedom is permitted within the vast circle of God's sovereignty, and he explains it with an illustration of a transatlantic ocean liner going from New York to Liverpool, England. The passengers on the ship have a certain amount of freedom—they aren't chained to the deck or anything. But the captain is going to make sure they arrive in Liverpool, and there's nothing the passengers have to say about it. "In the same way, you and I have our little lives. . . . We've got a little freedom, all right, but remember, we can't change God Almighty's course" (p. 163).

God has His plans, and He's going to have His way (Nahum 1:3). When we move with the will of God, everything's fine, but when we get out of God's will, we're in trouble.

The devil has also been given a measure of freedom by God, and he uses it to interfere in God's plans, but even a being as powerful as Satan cannot stop the course of God's sovereign will. Tozer suggests (along with many other Bible commentators) that when Satan fell, it may have occurred between verses 1 and 2 of Genesis 1. The destructive force of Satan's rebellion and downfall left the earth "formless and void." But God re-created the earth. Satan's attempts to derail God's plans were thwarted.

Then Satan orchestrated the fall of Adam and Eve. (Milton in *Paradise Lost* suggested that Satan tried to get back at God by tempting man to sin.) When man fell, it looked like he was lost forever. But God brought the second Adam—Jesus Christ—and started over again. God always has His way.

God wanted to take His people to the Promised Land. Pharaoh wouldn't let them go; God sent the plagues and got His people out. He always has His way.

When Jesus was born, He was one tiny baby against the whole Roman Empire. Before too long, the Roman Empire had collapsed, but that baby became the Man who died for all mankind and is worshiped by believers around the world.

Joseph Stalin, an early leader of the Soviet Union, once boasted, "We will pull that bearded god out of the sky." But by the time Tozer was preaching this, Stalin was dead, and today the Soviet Union does not even exist.

Tozer concludes his examples of the unalterable progress of God's will with Revelation 4:1-3. The rainbow that circles the throne, he says, represents immortality and endlessness. "No one can destroy God" (p. 167).

Sovereignty in the Crucifixion

When Jesus walked the earth, they tried to make Him king by force (John 6:15), but He said no. So they crucified Him. The disciples must have seen this as a failure on Christ's part. They never thought Jesus would die. Then on the road to Emmaus they met a Man who explained it all to them, and they realized it was Jesus (Luke 24:13-32). Jesus was raised from the dead. God had His way again.

What about today? Though we are in a difficult period of history, we can rest assured that God still has His plans and will carry them out. What are these plans? Tozer specifically mentions two: first, God will fulfill His promises to Israel; second, a ransomed company will be called and glorified.

God's sovereignty in calling a ransomed company is seen in the progress of world missions in the twentieth century. After WWII, many doors seemed to be closing all over the world. But God's plan to have a people from every tribe and tongue at the throne (Revelation 5:9) could not be thwarted. Tozer didn't even have to tell his audience that some of the greatest advances in world missions were occurring at the time he was speaking. Today there are similar doomsayers about the spread of the gospel in the twenty-first century; like Tozer, we need to trust that God's plans are sovereign.

One of God's sovereign plans for the future is that sinners will be cleansed from the earth (Psalm 104:35). The wickedness that is so firmly entrenched in much of our world seems to be here to stay. Yet God in His grace is keeping the human race from destroying itself. He will make a new heaven and earth "wherein dwelleth righteousness" (2 Peter 3:13).

But what about unforeseen circumstances? With God, there is no such thing; He knows the end from the beginning (Isaiah 46:10). What about accidents? God's wisdom prevents an accident. His orders cannot be countermanded, because there is no authority higher than Him. He cannot fail because of weakness because He is omnipotent.

Therefore, we who have given our lives over to the Sovereign Lord of the universe have nothing to fear. God is in control and will work out His will in our lives. As Tozer puts it in one of his editorials from *The Early Tozer: A Word in Season,*

> The life of the Christian is bound up in the sovereignty
> of God, i.e., His complete freedom in His universe,

His full ability to carry out His plans to their tri-
umphant conclusion. Since he is a part of God's eternal purpose, he knows he must win at last, and he can
afford to be calm even when the battle seems to be
temporarily going against him.

But this sword cuts both ways. If God has allowed
us a measure of personal freedom, and there are no
accidents, then when you walk against the will of
God and find yourself in hell, it's your own fault—
you *chose* to go there. No one ends up in hell—or in
heaven, for that matter—by accident. Those who end
up in hell may be surprised to be there, but they
shouldn't be; the road to that place was their choice.

Apply God's sovereignty and man's free will to consecration, the deeper life, obedience. It's not an op-
tion in the Christian life to be fully surrendered to
God; it's a choice, and if we don't make the choice
for God, we're making it against God. "If we're opposing God we can't win. But if we surrender and
come over to God's side, we can't lose" (p. 173).

But it's our choice. If we choose wrong, God will
let us do it, and we'll be on the losing side. And if
we choose right, we'll be on the winning side. It's entirely voluntary—"heaven will not be filled with slaves"
(p. 174).

If you can't surrender to God, you're choosing the
losing side. Give Him everything. "Choose Christ's
way, because Christ is Lord and the Lord is sovereign. It's foolish to choose any other way" (p. 174).
Don't strive against Him (Job 33:13).

LESSON PLAN—Group Study

AIM: To help my students understand and appreciate God's sovereignty and how it highlights the importance of serving Him fully.

Introduction

Have several members of the group read the Scripture passages at the beginning of the chapter (Deuteronomy 4:39; 32:39-40; Job 12:9-10, 16-17; 33:13; Jeremiah 18:6; Daniel 4:3, 35; Nahum 1:3). From these verses, lead the group in creating a definition of God's sovereignty.

Tozer tells us that God is absolutely sovereign—and yet, there are things He *cannot* do. What does he mean by that?

Because God has absolute freedom, how should Christians live their lives? Discuss what it means to be "carried along in the current" of God's sovereignty.

God's Sovereignty and Free Will

Ask the group what the apparent contradiction is between God's sovereignty and man's free will. How does Tozer resolve it?

Read Tozer's illustration of the passengers on an ocean liner (pp. 162-63). Does this answer the difficulty between sovereignty and free will?

Tozer refers to a number of events from biblical and modern history that show God's sovereign plans triumphing over Satan's schemes. Ask the group if they can think of others.

Sovereignty in the Crucifixion

How do unforeseen circumstances and accidents affect God's sovereignty? Discuss what the Christian should do when God's plans don't seem to be working out.

Tozer tells us that a correct understanding of God's sovereignty means that our personal choices are all the more crucial. Why is this?

Closing

1. Have everyone bow their heads. Ask them to think about what areas of their lives may be on the "losing side"—where they have chosen against God.
2. Assign reading of chapter 9 for next week's class.
3. Close in prayer, asking specifically that as children of a sovereign God, we might learn to choose the "winning side."

Chapter 9:
God's Faithfulness

Personal Study

Supplementary Material: A. W. Tozer, *Jesus, Our Man in Glory* (Moody).

Tozer begins the chapter with this definition: "Faithfulness is that in God which guarantees that He will never be or act inconsistent with Himself. . . . He will always be true to Himself, to His works and to His creation" (p. 176). Reread the various Scripture passages at the beginning of the chapter and see how they fit in with this definition. This is one definition that I might have wished Tozer had elaborated upon more fully. I would like to have seen or heard his explanation of how it applies to our relationship to God and to the promises in His Word. But like other definitions of attributes that Tozer gives, this is a bare-bones, boiled-down description; it only makes complete sense as we hear the rest of what he has to say about it.

"God is His own standard," Tozer declares (p. 176). This means He doesn't imitate or get influenced by anyone. In an age where "it isn't what you know, it's who you know," the idea of a Being who cannot be influenced is hard to fathom, but as Tozer says, "Nothing can force God to act otherwise than faithfully to Himself and to us—no person, no circumstance, nothing" (p. 176). If someone could influence God to do something He did not plan to do, or be something He isn't, wouldn't that person be greater than God?

My first question when I read Tozer's definition of faithfulness was, "How is this different from immutability?" Tozer doesn't directly answer this question, but he does recognize the close connection between the two. He says God's perfection "secures" His immutability—in other words, since God is perfect, He's not going to change, because when you're perfect, there's no place to go but down! Tozer also says God's faithfulness "secures" His immutability, "because God can never cease to be who He is and what He is" (p. 177). Perhaps what he means is that God's faithfulness is an immutability of *personality,* while His perfection is an immutability of *nature.* If that distinction makes sense to you, fine. If not, don't worry about it.

If it's hard to understand this, it's because the discussion of God's attributes is bedrock theology. Nuclear physics is hard to understand too, and it's the bedrock of physics, the basic building blocks of the natural world. You need to get back to the basics when life brings you trouble. When your life is shaken to the roots, you want to know they are sunk in the bedrock. "You can live on froth and bubbles and little wisps of badly understood theology—until the pressure is on. And when the pressure is on, you'll want to know what kind of God you're serving" (p. 177).

All that God says and does is in line with His various attributes. One attribute cannot be exalted above another: "We see God full-rounded, in all of His perfection and glory" (p. 178). Otherwise, Tozer warns, we end up seeing God "lopsided." If all we see is God's justice, He looks like a terror and a tyrant. If all we see is God's love, He looks sentimental and spineless. If all we see is God's grace, He appears to be blind to morality—to be unholy. But God is just and loving and full of grace—all of these, infinitely and at the same time. And that's what makes Him faithful. "Our God will always be true to His nature, because He is a faithful God" (p. 180).

Faithlessness is one of the greatest sources of pain in the world, but God will never be faithless. Tozer calls on the promises in God's Word to testify to His faithfulness. He quotes Genesis 8:20-22 (the promise that the daytime, the nighttime and the seasons will never cease) and 9:8-11, 14-16 (the promise that the world will never again be destroyed in a flood) to assure his audience that they need not be worried about one of the major concerns of the middle of the twentieth century: the threat of nuclear war. There is no danger of the human race being wiped from the face of the earth, because God has promised that nature will continue on as it always has—and God is faithful to fulfill His promise. Psalm 105:8 is a related promise: God will remember His covenant forever. And Matthew 5:18 says that heaven and earth will not pass away "till all be fulfilled."

It seems to me that the promises in God's Word are what make His faithfulness visible to us. I think Tozer would agree with that. Consider, for example, what he says about God's promises in *Jesus, Our Man in Glory*:

> God's total faithfulness is a vibrant, positive message. . . . Let me share a conclusion I have come to in my study of the Scriptures. I have come to believe that all the promises of God have been made to assure us weak and changeable humans of God's neverending good will and concern. What God is today He will be tomorrow. And all that God does will always be in accord with all that God is!

God cannot change, so He will remain faithful; He is perfectly faithful, because He is perfectly everything. He never broke a promise, never talked out of both sides of His mouth, never overlooked anything or forgot anything.

From here on in the chapter, Tozer shows God's faithfulness in application to sinners, to the tempted and to strugglers. (As I suggested before, faithfulness is *relational*.)

God's Faithfulness to Sinners

God is a God of justice and will be faithful to "banish from His presence all who love sin [and] reject His Son" (p. 183). I'm sure there are some sinners who would prefer that God was not quite so faithful in this regard! There are some who hope that perhaps "God threatens but doesn't fulfill" (p. 183). God is, of course, very gracious and withholds His judgment; He is "longsuffering . . . not willing that any should perish, but that all should come to repentance" (2 Peter 3:9). But to those who refuse God's gracious offer of forgiveness, judgment is coming.

Then there's the other kind of sinner—what Tozer calls the "returning sinner," such as the Prodigal Son. For him the message is "Come unto me" (Matthew 11:28). God welcomes them in His arms!

We can be sure that whatever God promises, He will do. But believing and trusting God had become a scarce commodity in Tozer's day and are far less abundant now than we like to think. A common practice, according to Tozer, was to put many of God's promises into the future, only to be fulfilled in "the last days"—the way Martha said that her brother would rise on the last day, but didn't consider that Jesus could raise him then and there (John 11:24). For these people, "eschatology is a dustbin into which we sweep everything we don't want to believe" (p. 184). So we explain away our disbelief in miracles, healing, God's manifest presence, revival and many other things that might become "inconvenient" if we really take God at His word!

When Tozer speaks of a people who "believe in miracles tomorrow or yesterday, but we stand in a gap between miracles" (p. 185), he's obviously taking a playful jab at strict dispensationalists, who believe that we live in "the church age," in which the miraculous intervention of God is (for some unknown reason) suspended.

He doesn't ignore those on the other end of the spectrum, however. For those who want to "celebrate miracles by putting up big tents and advertising that we're going to have a miracle," he insists that "God isn't going to allow Himself to be advertised" (p. 185). But a balance is possible between the denial of the miraculous and the outright worship of it. We can have authentic miracles that will bring glory to God—if we only believe.

And if you are a sinner who wants to return, you have to believe that God is faithful to fulfill His Word. You have to believe that God promises to give rest to those who come to Him (Matthew 11:28) and that God will forgive our sins if we confess them to Him (1 John 1:9). We should read these verses, Tozer says, "with the thought that God meant exactly what He said there," and differences in translations all "add up to about the same thing" (pp. 185-86). The important thing to remember is that God wrote it and is faithful to fulfill it.

But what of the believer who has sinned? Tozer admits that he is uncomfortable with the idea of "sinning Christians," but they still exist—and the promises in the early part of 1 John are written specifically for them. Of course, Christians should not sin, and it's a serious thing if they do. But such passages as 1 John 1:9 and 2:1 show that it happens, and God has provided for it.

It also shows that if God "is faithful and just to forgive us our sins" it means that "justice has come over on the side of the returning sinner" (p. 187). (This echoes the chapter on God's justice in the first volume of *The Attributes of God*.) Nothing stands between you and God's very heart. If you confess your sins, God's justice is not against you, but for you!

God's Faithfulness to the Tempted

First Corinthians 10:13 promises to the tempted that God will be faithful to keep the temptation from being more than we can handle, and will provide a way to escape. "God's faithfulness is the way out" (pp. 187-88). Your temptation is "common to man," so it's nothing that God can't get you through if you trust Him. When we get tempted, we may think it's worse than anyone else's temptations—but God helped others make it through and He can help us too. We can trust His faithfulness.

God's Faithfulness to Strugglers

Some are strugglers, and God is faithful to them as well. They may have problems believing that God accepts them, that everything is all right between them and God. But they can trust the promise in Isaiah 54:7-9, which declares that God's anger is "little" and "for a moment" but His mercy is "everlasting." Though God may correct and chasten, He will never be angry with us again, it says in the next verse (54:10).

Though a struggler may have been unfaithful, in 2 Timothy 2:13 God promises to remain faithful.

(Some commentators actually think that "If we believe not, yet he abideth faithful" means He is faithful to *judge* us—I am so glad Tozer doesn't hold to that!)

For those of us who get discouraged and feel like we aren't getting anywhere in the Christian life, Tozer suggests that God may just be showing us how bad we really are! But we need not worry; God will finish the job He's doing in us (1 Thessalonians 5:24). Just as a hen has to sit on her eggs for a full twenty-one days before they hatch, sometimes God makes us wait, as He made the disciples wait for the Holy Spirit (Acts 1:4). But He is faithful to provide, if we just trust Him.

As Tozer ends with a prayer, he covers a wide variety of people in various circumstances that need to be reminded of God's faithfulness. Feel free to insert your name or that of a loved one as you read it over.

LESSON PLAN—Group Study

AIM: To help my students learn to trust in God's faithfulness, and be faithful to Him.

Introduction

Have various members of the group read the Scripture passages at the beginning of the chapter (Psalm 89:1-2, 5, 8, 24; 1 John 1:9; 2 Timothy 2:13; 1 Thessalonians 5:24). Discuss how God's faithfulness might be defined, according to these passages.

Read Tozer's definition of God's faithfulness (p. 176). How does it compare to the group's definition?

Discuss how God's faithfulness is related to His immutability (you may want to prepare for leading this discussion by referring back to chapter 5).

Ask the group how an understanding of God's attributes, especially His faithfulness, can keep us from becoming "lopsided" Christians.

How does a study of some of the promises in God's Word help us understand and appreciate God's faithfulness?

God's Faithfulness to Sinners

What are the two types of (non-Christian) sinners identified by Tozer? How is God faithful to both of them? How is God faithful to "Christian sinners"?

Ask a mature Christian (possibly ahead of time, to allow him to prepare) to share briefly how God was faithful to lead him to Christ or to restore him when he was caught in a sinful habit.

God's Faithfulness to the Tempted

Read 1 Corinthians 10:13. Ask the group to identify ways that God is faithful to help us in temptation.

Ask a mature Christian (possibly ahead of time, to allow him to prepare) to share briefly about a time in his life when God was faithful to deliver him from temptation.

God's Faithfulness to Strugglers

Read Isaiah 54:7-10, 2 Timothy 2:13 and 1 Thessalonians 5:24. Ask the group how these passages speak to the three kinds of strugglers mentioned by Tozer.

Ask a mature Christian (possibly ahead of time, to allow him to prepare) to share briefly about how God was faithful to help him at a time in his life when he was struggling.

Closing

1. Read aloud the closing prayer at the end of the chapter, asking the members of the group to silently insert their names or the name of a loved one wherever appropriate.
2. Assign reading of chapter 10 for next week's class.
3. Close in prayer.

Chapter 10:
God's Love

Personal Study

Supplementary Materials: A. W. Tozer, *The Next Chapter after the Last* (Moody); C. S. Lewis, *The Great Divorce* (Macmillan); Lady Julian of Norwich, *Revelations of Divine Love*.

This chapter begins with a single Scripture passage: 1 John 4:7-21. Read through these fifteen verses three or four times and jot down some of the simple truths that John shares about God's love. Tozer says that God's love is the hardest of all His attributes to talk about. It's amazing to hear him say that, considering how difficult he said it was to speak about many of the others. As with other attributes, he views this as trying to "comprehend the incomprehensible" (p. 196).

Tozer says "God is love" is not a definition. This is a crucial point. It means that you cannot invert the statement and say "love is God." Why? Because it leads to a sentimental pantheism incompatible with Scripture that is the confused theology of "crackpot poets and religious people" (p. 196). John's declaration that "God is love" doesn't mean God is to be equated with love, or that God is love "in His metaphysical being" (pp. 196-97). God's essential being is inexpressible and incomprehensible.

If we thought that God and love were the same, then we could worship love, and "we would be worshiping an attribute of personality and not the Person Himself" (p. 197). First John also says that God is light (1:5) and God is life (5:20), "but we don't try to limit His nature to just light or life!" (p. 197).

What "God is love" means is that love is one of His essential attributes, and that all love comes from God, and He does nothing except in love. God is the source of all love, but God's nature is not limited to love—there are no limits on God's nature.

Someday we will know as we are known (1 Corinthians 13:12), and we will find that "even the damning of a man is an expression of the love of God" (p. 197). As was said before in previous chapters, God's attributes do not fight with each other or contradict each other. They are all wrapped up in His perfect unity of being.

Tozer expresses some misgivings as he attempts to discuss the love of God; as a botanist pulls apart a flower to analyze it, Tozer is afraid of destroying the bloom in the interest of learning about it.

Love Is Good Will

Love is characterized by "good will" toward the one loved, as the angels said to the shepherds (Luke

2:14). In other words, if you love someone, you "will good" for them—you don't want anything bad to happen to them.

This is Tozer's way of explaining the verse, "There is no fear in love; but perfect love casteth out fear" (1 John 4:18). This passage is puzzling to many, but Tozer's explanation makes perfect sense, especially when you read the verse in context. If we know God loves us, we know He wants the best for us, so we have no fear in His hands—just as a lost child loses his fear when he finds his mother and runs into her arms. He knows she won't let any harm come to him. Also, the context of this verse is talking about judgment, and we know that God in His love—His "good will" toward us—has delivered us from judgment through the death of His Son on the cross for our sins.

Tozer doesn't waste our time or insult our intelligence with a sickly-sweet view of life. He freely admits that there is every reason to be afraid in this dangerous world—if you haven't placed your trust in God. He scoffs at books that purport to show how to conquer fear, when their only advice is to convince yourself that everything is rosy and there is nothing to be afraid of. "If you believe you're in the hands of chance, of course there's something to be afraid of, and you're a fool if you're not afraid" (p. 200).

All right, maybe you don't believe in chance; maybe you believe in God. But if your sin stands between you and God, you've still got a lot to be afraid of! Hebrews 10:26-27 can send a shiver down your spine if you're not right with God. But if you've re-pented, you have a clean slate with God. You're no longer in the hands of men, but are in God's hands, and He loves you and wills good for you. So you have nothing to fear.

Love Is Emotional

Because God loves us, He "identifies emotionally" with us, Tozer says (p. 202). That seems like a per-fectly reasonable statement, but for some reason it jars my concept of God to think that He "gets emo-tional" over me. Perhaps I'm thinking of a syrupy, melodramatic attitude that was never Tozer's intent at all. And his illustrations of a father dying for his child or a mother being "nursed to death" by her baby are examples of noble self-sacrifice, with no hint of pretense.

This melodramatic attitude appears to be what Tozer means when he complains about songs that have Jesus saying, "Oh, what a hero I was and you don't appreciate it! Too bad for Me." I can agree with him, even though I am not familiar with any such songs. I also agree with him that some Good Friday services can be morbidly unhealthy, if we think we are empathetically "experiencing" Christ's passion. When Peter spoke of being "partakers of the [Christ's] sufferings," he was talking about persecu-tion (2 Corinthians 1:7).

But there is a proper way to meditate on Christ's sufferings. Tozer touches on it in *The Next Chapter after the Last:*

The believer who complains against the difficulties of the way proves that he has never felt or known the sorrows which broke over the head of Christ when He was here among men. After one look at Gethsemane or Calvary, the Christian can never again believe that his own path is a hard one. We dare not compare our trifling pains with the sublime passion endured for our salvation. Any comparison would itself be the supreme argument against our complaints, for what sorrow is like unto His?

A woman in labor forgets her pain after the baby is born (John 16:21), because "she emotionally identifies with her child. Whatever prospers her child, prospers her; whatever hurts her child, hurts her" (p. 203). God feels the same way about us. That was the reason, according to Milton in *Paradise Lost,* that the devil decided to make mankind fall—he knew it was the only way he could get back at God. And the devil succeeded in hurting God, because God loves mankind, made in His own image. "Our sins are an emotional wound in the heart of God" (p. 204).

Does it seem strange that God would love us so much? The psalmist was puzzled over it as well: "What is man, that thou art mindful of him?" (Psalm 8:4). When we suffer, God suffers along with us. God is also happy when we are happy. God's feelings toward us are like a bridegroom's feelings toward his bride, or a mother's toward her baby.

In the first chapter of Genesis, you can sense God's pleasure in His creation. He declared it "good" as He made it; when mankind was made He declared it "very good." Read Psalm 104:31 and Zephaniah 3:17 the next time you are feeling down about yourself. Have you considered that God *rejoices* over you? Have you considered that you make Him *sing for joy?*

Why then, Tozer asks, is there such a lack of warmth and enthusiasm in our worship of this God who is the Lover of our soul? His answer: We don't go deep enough in our relationship with God to catch a glimpse of His loving heart. "We get just enough religion to make us miserable. If we would go on, we'd find God's love" (p. 207).

The Christian life is not defined by what you don't do. It's a love relationship. He wants us for His bride; He wants to be our *Ishi* (Hosea 2:16), or "husband." Our maiden name was "Adam," but God became our husband and gave us the married name of "Christian."

Love makes everything all right, Tozer says. Marriage and families would be mechanical and burdensome if it were not for "the lubrication of love" (p. 209). If you love someone, they aren't a burden. That's how God feels about us. He is not to be pitied; He was happy to come down and die for us!

Since love is an attribute of God, you can be sure that it corresponds to the other attributes. God's love is infinite, eternal, immutable, etc. His thoughts toward us are loving all the time. He loved us before we were born—it was for love that Christ died for us (Romans 5:8). That same love protects us as well (Hebrews 7:25). Tozer uses God's love to defend the security of the believer: "God always keeps that which He loves" (p. 210).

But there are sinners who "love hate and hate love," who continually despise and reject God's love. They could never be happy in heaven, which is permeated by God's great love. Tozer illustrates this with the story of the street urchin who couldn't stand living in a beautiful large mansion and ran away to the street again.

It reminds me of the characters in C. S. Lewis' fantasy novel, *The Great Divorce*. They are residents of hell who are given the opportunity to visit heaven—but they hate it, because heaven isn't made for the likes of them. "Heaven will not be heaven to the man who does not have the love of God in his heart" (p. 212). Lazarus went to heaven and the rich man to hell (Luke 16:22-23) because "each man went to the place that he had been conditioned for" (p. 212).

How does a sinner become someone who is "made for heaven"? Through the new birth, in which "all things are become new" (2 Corinthians 5:17). We become "acclimated and psychologically conditioned to the kingdom of God" (p. 213). We love to sing and worship, to read the Word, to pray. We belong in heaven. And people who go to hell belong there by nature. "The gravitational tug of their moral lives is toward hell" (p. 213).

This chapter is far too brief an overview of God's love. Tozer himself describes it as similar to taking a world tour and only having five minutes to tell about it. Perhaps you would like to study God's love further. I hope that the brief passage he quotes on page 214 from *Revelations of Divine Love* by Lady Julian of

Norwich is enough to whet your appetite for more. This ancient book is widely available; you can even find the text of it on the Internet.

The one who is immersed in God's love is impervious to the attacks of the world, the flesh and the devil. And the one who is far from God doesn't realize that God still loves him and is seeking to draw him back. If you feel far from God, come to your senses like the Prodigal Son did, and go back to your Father (Luke 15:20). You'll find that God welcomes you with open arms.

LESSON PLAN—Group Study

AIM: To help my students understand and trust in God's love for them so that they may draw nearer to Him.

Introduction

Have a volunteer read 1 John 4:7-21. Using a whiteboard or overhead, compile (with the help of the group) a list of the characteristics of God's love as explained by John.

What does Tozer mean when he says that "God is love" is not a definition?

Love Is Good Will

Read 1 John 4:18. Discuss Tozer's explanation of this verse. How does this explanation relate to the phrase "fear hath torment"? (Refer to a modern biblical translation if necessary.)

What does Tozer say is the main advice given in most books about how to conquer fear? Why is this advice inadequate?

Read Hebrews 10:27. Of whom is this passage speaking? In light of God's love, how do we know it is not speaking of us? (Refer back to 1 John 4:17-18 if necessary.)

Love Is Emotional

What does Tozer mean when he says that God "identifies emotionally" with us? How does this relate to the fall of man according to Milton in *Paradise Lost?*

Have volunteers read Psalm 104:31 and Zephaniah 3:17. Discuss what these two verses say about God's attitude toward us.

What, according to Tozer, is the cause of a lack of warmth and enthusiasm in our worship? How can we cure this malady?

What reason does Tozer give for a sinner to be unhappy in heaven? How can a sinner become someone who is "made for heaven"?

Read the story of the Prodigal Son (Luke 15:11-32). Discuss what characteristics of God's love are displayed by the father in the parable.

Closing

1. Bow together and pray for prodigals. Ask anyone who knows a prodigal to raise his hand. Also include a time of silent prayer for anyone who senses that he is estranged from God.

2. Explain that next week's class will be a review of the entire book.
3. Close in prayer.

Review

This lesson is designed as a review at the end of your study. The aim is simply to discern what impact the lessons have had on you (and on your students, if this is a group study) and to review the main points again.

Testimony Time

The best review might be to determine what you have gotten out of this study. If this is an individual study, write down your thoughts in a journal. If it is a group study, do it in a group discussion. Share a significant lesson the Lord has taught you or the most important thing you have learned through this study. Allow as much time as you need for this valuable exercise.

Review

Feel free to emphasize the points you feel are most needed. What is provided is simply the major points each chapter made and some statements or related Scriptures about each point.

Introduction—God's Character

- A worthy concept of God is crucial, because He is the cause behind all things and the only One who can give meaning to our existence.
- Mankind fell as soon as we lost a right concept of God (see Romans 1:21-28), and studying God's attributes can develop faith and trust in Him (see Psalm 9:10; the word *name* denotes God's character and attributes).
- Studying the attributes can help bring revival. Our Christianity "is thin and anemic, without thoughtful content, frivolous in tone and worldly in spirit" (p. 8).
- "I want a vision of the majesty of God. . . . I want to live where the face of God shines every day" (p. 13).

Chapter 1—God's Self-Existence

- "God has no origin. . . . He is the Cause of all things, the uncaused Cause" (p. 22).
- God, the great Originator, created us to revolve around Him, like planets around the sun. "Then one day, the little planet said, 'I'll be my own sun. Away with this God.' And man fell" (p. 28).
- Read Galatians 5:19-21. We call such things sin, but in truth they are only manifestations, symptoms of the underlying disease: self.
- We have usurped God's throne. Being born again means getting off the throne and returning to the purpose for which we were made: to worship, glorify and love God, and to be objects of His love.

Chapter 2—God's Transcendence

- The word *transcendent* means "to rise above," and means that God and His ways are infinitely far above us.
- "God is just as far above an archangel as He is above a caterpillar. . . . God is of a substance wholly unique" (pp. 39-40).
- We think we understand God, that we've got Him down pat, but "Lo, these are parts of his ways: but how little a portion is heard of him?" (Job 26:14). God is infinitely beyond our finite minds.
- Ironically, at the cross—the lowest point in Christ's life—is where we can reach the transcendent God. And just as ironically, we can't meet the One who rises above everything until we come down—until we humble ourselves before His cross.

Chapter 3—God's Eternalness

- Read Isaiah 57:15 and Psalm 90:2, reflecting on the fact that the very nature of deity is eternal—it's what makes Him God.
- What if God were *not* eternal? How could a temporal God be the creator of everything? If He came into existence at some point in time, aren't we tempted to ask, "Then who made God?"
- God dwells in eternity, outside of time (see Isaiah 46:10).
- Only He who is "from everlasting to everlasting" can fill that longing for eternity in our hearts (see John 11:25-26). "Why can we believe in our own

immortality? Because God is eternal. . . . We can look forward with calm restfulness to the time that shall be" (p. 74).

Chapter 4—God's Omnipotence

- The root meaning of both *omnipotent* and *almighty* are exactly that: God has all the power there is. The Bible never uses these words to refer to anyone but God.
- "There isn't any power anywhere that doesn't have God as its source. . . . And the source of anything has to be greater than that which flows out of it" (pp. 78-79).
- Like a fly in an airplane, worrying about whether the plane can carry its weight, we actually worry that the Almighty God of the universe might not be able to handle our problems! But God sustains all things by His power (Hebrews 1:3).
- We shouldn't hesitate in our prayers to ask God for "hard" things, because there aren't any "hard" things for God (see Genesis 18:14).

Chapter 5—God's Immutability

- *Immutability* means "not subject to change." God simply never changes. Change is not even possible with God. "God never differs from Himself" (p. 97).
- A perfect being cannot get better, nor an infinite being get greater; neither can a holy and righteous God become worse.
- So how can we know what God is like? Look at Jesus Christ (John 14:9).

- When we turn to Him in our need, isn't it wonderful to know that He never changes? He is with us always (Matthew 28:20), ready to take us in, whatever our need.

Chapter 6—God's Omniscience

- There are two facets to God's omniscience. Psalm 147:5 tells us that God understands all data, knowledge and facts. Hebrews 4:13 says that no creature—including us—is hidden from His eyes. He sees right through us.
- Our knowledge, especially of God, is very limited; God is ultimately ineffable (inexpressible in words), inconceivable and unimaginable.
- We need not worry, because God knows it all, and you cannot "drift beyond His love and care" (p. 127).
- We should always be ready to confess our sins, our doubts and our fears to Him; there's nothing we can hide from Him, anyway!

Chapter 7—God's Wisdom

- "If I tried to prove that God is wise, the embittered soul would not believe it anyway. . . . And the worshiping heart already knows that God is wise and does not need to have it proved" (pp. 132-33).
- His perfect wisdom plans for "the highest good, for the greatest number, for the longest time" (p. 141).
- Redemption was accomplished in His wisdom (1 Corinthians 1:24; 2:7); salvation through faith was by His wisdom (1 Corinthians 1:21); and in

the consummation, His wisdom is also revealed (Ephesians 3:10).

- Will we accept God's wisdom or go our own way? The essence of sin is the concept that "I turn to my way because I think it is wiser than God's way" (see Isaiah 53:6).

Chapter 8—God's Sovereignty

- Sovereignty means God is "supreme over all things, that there is no one above Him, that He is absolute Lord over creation" (p. 154).

- As children of a God who is completely free to do as He pleases, we should be restful and peaceful, free of worry and care. In His time and by His will, He is carrying out His eternal purposes (see Nahum 1:3).

- The small circle of man's free will is permitted within the vast circle of God's sovereignty (see Joshua 24:15).

- "If we're opposing God we can't win. But if we surrender and come over to God's side, we can't lose" (p. 173).

Chapter 9—God's Faithfulness

- "Faithfulness is that in God which guarantees that He will never be or act inconsistent with Himself. . . . He will always be true to Himself, to His works and to His creation" (p. 176).

- All that God says and does is in line with His various attributes. "Our God will always be true to His nature, because He is a faithful God" (p. 180).

- God demonstrates His faithfulness through the promises in His Word.
- God is faithful to His promises to sinners (2 Peter 3:9; Matthew 11:28), to the tempted (1 Corinthians 10:13) and to strugglers (2 Timothy 2:13; 1 Thessalonians 5:24).

Chapter 10—God's Love

- "God is love" (1 John 4:8) is not a definition of God; it means that love is one of His essential attributes, that all love comes from God and that He does nothing except in love.
- If we know God loves us, we know He wants the best for us, so we have no fear in His hands (1 John 4:18).
- Because God loves us, He "identifies emotionally" with us, like a bridegroom feels toward his bride, or a mother toward her baby.
- If you feel far from God, come to your senses like the Prodigal Son did, and go back to your Father (Luke 15:20). You'll find that God in His love welcomes you with open arms.

Conclusion

- This quote from *The Attributes of God Volume One* summarizes the whole point of this study:

  Christianity at any given time is strong or weak depending upon her concept of God. And I insist upon this and I have said it many times, that the basic trouble with the church today is her unworthy conception of God.

• Close in prayer, asking that this study would help each person have a more worthy concept of our great and wonderful God.

More from A. W. Tozer:

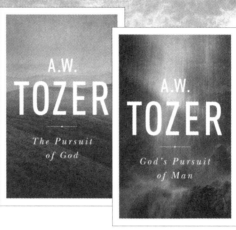

TITLES BY A.W. TOZER